The Book Of Daniel

The Book of Daniel

The Book of
DANIEL

—–— H.H. CHARLES —–—

CONTENTS

FOREWORD
SECOND CENTURY BCE

In Babylon there lived a man named Joakim, who married a very beautiful and God-fearing woman, Susanna. Joakim was very rich and had a garden near his house. At this time, two elders of the people were appointed judges. And many people brought their cases to them when they were at Joakim's house.

When the people left at noon, Susanna used to walk in her husband's garden. Two old men saw her every day on her walks and began to lust for her. Though both lusted after her, they did not tell the other for fear of revealing their lust for her. Day by day they watched her and then one day, parted saying they were going home as it was the noon hour. Time to eat the mid-day meal. But after they parted, both turned back to the garden. When there, they admitted their lust and agreed to look for an occasion when they could meet her alone.

One day, while they both were waiting for an opportunity, Susanna entered the garden with two of her maids as was her custom. Because the weather was warm, Susanna decided to bathe believing no one else was in the garden. The two judges watched her, hidden from her view and overheard Susanna tell her maids, "Bring me oil and soap and shut the garden doors while I bathe."

Her maids did as they were told, leaving the garden by a side gate. As soon as the maids left, the two old men left their hiding place and hurried to her.

"Look," one said, "the garden doors are shut, and no one can see us." The other quickly implored, "Give into our desire. Lie with us."

Susanna's face showed shock and disbelief. So they added, "If you refuse, we will testify against you that you dismissed your maids because a young man was here with you."

Susanna was dismayed. "I am trapped. If I yield, it will be my death. If I refuse, I cannot escape your lies. But better that I suffer your lies knowing I have no guilt."

They moved toward her and she screamed and one of the old men then shouted at her while the other ran to open the garden doors. When the people in the house heard the cries from the garden, they rushed by the side gate to see what had happened to her. When they arrived, the old men accused her as they had threatened her.

The next day, the people and the two elders came before Joakim. The two elders ordered, "Send for Susanna, the wife of Joakim."

She came as bidden accompanied by her parents, children and relatives. When she arrived before her husband, she radiated delicacy and beauty, but was veiled. The two judges ordered her to uncover her face so as to sate themselves with her beauty.

Both judges now rose and laid their hands on her head and made their accusations.

"As we were walking in the garden alone, this woman entered with two maids and shut the doors of the garden, dismissing her maids. A young man, who was hidden there, came and lay with her. When we, in a corner of the garden, saw this crime, we ran toward them. We saw them lying together, but the man we could not hold, because he was stronger than we. He opened the garden doors and ran off. Then we seized this one and asked who the young man was, but she refused to tell us. We testify to this."

The assembly believed them because they were elders and judges of the people and Susanna was condemned to death.

Susanna swore her innocence and that the testimony against her was false. As she was being led away, a young man named Daniel, cried out.

"I will have no part in the death of this woman."

The crowd asked him, "What is this you are saying?"

He walked into their midst and continued, "Are you such fools to condemn a woman without examination and without clear evidence? Return to the house for her accusers have testified falsely against her."

The people returned, but the elders approached him and said, "Come sit with us and inform us of what you know, since you assert to have the wisdom of old age."

Daniel ignored them and in a loud voice, stated, "Separate these two old men far from one another that I may examine them."

It was done as he said.

Then he called one of the elders and said, "How you have grown evil with age! Your past will now come to term – passing unjust sentences, condemning the innocent, freeing the guilty. But this time, the innocent and the just you shall not put to death. Now then, if you were a witness, tell me under what tree you saw."

"Under a mastic tree," the first elder to be called answered.

Dismissing the first elder, Daniel ordered the second one to come forward.

"Now then, tell me under what tree you surprised them together."

"Under an oak," the second elder replied.

The crowd drew a collective breath and began to murmur among themselves when Daniel turned and addressed them all.

"You have heard the lies of these two wicked men. Those lies will cost them their heads."

The whole assembly cried and rose up against the two elders, for by their own words Daniel had convicted them of perjury. According to the law of Moses, the assembly inflicted on them the penalty of death they had plotted to impose on Susanna. They were both stoned to death.

CHAPTER 1
THE FORGOTTEN

In a lengthy opinion, the state's death penalty for capital crimes was struck down. Along with the murderer whose death sentence was commuted, so too were the death sentences of the murderers convicted and sentenced to die years earlier. For Jed Summers, the decision inflicted anew the agony he suffered from the ritualistic rape and murder of his wife and daughter five years before. The scene of their nude and bloody bodies surrounded by demonic symbols once again was made vivid in his mind. Knowing that the man that had so violated his love ones would forfeit his life provided no real solace at first. His anger and hatred was not assuaged by the jury's guilty verdict of aggregated murder. Their murderer was still alive, unremorseful and even defiant. When the jury came back a few weeks later and imposed the death penalty, he was still alive, still defiant. He smirked when he heard the jury pronounce the sentence of death. Then he was led away. And Summers knew that he would remain alive for years, decades, before he would forfeit his worthless existence in payment for the innocent lives he first violated and then brutally ended.

As time passed, Summers slowly resigned himself to the realities of the limitations of the law to obtain justice for the victims and their survivors. He knew that no one who had not suffered what he was forced to suffer could ever understand the helplessness, shame, anger and disgust he had to live with every day. They could not know that his feelings of shame and disgust were directed at himself, borne of the helplessness he was forced to accept that he was not around to protect his loved ones; to die in their place if necessary. His anger at himself was nearly equal to his anger at the murderer and at the legal system which not only tolerated such a heinous creature's continued existence, but which would provide him with food and shelter for years to come.

He became aware of those people and organizations that opposed the death penalty and sought to outlaw it. He feared their success, but was aware that his state law provided for capital punishment. He did his best to ignore media accounts of protests at prisons around the country when a convict's execution date had been set. He ignored appeals to the Supreme Court and state supreme courts seeking stays of execution. He couldn't understand how these organizations, the lawyers and others took up the cause of criminals convicted and sentenced by a jury of their peers. There was not a moment's thought of how their efforts affected the victims, their families, the survivors. It tortured him that with the passage of time, the horror of the crimes committed by these fiends faded. In its place came a concern for taking their lives. Why did they ignore the logic that the punishment must fit the crime? If a life, or lives, are taken, if they are taken in horrible ways, what principle supports defending the life of the person who took those lives and, in the killing, the last remnants of their human dignity?

Now the state supreme court had flipped and overruled the legislation that had been on the books for centuries. The horror and pain of his losses came thundering down on him anew. He was plunged back into the cesspool of self-recriminations, anger, hatred, frustration. He had no idea what to do. But he was afraid of what he might decide to do.

CHAPTER 2
STARTING ANEW

It was a year and a month after Chris Knight and Kelly Young had been rescued from the hit woman hired by the gun extremists in their attempt to stop Chris' attack on the unbounded interpretation of the right to bear arms under the Second Amendment. In the weeks immediately following, they had retreated to Chris' apartment, neither one wanting to be apart. Chris kept up with his law practice from his den and also worked on completing his action for a declaratory judgment seeking a better interpretation of the Second Amendment based on the many records from the earliest days of the republic. He found it both astounding and disappointing that the broad interpretation of the Second Amendment had ignored these writings made by the most pre-eminent members of the Founding Fathers.

Kelly had suspended her practice for the time being. She needed to get back her own equilibrium and peace of mind after the harrowing experiences they had been through.

It was a Tuesday morning, Chris had risen early and was in the kitchen making coffee. Kelly was still in bed but awoke to the aroma of the coffee, got up, did a quick brush of her hair and joined Chris. Chris turned when she entered the kitchen, and said, "Good morning, sleepy head." Kelly saw him smile.

"What?" she said in response.

"What, what?" Chris asked in return.

"You've got this goofy... but sweet smile on your face. That's what."

"Yes. You know why, my love?"

Kelly laughed, "No. That's why I asked."

"Kelly, it's time."

"It's time for what?" Kelly asked. "Quit being so mysterious."

"I know the last several months have been draining on both of us. We've coped. But, it's time the recent past be put away."

"Hmm," Kelly said. "I don't disagree. What do you have in mind?"

Chris went over to her and took her into his arms. She looked up at him giving him a puzzled look. She was about to say something, but Chris put his finger on her lips.

"Will you marry me?" he asked.

Kelly drew back, "What?"

Chris again put his finger on her lips, and said, "It's time Kelly. I don't want to be without you and I think you feel the same. I've been thinking about us for a long time. Where would we be going? I had to ask myself about whether I could make such a commitment again. Then all hell broke loose around us that didn't end until a few months ago. Since then, I've been able to think about the future. Our future. And I want that future to be as husband and wife."

"Wow! Good morning to you too!" Kelly managed to respond.

"Will you?" Chris asked.

Kelly turned away from him for a moment and then turned back.

"You're sure of this Chris?"

"Yes. More than sure."

"Then my answer is, 'yes.'"

"Great!" And Chris put her into a bear hug and kissed her.

Releasing her, he said, "Here's what we'll do. We'll go off somewhere after the ceremony. Have a real honeymoon. When we come back we can restart our lives and work as man and wife."

Six months' later, Chris' lawsuit over the interpretation continued pending before the court. But, as a result of the suit, Chris decided there were other issues with broad implications for the public's interests arising from other provisions of the Constitution. When tax laws are passed that decidedly provide windfalls to the wealthy while increasing the burden on other taxpayers, is there a question raised under the Equal Protection clause? When political candidates appeal to the religious beliefs of voter blocks is there a violation of the First Amendment's requirement for the separation of church and state? When members of Congress encourage direct disobedience to federal environmental regulations; refuse to act on Presidential nominees; enact meaningful gun control laws, have they violated their oaths of office?

Then another issue hit closer to home. A decision by the state Supreme Court to not only abolish capital punishment, but to apply its ruling retroactively commuting the death penalty for murderers convicted years earlier and awaiting their fates on death row. The decision implicated the Eighth Amendment's ban on cruel and unusual punishment. When announced, the decision not only stirred Chris' interest in its public interest ramifications, but Kelly's professional concern over the impact such a change would have on the survivors of the victims of those that had been sentenced to death.

They decided that their concerns could be aired by posting their comments and insights on their respective web pages. The response to Dr. Young's posting was almost immediate.

CHAPTER 3
SURVIVOR

The call came into Kelly's cell phone. She had not yet fully resumed her practice and hadn't reopened an office. She believed that by using her web site to post her comments and general advice, it would allow her to ease back into her practice on her own terms and in her own time. She could screen calls she received and up until now, she would advise that she had not yet decided to reopen her practice and provide references to other grief counselors. This time when she answered and listened, her response would be different.

"Hello."

"Is this Dr. Young?"

"Yes. Can I ask why you called?" Omit?

"I found your web site. I've been reading your postings. I think you may be able to help me."

"I see. But I haven't reopened my practice. I can give you some references if you like."

"No doctor, I think I need to speak with, meet with you. I just ask that you hear me out."

The tone of the caller's voice evoked sympathy Kelly could not ignore.

"I won't make any promises, Mr..., Mr...

"It's Jed Summers.

"Mr. Summers. I'll listen. No promises. Go ahead. Just be as brief as possible."

"Thank you, doctor. My wife and young daughter were murdered. Worse than murdered."

"I am sorry. Was this recent?"

"No. it was five years ago. But...but it seems like ..."

"I understand Mr. Summers. Please continue if you can."

"The murderer was tried and convicted and sentenced to death. At the time, his sentence provided a small sense of justice. But as time passed the horror of his crimes started to seep back into my consciousness. I tried to ignore them, change whatever I was doing to distract myself – tried to stop re-living the horror."

"You've had no success at all as a result of your attempts?" Kelly asked.

"I have had some. As more time passes, I have improved. But I still have problems."

"I understand Mr. Summers. It takes time to overcome tragic experiences. The amount of time varies depending on the individual and what he or she must deal with. But you seem to be making progress [said you were]. Has something changed?"

"Yes. It's why I called you."

"I see. What has changed?"

"Perhaps you have seen the newspaper reports about the court's decision overturning the death penalty."

"Yes. I saw some."

"Well you know then that the penalty was commuted not only for the person whose case was on appeal, but the penalties were commuted for all those whom were given the death penalty for their crimes."

"And?"

"One of those whose sentence was commuted was the one who violated and murdered my wife and daughter."

"I see. Mr. Summers. I am sorry. But how do you think I can help? There are other highly qualified counselors and I could give you their names."

"Doctor. I've done my research not only on you, but Chris Knight. I understand he is an attorney and you have worked together before."

"That's right. But I need to tell you we are married now."

"Oh… Con…Congratulations!"

"Thanks. But…"

"It makes no difference doctor. I may have need of his services as well."

Kelly didn't like the sound of this, but said, "I see. Are you in some kind of trouble with the authorities?"

"No. No I am not. But that's my problem. I'm afraid that may change. It's why I looked you up and called."

"I see. What's you address? I will think this over. I will write you of my decision promptly, that much I can assure you. I cannot assure you I will take you as a patient. And even if I did, if you need an attorney to advise you now or in the future, you would have to make arrangements directly with my husband or whomever you might chose to represent you. Do you agree with these terms?"

"I do."

After Kelly took down Summers' address, she hung up and went to talk with Chris.

CHAPTER 4
PAYBACK

It was three am. The rain fell softly… steadily. The leaden sky hid the moon. A figure moved slowly… quietly… through the blackness… unseen… making no sound.

The figure approached the patio door at the rear of the stately townhouse in the upscale community know as Crest Point. The junction box was on the wall just to the right of the door. A small "snapping" sound and the padlock was removed. No sound was made when the main electrical circuit was cut throwing the house into total darkness but for the small pen light shown on the lock of the patio door. A few expert "picks" and the door slid open. The figure entered silently and proceeded upstairs to the master bedroom.

Just outside the door, the figure stopped and listened. The only sound was the soft breathing coming from the large bed to the right of the windows. The black cloaked figure removed the Glock from his pocket, twisted the silencer in place and advanced until standing over the recumbent figure of the Chief Justice of the state Supreme Court. With one gloved hand he seized the throat of the victim and with the other jammed the barrel of a gun into his mouth.

"Lay still. Move and you die." Releasing the man's throat, he flashed the pen light into the terrified eyes of his victim. All the Justice could see was the outline of a hulking black figure looming over him. His fright and panic caused him to soil himself.

With the barrel of the gun in his mouth, the figure said, quietly, "This is payback." With that he fired once. Thwat was the only sound. The victim's body tensed. Then it relaxed. The Justice lay motionless.

The figure pocketed the weapon and took out a card and placed it on the dead man's chest, turned and left.

The morning was gray and raining when Sheldon Morris, law clerk to the Chief Justice of the Supreme Court, arrived at his usual early time. It was the Monday following the Court's decision a week earlier to declare the death penalty unconstitutional, commuting the sentences of those on the state's death row. The decision created the expected reactions of the media and the public. Despite the uproar that decision caused, Morris knew the Chief Justice had at least two more important decisions to address this coming week. He expected therefore that the Chief Justice would arrive promptly at 8 AM as he always did. When it was half pass eight, Morris called the cell phone of the Chief Justice. Only he and a few equally close confidants knew his number.

There was no answer. Morris was surprised but not unduly concerned and left a message. When 9 AM came and went without a return call or the arrival of the Chief Justice, Morris called the Court's security office and asked them to go to the Chief Justice's home to check on his whereabouts. A little more than an hour later, Officer Gaines called Morris and said no one had answered the door and the Chief Justice's car was still in the garage. Morris said, "You have to get into the house. I'll take the blame for it. But you have to get in there. This is very worrisome."

That afternoon, the local news channels hyped their own versions of "Breaking News."

This just in. Court security officers found Chief Justice Bertram Baker in his bed this morning. He had been shot. Police have been searching the house and surrounding area but have issued no statements about what may have happened. Justice Baker most recently made news when the Court declared the death penalty unconstitutional and thereby commuting the sentences of those waiting on death row to life imprisonment without parole. As soon as we know more, we will bring the information to you. This is Bert Keene, Channel 10.

At the eleven o'clock news, Bud Vincent, Channel 10's anchor reported:

The police have released some new facts about what their investigation uncovered about Justice Baker, found shot to death in his bed this morning. This is what Police Captain Sharon Wilcox told Channel 10's Bert Keene.

When Justice Baker failed to show at court up this morning as scheduled, and failed to respond to calls from his law clerk, Court Security personnel were dispatched to Justice Baker's residence in Crest Point. They arrived around 10:30 AM. They found his car in the garage but no one answered when security personnel attempted to rouse someone in the house. When this was reported to Sheldon Morris, Justice Baker's law clerk, they were told to gain entry and call the police. When we received their call, we dispatched a team who arrived at about 11 AM.

By that time, court security personnel had gained access through a patio door in the rear of the house that had apparently been pried open. Their search led them to Justice Baker's bedroom where they found the Justice lying on his back in his bed. He had been shot once in his face. Police declined comment on whether the shooting had the characteristics of an execution style murder. Captain Wilcox did reveal they had found a small card, the size of a business card on the floor next to the bed where they found the Justice. He refused to say what, if anything was on the card.

Public Defender, Fleming Richards, didn't graduate from a prestigious law school. Even then his class ranking was mid-level. He had to take the bar twice before he passed. He had no choice but to hang out his shingle as a lone practitioner. While he built something of a practice, his income was anything but steady. He applied for and was accepted as a public defender. At least he would have a steady, more predictable income. So, up until now, he labored in obscurity. Defending those who could not afford counsel. Those "clients" who were poor, mentally challenged, uneducated, jobless, homeless, but, who wittingly or not, got caught up in the criminal justice system.

He had one passion on which he allowed himself to spend more than a prudent amount of his income. African art and artifacts. The art work, small sculptures, carvings, various tools, vases, cooking implements made all the solitary hours he had to spend in his office more bearable.

He had almost saved for the cost of a trip to Africa, but he hadn't yet decided exactly where he wanted to visit. It was a vast continent and the diversity of its peoples, mores and environments made it a difficult choice.

But now, unexpectedly, since his 15 minutes of fame had arrived, he could do some serious planning. Having been appointed to defend the accused in a murder case that he not only lost, but against whom the jury returned the death penalty, his success on appeal garnered the spotlight. The fact that his appeal not only won a reversal of the death penalty for his client, but resulted in a precedent setting legal milestone made him the darling of both the local and the national media as well. He was also recognized by various anti-capital punishment organizations. He was street smart enough however to know that the chances his current fame would last were very iffy. Little did he think that a far worse fate awaited him.

It all started, as most unexpected tragic events do. He arrived at his office. Got a cup of coffee. Each time he did, he "dreamt" of having a secretary and having her bring a steaming cup to his desk. But alas, that was not the life of a public defender. He retrieved his mail. Sat at his desk. Sipped his coffee. The usual. Various notices, bills, junk mail. Then a knock on the his door.

"UPS. Package for a F. Richards."

The delivery man entered and placed a package 36 inches high, a foot wide on the floor in front of his desk.

"Are you Mr. Richards?"

"Yes. Why?"

"We normally don't inquire, but we were told not to deliver to anyone else and to make sure we had delivered it to you."

"Well I'm your man."

"Ok. Sign here."

Richards initialed the delivery slip, was given a copy and the UPS man left.

"Now what is this I wonder," Richards thought to himself.

The phone rang before he could open the package. But he was too curious to wait, so he put his cell phone on speaker and cut the package opened. He found an envelope inside that he opened – it was a description of the contents.

This is a replica of an African Battle Shield. It is based off the Zulu Shield with the exception of the fur on the shield. Traditional Zulu shields use only cow hide but to enhance the aesthetic zebra print fur was substituted. The shield measures over 36 inches from the "Mgobo" (the center pole), and is wrapped with feathers. The shield proper is made of wood, 24 inches high and 13 inches wide. The "Assegai" or spear is 3 feet long with a 4 inch blade. The ball club, the "Knob-Kerrie," is also three feet in length. For display, the shield is self-standing or can be hung from a wall.

Richards said, "Let me call you back. Something came up. I'll get back to you in a bit."

With that he ended the call and started to unwrap the shield. When he pulled the shield from its wrappings, he gasped in his excitement, inhaling what he assumed was dust from the protective covering but it was enough to make him cough. He took a sip of water then raised the shield to admire it, rubbing his hand over the soft black and white fur. He looked around for a place to put it. At first he stood it in a corner of the office away from his desk. But that was not a place prominent enough for such a rare artifact. He held it up against the walls on either side of the doorway. But those spaces were unsatisfactory as well. Then he turned and looked at the wall behind his desk where he hung his diploma and state bar license.

"That's it," he thought to himself. "This goes right behind my desk. I'll see it each time I enter the office and so will everyone else. I can always swivel around and admire it whenever I want. What a great surprise."

Then he caught himself and turned back to the wrapping and looked for a card or letter that would identify who had sent this. Rummaging around, he found an envelope and tore it opened. Again, some dust or powder floated up to his face and he coughed again. He pulled the card out and was puzzled. The card read – "Congratulations. You have saved not one but many from the fate they earned. May you not live to regret it. Then there was a series of letters, jumbled and incomprehensible - GHDWKZLOOEHF-HUWDLQDQGDJRQLXLQJ.

Fleming mused to himself, "A practical joke? A serial number perhaps. There are so many numbers now with the Internet and all."

He put the card in his desk drawer. He took the shield and arranged the spear and club the way they would be assembled on his wall behind his desk – stood back and admired his prize. Then he picked up the shield and held it with his left hand and slapped it with his right, several times to test its ability to withstand attacks. A small cloud of dust sprayed into is face making him cough and gasp.

CHAPTER 5
PTSD

After talking it over, Kelly and Chris decided to meet with Jed Summers. Kelly would speak with him first. Then if it appeared he needed to speak to an attorney, Chris would meet with him later at his office. Summers arrived at their apartment at noon. Kelly answered the door.

"Mr. Summers?"

"Yes. Doctor Young...er Knight?"

"Professionally, it's still Doctor Young. Come in."

Summers entered.

"We can talk in my office, just to your right."

"Thank you."

Summers entered the room and took a seat on the couch in front of Kelly's desk. Kelly sat behind her desk and took a moment to view his person and body language. He was nervous and seemed uncertain.

"Mr. Summers, it would be best if you could relax. There's nothing here to be nervous about."

"I know. I asked for the meeting... your help. It's just that ... that..."

"Take you time. Would you like something to drink, coffee, tea, water?"

"Yes, some water. Thank you."

"I'll be right back."

Kelly went to the kitchen and brought back a bottle of Evian and a glass.

"Thanks. The bottle is fine," Summers said.

"Now. Would you like to start?"

"Yes. Okay. As I told you over the phone when we first spoke, the recent court decision resurrected emotions the passage of time had lessened, but not erased. Then the decision came down and the anger, frustration, hatred started coming back. I didn't sleep well. I don't sleep well. I have night-mares. The images… images of my… my…"

"I know. You don't have to say, Mr. Summers."

"Those are horrible of course. But there are new ones and they fright-en me."

"What are those, Mr. Summers?"

"I see the TV news shots of the Supreme Court. Then I see the pho-tos of the judges. When I see the photo of the Chief Justice, I approach him. He looks at me with fear in his eyes. He throws his hand up in front of himself. Then I wake up in a cold sweat. I get up. Afraid to go back to sleep. I walk around the house in the dark and the quiet. I still see his face. It doesn't go away even though I'm awake. Well, not really awake or not fully so. It's more like I'm in a daze. Most recently, I've wandered into the kitchen. I go to the drawer with the kitchen knives and I pull out a butch-er knife. I hold it. My grip tightens. I feel an urge to thrust it. Then, I seem to awake. I drop the knife and when it clatters to the floor, I do awake. But I'm shaking."

"How long has this been going on, Mr. Summers?"

"It started about a week after the decision was announced."

"Does this happen every night?"

"No. There are nights when I have no dreams at all. Most of these are when I drink."

"Did you always take a drink before you retired before?"

"My…my wife and I usually drank wine with dinner. And I might have a night cap. But now when I drink, I drink a lot. I know I'm trying to anes-thetize myself to avoid having these dreams. Since it works, I keep doing it, but not every night. And when I don't, the nightmares return."

"I see. Your problem is serious. On the other hand, it is not unique."

"How so?"

"Most of us are aware of PTSD, have heard of it, but mostly in con-nection with military veterans returning from combat. The most recent ver-sion of the DSM-5 however recognizes the stress of individuals exposed to aversive details of traumatic events such as particularly violent or accidental experiences of family members."

"I'm sorry, doctor, DSM-5?"

"It stands for Diagnostic and Statistical Manual of Mental Disorders. It's the newest release in this area by the American Psychiatric Association."

"Mental disorders?"

"Don't be concerned. It doesn't mean what you might think. The kind of trauma experienced from particularly violent experiences of family members, the kind you had can and does shatter a person's world. I hardly need to tell you that. But the results for example are that things that were once safe can become dangerous and everyday life difficult to manage. You exhibit some of the common behavioral symptoms."

"Meaning?"

"Re-experiencing the trauma through flashbacks or nightmares. Negative cognitions and moods such as a distorted sense of blame. Arousal meaning sleep disturbances. Your problems suggest that from the recent court decision you are re-experiencing the loss of your family – a loss that was unfortunately more traumatic than most losses. I hope you see that while the difficulty is referred to within the professional literature as mental disorder, it doesn't have the connotation the public associates with such words."

"You're telling me I'm not crazy?"

"Not my words, but if it helps you understand that your condition has a cause, a terrible cause, it is not because there's something wrong with you. Just the opposite. Given the trauma you experienced, your reaction could be described as normal."

Summers sat there for a moment and looked away.

"Of course there are treatments for my condition doctor?"

"Yes. First you need someone with clinical expertise and experience working with those who have PTSD. I have those qualifications. Such qualifications are used in a treatment program, one that can be intensive such as a four times weekly psychodynamic psychotherapy. There are also medications that can be prescribed."

"Then you can help me?"

"I could, but the best course may well be to enter into a therapeutic community program. That means there would be others with PTSD symptoms you would meet with under the supervision of a psychotherapist with experience in recognizing the specific treatment dilemmas involved in working with someone with PTSD."

"Do I have to join such a group?"

"The benefits are that you will increase your opportunities to learn about yourself being in a therapeutic community. There you can learn how others affect you and how you affect others. This should result in being able to shed unproductive roles."

"I'm not sure I fully understand. I mean I understand that my PTSD would result from the loss of my family and how that happened. And I think I understand that this court decision has led to my re-experiencing that trauma. I guess my question is, why do I have these nightmares that include the judge who was responsible for the decision."

"Well, that's a question best left to be explored in your therapy sessions. But, your nighttime wanderings, your images of the judge and your episode with the knife in your kitchen could be an extension of your reactions to the original trauma. In other words, the decision and those responsible for it have exposed you to new aversive details of the original traumatic events. You seem to have made progress in putting your world back together only to have it shattered once again. It's logical that you would focus on this new cause – the decision and the judge or judges who rendered it."

"I understand things better now. But it leads me to another concern. In my condition, am I likely to seek revenge? I mean how long would these therapeutic sessions you spoke of take? I assume the time frame is indefinite, but would be lengthy. What if I keep having the episodes and one day, night, they push me over the edge?"

"I've only just met you, but I can tell you this. Most of us are not prone to violence, even when severely traumatized. What I'm saying is I am not getting an impression that you would act out your nightmares. But what I'm also saying is that the sooner you begin therapy, the better."

"I see. I'll think about this. Can I get back to you?"

"Of course. But again, the sooner the better."

Summers rose, shook Kelly's hand and left.

Chris walked in after Summers had left and asked how things went. Kelly said, "The man has been through hell. And this court decision has dragged him back into it. He has to deal with his PTSD all over but with new torments. He's going to struggle with that. And his new burden is whether his disorder might so overtake him that he'll do something awful."

"Like what do you think?" asked Chris.

"Well, when he first called, he said he wanted to know if you were available to represent him. That tells me, he is concerned he may seek revenge and if so would need a defense attorney."

"Well, let's hope that doesn't happen," Chris said.

"Agreed."

CHAPTER 6
THE DOYLE FACTOR

Captain Wilcox was taking a lot of heat to get a quick arrest for the murder of Chief Justice Baker's murder. The homicide division's bullpen was more than usually crowded because Wilcox gathered all the divisions' detectives on duty.

"I know all of you are working other cases. But you know that the murder of Justice Baker is bringing a lot of heat to get the murderer – if not today, then tomorrow."

The detectives looked at each other and grinned. They had all been down this road before. It wasn't their first time working a high profile case. But they had to admit, this one was a doozy. None could remember a judge being murdered, and certainly not in his own bed. Execution style.

"Gaines, you were the first on the scene at the Justice's house and you found the body. Summarize what you found."

"Justice Baker as you all know was in his bed. I found him, what was left of him on his back, soft tissue, bone, blood scattered behind and to his sides. There was no evidence of a struggle or any resistance. Next to the bed was a night table with a book he was reading. He was alone in the house. His wife died two years ago. The bullet passed through his head. His front teeth were chipped, meaning the killer shoved the gun in his mouth. We recovered the bullet buried in the mattress. It was from the new Glock 42. It's the smallest Glock made so it could accommodate conceal carry or pocket carry. Thirty-eight caliber. That's about it. No finger prints. We do know the patio door was jimmied open, but again no prints. The patio's concrete so no foot prints. It connects to the driveway. The killer must have come in that way and left that way because we found no footprints in the yard. That's about it."

"Gaines! There was another item I recall," said Wilcox.

"Oh, yes ma'am. I forgot. We did find a card, size of a credit card or business card on the floor next to the bed. It had blood on it and some letters that don't spell anything – at least not in English."

"Do you have the card with you? Can you read the letters?" asked Detective Edwards.

"The card's in the evidence room. But I copied the letters on some papers. I'll pass them out now. Anybody get an idea what they might mean, let me or the Captain know."

The letters Gaines had copied read – BRYPDHHHDEEGGIFLWL-RQISUZLLFLXKLWLVTCBFCFN.

"Could be some kind of code," suggested Officer Whitman.

"We thought of that. Actually thought we had it solved using Julius Caesar's Cipher, but that hasn't worked. At least not yet. Our code crackers are still working on it. Pretty sure they'll solve the puzzle."

Detective Edwards spoke again. "Have we thought about why this Justice was murdered?"

Wilcox, asked, "What's your point Detective?"

"When judges, prosecutors, or cops are murdered, the logical place to start looking is for the perps they sentenced, prosecuted or arrested. Have we started on that search?" Edwards responded.

"We haven't as it happens," Wilcox admitted. "But going down that path doesn't seem promising. Justice Baker was appointed to the State Supreme Court over fifteen years ago. He hasn't presided over a criminal trial in nearly twenty years. Doesn't seem likely that someone held a grudge that long."

"Maybe not," Gaines offered. "But couldn't that be because the perp just got out of prison?"

"We'll run the records. Shouldn't take that long and it would cross off a line of inquiry if nothing turns up."

"Captain?" Edwards again.

"Yes, Dan. What?"

"Well, Lou's idea about someone the Justice may have sentenced long ago, prompted another theory somewhat along those lines."

"Okay. Let's hear it," Wilcox questioned.

"What if we focus on the recent past? That is, the recent decisions that came down from the Supreme Court that are controversial. Ones that one group or another have protested."

"You mean like those protesting over abortion or immigration?" Officer Whitman asked.

"Yes. Of course those cases are before the U.S. Supreme Court. What recent cases have been controversial that Justice Baker played some part in?" Edwards responded.

"That's easy. Sort of," Captain Wilcox said.

"How so, Captain?" Edwards wanted to know.

"The most controversial decision, or at least the one that got headlines and national attention as well, was Justice Baker's, the Court's decision, holding the death penalty was unconstitutional. But, that decision commuted the execution of not only the defendant before the court on appeal, but the others sitting on death row. Seems to me none of those would want Justice Baker killed. Besides, they are all in prison. The only way they could be involved would be to have help from the outside. And why would their families, cronies, or anybody, however associated with them, want to kill the Justice for, in effect saving their lives?"

"You're absolutely right, Captain. What you just pointed out suggests we might be looking in the wrong direction insofar as who was affected by the Court's decision."

"You mean the victims of these felons, Dan?"

"Yes, Captain. Like Sherlock said, or was it Arthur Conan Doyle himself who advised, 'Once you eliminate the impossible, whatever remains, no matter how improbable, must be the truth.'"

"So your suggesting that since there is little likelihood that the murderer is someone Justice Baker sentenced some decades ago; that the death row inmates and their families and others would have little reason to murder the Justice who just commuted their death sentences; and that the most recent ground shaking decision issued by the Court that Justice Baker serves as

Chief Justice is that decision, while improbable, the likely truth is that one of the survivors of the victims of the criminals sentenced to death could be Baker's murderer?"

"Well, Captain there is a certain logic to it," Edwards commented.

"Okay. I agree," Wilcox said. Let's get to work on compiling what information and records we have on the survivors. But this has to be kept totally under wraps. If the press gets ahold of this, we'll be raked over the coals as a bunch of heartless bastards worse than the criminals convicted and sentenced to death. Edwards, this was your idea. Take Gaines and Whitman on your team and begin your investigation. I'm going to assign Trainor, Lister and Rogers to look for possible third parties who wanted Justice Baker dead or if we have a nut cake on our hands who likes to murder high ranking government officials. That's all gentlemen. Let's get to work."

CHAPTER 7
AN AGONIZING DEATH

It [had been] was two days since Public Defender Fleming Richards had received his prize African Zulu Zebra shield and weapons. The day before, he hung it behind his desk as he had planned. He was well-pleased. But he was annoyed at his shortness of breath. It started the day he hung his prize, but was getting worse. At the worst times, he felt as if his head were being held underwater, allowed to bob up, and then pushed under again. Now, two days later, his joints ached and seemed on fire. He could not keep his breakfast down. He assumed he had caught a flu bug and knew he should see a doctor.

But it was a bad time to be away. The Supreme Court had rejected the prosecutions' motions to reconsider its decision to eliminate the state's death penalty, but the fate of capital punishment in the State technically remained unsettled. The prosecution filed a motion in another case to make the arguments they would have made if the court had granted the reconsideration motion. And Richards knew it would be highly unusual and surprising for the court to reverse itself on such an important issue in a short period of time. Now, the bogey factor of the murder of Justice Baker greatly changed an already highly charged atmosphere. Moreover, with Baker's death, the makeup of the court changed. Justice Baker who led the 4-3 majority to abolish the death penalty was gone and his replacement had yet to be seated.

Having become a noted attorney after all the years slaving in obscurity, becoming the "darling of the press" for more than the standard fifteen minutes of fame, Richards cursed his aches and pains, but decided he'd endure and make sure he remained center stage. He cleared his throat and shook his head and took a deep breath. His phone rang. He answered. He had a visitor.

"Who is it and what does he want? I'm busy now."

The voice of the shared receptionist answered, "He said his name is Charles Leighton. He says he was in the neighborhood and though he'd stop by. Said something about a package he sent to you a few days ago and wanted to see if you received it."

"Oh, alright. Just a minute. I'll let him in, in a minute. Just want to clear my desk of some papers. Ask him to take a seat."

"Right," said the receptionist and hung up.

Richards shoved some papers about the case in his middle desk drawer, straightened his tie, walked to the door, opened it and welcomed Mr. Charles Leighton.

"Come in Mr. Leighton. Pleased to meet you. I don't believe we have met before."

"No Mr. Richards we have not."

"What can I do for you? You told the receptionist something about a package?"

"Yes. Yes, I did. And I see you did receive it," Leighton said as he motioned to the Zebra shield behind Richards' desk. "You! You sent that to me. Thank you. But why? We haven't met before."

"I appreciate your recent work. Getting the death penalty overturned. Stellar result."

"Well, thanks. But how did you know …"

"About your love of African art and artifacts? There are few things one cannot find out online these days. It didn't take long to learn of your passion for such things."

"I see," Richards said as he took a deep breath and sat down behind his desk. He hacked into some tissues and couldn't avoid spitting.

"I'm sorry …"

"You're not feeling well Mr. Richards?" Leighton asked.

"No. I apologize … I"

"No need to Mr. Richards. I found out what I came for. I'll be leaving now. Don't get up. I'll see myself out. Take care Mr. Richards. But alas, it's clear it's already too late. Goodbye."

"What… wait, stop!"

But he couldn't get his breath and as he tried to rise to go to his door, he spit up worse than before. He dialed the receptionist, "Come... come here, please!"

Before she could answer she heard a sound like someone falling. She said into the phone, "Mr. Richards, Mr. Richards, are you okay?"

When there was no answer, she hurried to his door and went in. She gasped and ran back to her desk and dialed 911.

The EMT arrived. They found Richards on the floor behind his desk. His face had ballooned beyond normal recognition. When they tried to maneuver him to get him on the gantry, he cried in pain. The EMT had him at the emergency room at Mercy Hospital twenty minutes after they arrived on the scene. Unfortunately, the doctor on duty was still in his internship. He had little idea what was causing the symptoms of the man that had just been wheeled in. He guessed sepsis and ordered blood and a chest X-ray. Before the X-ray could be taken, Richards had a seizure. The doctor then sedated him and then inserted a tube in his larynx to protect his airways. He was rushed to the radiology department where a spinal tap was taken under fluoroscopy. All of this took several hours during which Richards had not regained consciousness. By this time, Doctor Sam David, the head of Emergency Medicine had arrived. He was told Richards's spinal fluid had been taken to the lab and went there immediately.

Doctor David hurried to the lab. Put the spinal fluid under the microscope.

"Doctor Swift, you admitted the patient?"

"Yes, Doctor."

"Okay. This is unusual. I see a bacillus in his spinal fluid. When you think of all the bacilli that can cause somebody to be ill, there are probably three or four. Unfortunately, anthrax is one of them. If this is anthrax, we may be too late. Or, more accurately, our patient is too late."

"I'm not sure I'm following doctor," Swift questioned.

"If this is anthrax. I should say, if this is inhaled anthrax, the critical necessity is to get treatment as soon as possible. Survival depends on getting the appropriate antibiotics before the bacteria [releases] have released so much toxin that the body cannot recover. If not treated in time, almost all victims suffer a tortured death. One organ after another is decimated — the lungs, the kidneys, the heart — until life is literally sucked away."

Richards died the following morning. Given the circumstances, his death was reported to the police, the Public Defender's Office and the Center for Disease Control. The report to the police department was forwarded to Detective Edwards. When he received it, he contacted the CDC to inquire about the anthrax poisoning.

"Hello, this is Detective Mark Edwards with the state police homicide division. I need to speak with your department that knows about anthrax poisoning."

"Please hold, I will see if someone in the department is in today."

A few minutes later, Edwards was put through.

"Hello. This is doctor Sam David. You/re Detective Edwards I've been told."

"Yes that's correct doctor. Am I correct that you are familiar with anthrax poisoning?"

"Yes, that's correct. What is your interest detective?"

"We've just received a report that a person died yesterday morning from being infected with anthrax. Male, African-American, age 45. According to the report we received, he was admitted to the emergency room of Mercy Hospital here at about four p.m. two days ago. That means he died not long after he was admitted. An autopsy is being performed, but in all likelihood, the anthrax was inhaled."

"I see. That would explain the short period between the time the deceased was admitted to the hospital and his death," Doctor David informed Edwards.

"Can you elaborate on that, doctor?"

"If the anthrax was inhaled it is fatal 80 to 90 percent of the time if not treated as soon as the first symptoms appear. If not treated in time, death can occur within twenty-four to thirty-six hours. It seems that is what is likely to be the case here given the time frames you've mentioned."

"How would someone inhale anthrax? Would they know they were doing so?"

"Most doubtful, if not impossible. The anthrax germs are odorless, tasteless and lethal quantities can be so tiny they can't be seen. Every three seconds or so, we inhale and exhale about a pint of air. When inhaling, the air commonly carries with it floating incidentals – dust, bacteria and other microscopic particles. A particle larger than 5 microns, a micron is one millionth of a meter, would be unlikely to be blocked and would not reach deep into the lungs by the respiratory tract's mucus and filtration hairs. An anthrax spore may be one micron wide and two or three microns long, just the right size to reach deep into the respiratory pathway."

"Could someone use these spores if they wanted to kill someone?"

"Yes and no, detective."

"Can you explain that answer?"

"Short version is that anthrax spores have been placed in the mail and some of those who received the posts did inhale and died. In such an instance, the anthrax was used as a murder weapon. On the other hand, some died from inhaling anthrax accidentally."

"Can you give some specifics about each of these?"

"Yes. You may remember the anthrax scare in 2001. It is known as Amerithrax, the case name given it by the FBI. It occurred over the course of several weeks beginning on September 18, 2001, one week after the September 11 attacks. Letters containing anthrax spores were mailed to several news media offices and the offices of two Democratic U.S. Senators. In this case, five people died and 17 others were infected. Anthrax here was the murder weapon."

"And a case in which anthrax wasn't intended to murder anyone?"

"There are a couple and they show the difference. One woman among a group was attending a drumming session – drums being played. She had gastrointestinal anthrax. Spores were found on two of the African drums and an electrical outlet in the room. The theory was that she swallowed the spores that were aerosolized, made airborne, by the drumming. The anthrax detected on the drums was a naturally occurring strain. That is, animals that ingest contaminated soil can pass the disease to people who handle their hides. The drums at this session were from animal hides. Then two people in 2007 were treated for cutaneous anthrax, spores reaching a cut or wound, traced to animal hides. Again used to make African drums. The year before a drum maker in New York contracted inhalation anthrax. He was lucky. He survived."

"In the case we are investigating, the medical report concludes the anthrax was inhaled. But, the victim could also have swallowed some spores if they have been released by some action?"

"Yes, but given the shortness of time between contracting the infection and death, it points more to inhaling than digesting."

"Thanks, doctor. I think that's all for now."

"Did what I tell you persuade you whether the death was accidental or not?"

"Too soon to tell. But with what you did tell me, we have a much better chance of making that determination. Goodbye!"

Edwards called Gaines and Whitman and told them to join him in Captain Wilcox's office. Ten minutes later the three detectives met in her office.

"Something new Mark?"

"Yes."

"Is it about Justice Baker's murder?"

"Yes."

"Let's have it, then."

"This may be coincidence. But that's hard to swallow."

"What?" Wilcox asked.

"We got this report about the death of the public defender that won the appeal that overturned the death penalty, Fleming Richards. He died at hospital after being taken there by the EMT boys after collapsing in his office. He was in very bad shape when he arrived and was dead within twenty-four hours. It was diagnosed as anthrax poisoning. It appears he inhaled enough spores to kill him. Which they did."

"I'm not seeing an immediate connection to the Baker murder," Whitman observed.

"Let me start this way," Edwards said. "There's a landmark decision overturning the death penalty. The Chief Justice of the Court rendering the decision is murdered execution style. A few weeks later, the public defender attorney who was successful in making the appeal for his client dies of poisoning. Two major players linked to a major legal case are dead. One we know was murdered. The other, in my opinion, was also murdered."

"Coincidence? I don't mean the murders. I mean the deaths. The Justice was shot in his bed. The attorney was poisoned in his office, but there's nothing to indicate he was poisoned by another. Certainly the deaths of two of the principals in a short time is cause for question. But if it's the same murderer, why not just shoot the attorney too? It's a lot more certain than using anthrax. My take is it could as easily be a coincidence. Totally unrelated?" asked Whitman.

"I agree in general, Lou. But it bears a hard look. The relationship of the two victims is too bizarre to ignore. What we need to do is search Richards office and home and talk with his receptionist and any others he was in contact with. What we're looking for is anything that might be infected with anthrax spores, someone that knows about anthrax, how to use it, how lethal it is."

Wilcox intervened. "I see the logic in your approach Mark. But even assuming there's probable cause to suspect Richards was murdered, it doesn't point to a possible suspect or suspects. It doesn't increase the chances that some survivor of the victims of those on death row is the murderer. Would you agree?"

"Yes. But it only means we are either looking for two murderers whose killings are unrelated happenstance. Or, we have one murderer seeking revenge for overturning the death penalty. If the latter, then the other question is whether there are other targets out there, targets somehow connected to that decision."

"You suggesting a serial killer?" Gaines asked.

"I'm not suggesting anything. That comes after we do our investigating into Richards death," Edwards responded.

"Fair enough," Wilcox said. "Get to work."

CHAPTER 8
PYRRIC VICTORY

The organization of Concerned Humanitarians Against State Executions, CHASE, called a special meeting of its Board of Directors to determine how best to capitalize on the Supreme Court's decision to abolish the death penalty. It was a goal many of its members often despaired of achieving. But that goal had been achieved in yet another state. But the battle wasn't completely over. It was recognized that the state legislature could overturn the decision. A worse, and even more immediate concern however, was the murder of Chief Justice Baker who wrote the majority opinion. But it was a narrow majority, only 4-3. A new justice would be appointed and there was no certainty that Justice Baker's replacement would agree with the reasoning and rulings of the decision. Strong dissents had been written and there was no certainty whether a majority of the public itself agreed with the decision.

Chairwoman of the Board, Caitlin Madison, had a prepared agenda. When all the Board members had arrived and taken their seats, she opened the meeting.

"We should all be gratified by the Supreme Court's landmark decision abolishing the death penalty in this state. Unfortunately, the chief author of that decision has been struck down in the most disturbing manner. Murdered. His death is incomprehensible and regrettable on many levels."

"Caitlin, do you have any details about Justice Baker's murder?" Board Member Ed Perry asked.

"No. Not really. I know only what I've read in the papers. Has anyone else been told or heard anything not publicly reported?" Madison asked as she scanned over the seated members.

No one responded. A few shook their heads.

"Okay. I didn't think so. The reports in the press do raise the question whether the Justice's murder was retaliation for the decision. But it's pure speculation. The police have indicated that there are no facts at this time to suggest a connection. They've stated that they are investigating this with no preconceived notions."

"What exactly does that mean, Caitlin?" asked Member Anna Vernon.

"My guess, it means the police have nothing to link the murder to the court's decision or Justice Baker's role in making it. They don't want to make such an assumption because it could result in the investigation starting down false paths. So, as of now, the murder is viewed as a random act. But I think that is not for public consumption."

"What's that mean?" asked Todd Webb.

"To me, it suggests that the police want the killer, if he murdered the Justice because of the decision, to believe they are not following that line of inquiry. Create a false sense of security until they can get further into the investigation. And, as I alluded to, they don't want to jump to any conclusions that would take them off on a wild goose chase."

"Well, you may be right Caitlin. But I've come across some news that may be relevant in defining the focus of the investigation," Perry spoke up.

"What's that Ed?"

"The Public Defender lawyer, you know, Fleming Richards, the counsel who won the appeal overturning the death penalty? He died."

"What? When?" came as a chorus of the Board.

"Don't know the details. I just heard he was rushed to the hospital with some kind of terrible affliction and died there. Rather quickly, I understand."

There was silence as the Board members looked one to the other.

Anna Vernon was the first to break the silence.

"I don't want to be an alarmist. But I don't like this at all."

"What are talking about Anna?" Todd Webb asked.

"We live in a society rampant with gun violence. We live in a society of little to no tolerance for any view that Mr. This or Mrs. That doesn't agree with. Too often, that lack of tolerance leads to violence. Abortion clinics. Resentment against law enforcement."

"Your point, Anna?" asked Caitlin.

"Assume for the sake of argument that the murder of Justice Baker and the yet to be explained death of Mr. Richards are connected. I mean the motive was to eliminate, get revenge against, the principals responsible for overturning the death penalty in this state. That, and all the attacks on abortion clinics, the nurses and doctors involved, makes this organization and its leaders, us, possible targets for the killer who murdered Justice Baker. If it is discovered that the death of Richards was not due to accident but was deliberate, was caused by some unknown source, then is it paranoid to think that this organization and its leaders, us, may become or are already targets from someone who supports the death penalty and seeks vengeance against our efforts? Because they have succeeded?"

Again, there was silence.

Todd Webb spoke first. "Anna, I can't totally discount your concerns. But, I for one don't want to start looking over my shoulder every day."

At this point, Board Member Oscar Royce, spoke.

"Ladies and gentlemen, Madam Chair Person. I regret I must leave. This meeting has been most enlightening. I will say, that I do not reject Anna's concern out of hand. Still, it seems unlikely. Good evening to all." And with that Oscar Royce took his leave.

Chairwomen Madison took over.

"Members, let's bring some things together and then adjourn. First, we have had a great legal victory. Let's not lose sight of that. Second, we have had not one, but two tragedies – the murder of Justice Baker and the death from unknown causes of the lead counsel that won the appeal and the decision overturning the death penalty in this state. As an organization that opposes the death penalty, we are well aware of the positions of our opponents. Going forward, we must be concerned that the victory that has been won is not overturned by the legislature either by writing a new law, or more realistically, appointing a replacement for Justice Baker that does not agree with the abolition of the death penalty."

"In addition, we have to recognize that in today's society, extremist views can have deadly results. While I don't for a moment believe that anyone on this Board, the organization or its members are in any real danger, Anna's concerns cannot be ignored. They also cannot affect our daily obligations and activities. Rather, we are to keep such concerns in the back of our minds and remain alert."

"What will help here is following the police's investigation. If that turns out that Justice Baker's murder was a tragic random act or some form of revenge for some actions he took as a judge and not related to his decision overturning the death penalty, we can breathe a sigh of collective relief. Similarly, if the tragic death of Mr. Richards is due to factors having nothing to do with his participation in the decision, again we can breathe a sigh of relief. But until we know more about these matters, remain vigilant, but avoid being paranoid" (said with a smile as she looked over the seated members).

"Ladies and gentlemen we are adjourned."

CHAPTER 9
DOUBLE AGENT

CHASE Board member Oscar Royce left the meeting and drove to City Central Park. He left his car in the lot and walked to the Fountain of Pegasus – a winged steed hovering over the circular pool home to large koi fish of varying hues – white/red, indigo, black with white, red and yellow markings. He sat on the bench at the back of the fountain because it was the most secluded. He pulled out his cell phone, dialed. It connected after the third ring.

"I just left the Board meeting. The discussion included concerns about the court decision being overturned, the replacement for the Chief Justice, that attorney Richards' death, and questions about whether they could be connected."

"Interesting," the voice on the other end of the call said. "Why was the question raised about the two deaths being connected?"

"One of the members was concerned that if they were, could it indicate a motive for the killings."

"A motive?"

"Yes. The attacks on abortion clinics, and their doctors or nurses were brought up. One of the Board members feared that if the deaths were linked, it could mean that someone or group that favors the death penalty could be responsible for both deaths. If so, the question raised was whether CHASE or other anti-death penalty organizations and their members could be targeted."

"I see. Have you decided on your next move?"

"Not fully. But it won't take me long. Has the money been deposited as agreed?"

"Not to worry. It was wired yesterday. Anything further? I have a meeting starting in a few minutes."

"No. That's all for now. Watch the papers and TV news. The next act should establish the necessary link."

"Goodbye."

"Goodbye."

Chester Gibbons was CEO of Universal Energy Corporation. But the days of massive profits were under siege. The price of oil had fallen so low that a lot of companies were in bankruptcy or about to be. Universal Energy was holding its own – for now. But the future was far from certain. A wave of bankruptcies and closures had swept across the oil business and even many hydraulic-fracturing companies were said to be at risk. Gibbons saw the opportunity for his company to help oil-and-gas explorers drill and frack wells as many other small, privately owned companies were doing making up a flood of new entrants in the energy business. But many were drying up as oil prices dipped to record lows per barrel. At least five frackers filed for bankruptcy, stopped fracking, or shut their doors altogether. Some industry analysts believed that number may be higher, and expect many more companies to follow suit or consolidate in a merger frenzy.

Oil-field service companies that help drill and complete wells are usually massive conglomerates—such as Schlumberger Ltd. and Halliburton Co.—with operations all over the world. But they too, struggle with low oil prices and had laid off 55,000 people around the globe. They also slashed their prices, so low that it drove out smaller players.

Some smaller companies rose to the challenge and took on the Schlumbergers and Halliburtons of the world. Universal Energy was one of those. It embraced wildcatting fracking, blasting a slurry of water, sand and chemicals down a well to break apart densely packed rock to unlock the oil and natural gas trapped there. The high-intensity technique has helped push U.S. oil production to its highest level in nearly half a century.

Gibbons had his company positioned at the beginning of the drilling boom, which began in the wake of the global economic recession. When it later picked up steam there were dozens of new outfits and plenty of fracking work from Texas to North Dakota. But today, the market has gone from cutthroat to nearly nonexistent in many oil-and-gas fields. So far this year, Gibbons saw the amount of fracking work fall by 40% from a year earlier, and the price of a frack job was down 35%. Like other small publicly traded oil-field service companies, Universal Energy debt trading was at distressed levels, trading at steep discounts.

Against this dire background, Gibbons had called a meeting with Don McCallum, his General Counsel, Leon Powell, lead outside legal counsel and Russell Pederson, UE's CFO.

After they were seated in the company's Board Room, Gibbons asked, "Russell, we'll start with you. What's the bad news?"

"Not a positive way to start this meeting, but unfortunately justified," UE's CFO responded gloomily. "Our shares have fallen more than 75% in the last year. This is about the same fix other companies find themselves in, but that's no comfort. Unless something good happens as many as a third of these companies will be gone by the end of next year. In addition to the already bankrupt companies, it appears that many others are currently insolvent or close to it. Many are clinging to hopes of a quicker rebound or just to make it to the upturn."

UE's General Counsel McCallum asked, "Do you have an idea when we might see an upturn?"

"Perhaps in a year. Who really knows? No one was expecting what has happened. Predictions are therefore unreliable, particularly favorable predictions."

"Russell, can we survive for at least a year?" asked Gibbons.

"To answer that, we have to hear from Mr. Powell. However, let me preface that by saying that the quick answer is that if the lawsuit to block fracking is sustained on appeal, odds are Universal Energy will fold."

"Well, gentlemen, as I've been the bearer of a gloomy outlook on this case for some time, as you may have surmised, things have changed, dramatically changed."

"You're referring to the murder of Justice Baker?" McCallum asked.

"Yes. I find it unsettling to say this, but all our experience and nosing about convinced us that Justice Baker would have been the fourth vote delivering the majority opinion upholding the injunction against any further fracking in the state. Now that he's no longer on the bench, the least we get is a delay. With the right new justice, UE may get a longer reprieve, maybe long enough to turn things around."

"I understand the delicacy of your circumstances, Leon," Gibbons acknowledged. "Officer of the court and all – professionalism, and so forth. The hard reality however is that an impediment to this company's survival has been, how shall I say this, removed. Terribly regrettable circumstances. But there's nothing to be done about it and nothing anyone could have. Perhaps the justices should think more carefully about letting death row inmates off the hook."

"Chester, are you suggesting Judge Baker's murder was a result of overturning the death penalty?" Powell asked.

"Hell, I don't know. But it has a logic to it. How would you feel if your family had been killed, their murderer convicted and sentence to death and then have him escape the punishment he deserves? Anyway, it's none of our affair. What is our affair is using the time we have to improve the position of this company."

"I agree Chester," said CFO Pederson. "When UEC started fracking five years ago there wasn't enough pumping equipment to complete all the new wells we wanted to drill. Then we grew and flourished. Today, we're still doing other oil-field work, but most of the company's fracking equipment is idled sitting in our garages."

"That's right Russell," Gibbons said. But I saw the writing on the wall earlier last year as the rig counts started to drop steeply week after week. Our getting out of the market as oil prices plunged was the right call. I was not going to lose money and tear up our equipment. Because all along it was planned to run in the future when pricing got better. That plan was not going to work if we were shut down by the courts. Now, we have more time. Perhaps a lot more time. We start by focusing on completing wells in more conventional, easier-to-tap locations than most shale operators. There's still demand for the work we do. And I know this will sound harsh, but if one of the survivors of the victims of some heinous crime decided to revenge his loved ones for the court's decision, may God have mercy on his soul. But there's no shame in our taking advantage of the opportunity created. I don't mean to sound so callous, but the reality is, if UEC is saved, so are all the jobs UEC makes possible. Tomorrow I'll get the ball rolling around here. We're still in business."

CHAPTER 10
PRO AND CON

As can be imagined, the Supreme Court's decision resulted in much public debate – a lot of hot air, some insights, and plenty of disagreement. Given the broad controversy the decision had raised and the uncertainty over whether the decision was sustainable or would be overturned by legislation or by the Governor's appointment and confirmation by the state senate of a new justice, the state bar association arranged for a public debate over the issue. The debate would be aired on the local educational TV channel. The Governor was asked to appoint an impartial selection committee that would select those who would participate in the public debate. The Public Affairs Manager of the educational channel would serve as host.

A selection committee of three was named – the Chairman of the state senate's Judiciary Committee, the Warden of the state prison system and the Attorney General of the state. After carefully sifting through a list of candidates compiled by suggestions solicited through newspaper postings, social media and TV and radio public service announcements, the panel members were named. Ed Perry, Board Member of CHASE. Christopher Knight, attorney whose recent focus on Constitutional law issues had garnered national attention, William Nightingale, a reporter who had attended executions. And surprisingly, Jed Summers, whose wife and daughter had been murdered by one of the felons whose death sentence had been commuted.

The selection of Summers was the most controversial. Some argued it was next to inhuman to make him the only participant who directly experienced the pain from the brutal actions that had taken his loved ones. And at first, Summers refused. But his therapeutic sessions had helped him cope with his loss and he came to the belief that the public disserved to hear from one so directly affected by the controversy over the death penalty.

The participants selected, the debate was scheduled for 9 PM the coming Wednesday.

Fifteen minutes before air time, the members of the panel took their seats in the studios of TV Channel 36. The moderator was Dr. Philip Riggs, from the Wright Institute in San Francisco.

The sign "ON-AIR" glowed red and Dr. Riggs faced the camera and opened the session.

"Good evening. We appreciate the viewers that have tuned in. Tonight's debate, perhaps a better term would be 'discussion' has brought together a panel of knowledgeable and committed individuals who have been willing to discuss perhaps the most serious facet of this country's legal system – capital punishment. The recent court decision of the state Supreme Court has of course ruled the death penalty to be unconstitutional. That the punishment of death constitutes cruel and unusual punishment that is no longer consistent with modern day mores. At least in this state.

"Let me first point out that no one from the prosecutor's office is attending. The court case is not as yet totally final and additional legal steps may be taken. As such it was not proper for them to participate at this stage. And in any event, this discussion is not about that decision *per se*. Tonight's discussion is about capital punishment – the death penalty. Is it effective? Is it fair? Where does society stand on the issue? Are there pros? What are the cons? With that preamble, let me now turn to our panel and have them introduce themselves."

The camera shifted to the far end camera left – Ed Perry.

"Good evening everyone. I am Edward Perry, Board Member of Concerned Humanitarians Against State Executions or 'CHASE.'"

"Good evening. I'm Christopher Knight, an attorney whose practice most recently has a focus on constitutional issues."

"My name is William Nightingale. I'm a reporter."

"I am Jed Summers. Many of you may know me because it was my wife and daughter who were murdered. Their killer was convicted and sentenced to death, but the recent court decision has commuted his sentence."

"Mr. Summers, your presence here is truly appreciated. It must be very difficult for you. I think we all admire your courage and truly regret your losses."

"Thank you Dr. Riggs," Summer responded.

"Let's begin then. Mr. Perry lead off for us won't you?"

"Thank you. I do find it somewhat uncomfortable to have Mr. Summers on this panel. But I understand the reason for it. Let me just preface my comments and participation by saying that CHASE's position against the death penalty understands the suffering of those who have lost loved ones. However, we think that the facts about this penalty demonstrate that its retention and use does little or nothing to compensate for the terrible tragedies resulting from criminal conduct.

"There are many reasons CHASE believes the death penalty should be abolished. With the audience and the panels indulgence, I will enumerate the following. There is a better alternative: life without parole. Those states without the death penalty convicted murderers to life in prison without the possibility of parole. For example, there are currently over 121 people in Oregon who have received this sentence.

"What goes hand in hand with the first reason is that the death penalty puts innocent lives at risk. Since the reinstatement of the death penalty in the United States in 1976, 138 innocent men and women have been released from death row, including some who came within minutes of execution. In Missouri, Texas and Virginia investigations have been opened to determine if those states executed innocent men. To execute an innocent person is morally reprehensible; this is a risk we cannot take.

"Race and place determine who lives and who dies. Those who kill whites are more likely to be sentenced to die than those who kill African-Americans. In some states, prosecutors from some counties are more likely to pursue the death penalty than others are.

"We pay many millions for the death penalty system. According to published reports the trials for three murder cases cost more than $1.5 million. Only one was sentenced to death. The two others, one of whom was found guilty of four murders, are now on death row. In a fiscal impact summary from the State Department of Administrative Services it was stated that the State's Judicial Department alone would save $2.3 million annually if the death penalty were eliminated. It is estimated that total prosecution and defense costs to the state and counties equal $9 million per year.

"Poor quality defense leaves many sentenced to death. One of the most frequent causes of reversals in death penalty cases is ineffective assistance of counsel. A study at Columbia University found that 68% of all death penalty cases were reversed on appeal, with inadequate defense as one of the main reasons requiring reversal.

"Capital punishment does not deter crime. Scientific studies have consistently failed to demonstrate that executions deter people from committing crime. Around our country, states without the death penalty have a lower murder rate than neighboring states with the death penalty.

"There is a better way to help the families of murder victims. Families of murder victims undergo severe trauma and loss which no one should minimize. However, executions do not help these people heal nor do they end their pain. The extended process prior to executions prolongs the agony of the family. Families of murder victims would benefit far more if the funds now being used for the costly process of executions were diverted to counseling and other assistance.

"The death penalty is applied at random. The death penalty is a lethal lottery: of the 15,000 to 17,000 homicides committed every year in the United States, approximately 120 people are sentenced to death. Less than 1%."

"Capital punishment goes against almost every religion. Although isolated passages of the Bible have been quoted in support of the death penalty, almost all religious groups in the United States regard executions as immoral.

"Mentally ill people are executed. One out of every ten who has been executed in the United States since 1977 is mentally ill, according to Amnesty International and the National Association on Mental Illness. Many mentally ill defendants are unable to participate in their trials in any meaningful way and appear unengaged, cold, and unfeeling before the jury. Some have been forcibly medicated in order to make them competent to be executed. Although the U.S. Supreme Court has decreed that people with 'mental retardation' may not be executed, some states have not yet passed a law banning the execution of the mentally ill.

"The USA is keeping company with notorious human rights abusers. The vast majority of countries in Western Europe, North America and South America — more than 117 nations worldwide — have abandoned capital punishment in law or in practice. The United States remains in the same company as Iraq, Iran and China as one of the major advocates and users of capital punishment.

"We are the 'State.' When the 'State' kills, we are participants. Would you choose to be the person that pulls the switch that snuffs out a human life?

"No civilian's job description should include killing another person. Corrections personnel involved in executions, like our military, frequently suffer PTSD from having to kill. Perhaps there is a reason to have a defensive military, but prisoners pose no threat to the well-being of our citizens. There is no reason to place the mental health of our corrections workers at risk simply to pursue vengeance.

"I want to thank this station and you Dr. Riggs for this opportunity to justify CHASE's position on why we must get rid of the death penalty."

"Thank you Mr. Perry. Next I would like Mr. Knight ..."

"Excuse me Dr. Riggs. May I respond before Mr. Knight?" asked Summers.

"Well, I see no reason why not, Mr. Summers. Please proceed."

"Thank you," Summers said. Taking a deep breath, the camera clearly catching his agitation, Summers began.

"I will try to be very honest. Therefore, I admit I suffer from PTSD from the murder of my wife and daughter. But what I want to say about Mr. Perry's points I hope is based on reason and logic and not an altered mental state due to the PTSD."

"Fair enough, Mr. Summers. Perhaps more than fair. Please proceed," advised Dr. Riggs.

"I will try and address Mr. Perry's points, by point.

Mr. Perry asserts that life without parole is a better alternative. He states there are currently over 121 people in Oregon who have received this sentence. I fail to see any relevance to these cold statistics. There is no detail about the nature of the crimes these people committed. That is, whether their crimes were premediated or due to some mitigating factors. Whether the crimes were aggravated, that is cruel, dehumanizing, or brutal.

"He next asserts that the death penalty puts innocent lives at risk. Then he asserts that since the reinstatement of the death penalty in the United States in 1976, 138 innocent men and women have been released from death row, including some who came within minutes of execution. But he disproves his own point. The innocent were exonerated. His statement that to execute an innocent person is morally reprehensible is a truism without any meaning. Of course it is, but it begs the question.

"Mr. Perry asserts that we, society, cannot risk executing innocents. That is no comfort to the survivors of victims brutally murdered and dehumanized. He is saying society cannot take the risk, but the risk is created, if at all, by the legal system and its processes. The solution to being sure that innocents are not executed is to be sure the legal system prevents such a risk.

"Mr. Perry asserts that race and place determine who lives and who dies. He says, 'those who kill whites are more likely to be sentenced to die than those who kill African-Americans.' Even if true, the fault is not with the penalty, but with its enforcement.'

"He next alleges that 'in some states, prosecutors are more likely to pursue the death penalty than others are.' He gives no specifics, no facts to support this. Perhaps there are. But unless revealed, this is just a baseless assertion that plays to the position being advocated.

"Next, he says society pays many millions for the death penalty system. He asserts millions could be saved on an annual basis if the death penalty were eliminated. There's no reasons given why this is so. If it is. But it's one sided. This is bogus without specifics provided as to the causes for the cost of enforcing the death penalty along with a cost comparison for incarcerating a criminal for life.

"Mr. Perry alleges that the poor quality of defense leaves many sentenced to death. Then he admits that 'one of the most frequent causes of reversals in death penalty cases is ineffective assistance of counsel.' He undercuts his own argument. Death penalty cases are reversed because of ineffective counsel.

"His statement that 'a study at Columbia University found that 68% of all death penalty cases were reversed on appeal, with inadequate defense as one of the main reasons requiring reversal' only underscores the sophistry of his argument.

"Mr. Perry's assertion that 'capital punishment does not deter crime', that 'scientific studies have consistently failed to demonstrate that executions deter people from committing crime' is meaningless. The death penalty is justified by the specific crime committed. Any penalty will not deter crimes. Has life imprisonment without parole deterred crime?

"The assertion that 'around our country, states without the death penalty have a lower murder rate than neighboring states with the death penalty' is presented in a vacuum. There is no evidence that the lack of the death penalty has any relation to a lower murder rate."

"Here, I have a right to take particular exception. The assertion that 'there is a better way to help the families of murder victims.' That 'families of murder victims undergo severe trauma and loss which no one should minimize. However, executions do not help these people heal nor do they end their pain' comes from what personal experience of Mr. Perry. His assertion that 'the extended process prior to executions prolongs the agony of the family' misses the point entirely. It is the failure of the system to make the process inefficient that causes the agony.

"His assertion that 'families of murder victims would benefit far more if the funds now being used for the costly process of executions were diverted to counseling and other assistance' is quite frankly insulting. How callous can one be to assert that money could in any way reduce the agony of having one's loves ones brutalized, dehumanized, killed, raped …'"

"Excuse me."

Summers sat back and took a deep breath. His eyes were watery. The anger and frustration apparent in his face.

"Take your time Mr. Summers. We understand, or at least think we do. Please take a moment."

On a commercial station, a perfect time for a commercial. But this being an educational station, the capture of the suffering obvious in Summers face was heart rendering and disturbing.

"Mr. Perry… Mr. Perry alleges that 'the death penalty is applied at random. The death penalty is a lethal lottery: of the 15,000 to 17,000 homicides committed every year in the United States, approximately 120 people are sentenced to death, less than 1%.' Where's the logic in this? Doesn't it establish that the death penalty is rarely used. It is highly questionable that these statistics warrant the conclusion that the penalty is applied at random. Rather doesn't it establish the opposite. That it is applied only when absolutely necessary."

"Mr. Summers. Let's take a break here. While this station does not have commercials, it does have messages of interest and importance to its audience."

"Of course. Thank you," Summers replied.

"We're back,' Dr. Riggs announced. We were hearing from Mr. Summers responding to Mr. Perry. Mr. Summers do you wish to continue?"

"Yes, yes I do. I'm sorry if I'm taking so much time."

"No problem Mr. Summers. Please continue when you're ready."

"Thank you. Where was I? Oh yes. It was asserted that 'capital punishment goes against almost every religion… almost all religious groups in the United States regard executions as immoral.' Again there's no proof of this. It's an unsupported assertion. But in my therapy, we covered this subject. What I learned is that the Catholic Church does not oppose the death penalty. The Old Testament delivered capital punishment for far less heinous crimes than are committed today. And this I found of particular relevance.

A stellar clergyman of the church, no less than Archbishop Fulton J. Sheen, whose influence and prestige extended far beyond Catholics advised, and I quote, 'the refusal to impose just punishment is not mercy but cowardice.'

"It is regrettable if as alleged that 'mentally ill people are executed.' That 'one out of every ten who has been executed in the United States since 1977 is mentally ill, according' as Mr. Perry cites, to Amnesty International and the National Association on Mental Illness. Obviously, mentally ill defendants are unable to participate in their trials in the same ways as others. And if it is true that they appear unengaged, cold, and unfeeling before the jury, that some are forcibly medicated in order to make them competent to be executed, abolishing the death penalty is irrelevant to these problems. It does cause these failures in the legal system. Indeed, as Mr. Perry admits the U.S. Supreme Court has decreed that people with "mental retardation" may not be executed. His allegation that 'some states have not yet passed a law banning the execution of the mentally ill' again places blame where it doesn't belong. Eliminating the death penalty has nothing to do with a state's failure to enact a ban on execution of the mentally ill. Moreover, there is nothing presented that mentally ill people commit heinous crimes.

"The assertion that "the USA is keeping company with notorious human rights abusers, that The United States remains in the same company as Iraq, Iran and China as one of the major advocates and users of capital punishment.' is truly stooping to the lowest level. No need to make more of a point than to point out that in this country the use of the death penalty can be and is debated, something that is impossible in the countries Mr. Perry slanderously compares us to.

"Next he asserts 'we are the 'State. When the 'State' kills, we are participants. Would you choose to be the person that pulls the switch that snuffs out a human life?' Mr. Perry has no right to ask this question, nor does anyone who has not had his loved one brutalized. I say no more here.

"Finally, he asserts that 'no civilian's job description should include killing another person. Corrections personnel involved in executions...frequently suffer PTSD from having to kill.' I suffer from PTSD and I am in therapy because of it. My PTSD was caused by the violent loss of my wife and daughter's lives. There is no support for what Mr. Perry asserts and even if there were, it has no bearing on the issue. Unlike survivors like myself, corrections personnel have a choice. They can refuse to participate in an execution, an execution of those guilty of heinous crimes. I had no choice in becoming a survivor. I had no choice about having to live the rest of my life with the burden of having lost my loved one in the worst way possible.

"The final 'excuse' (Summers using air quotes) made by Mr. Perry is 'that prisoners pose no threat to the well-being of our citizens.' Mr. Perry perhaps forgets or is oblivious to the recent escapes of convicted felons from two supposedly top security prisons. Fortunately, in both cases the felons were caught before they could harm anyone else, but the cost of the efforts to recapture them and the fear their presence created were immense. Criminals, the worst of them, the ones that deserve the death penalty don't change.

"I have nothing further to say. Thanks for letting me speak."

"Thank you Mr. Summers," said Dr. Riggs. "We'll take another break here for some important messages. When we come back, we'll be hearing from Mr. Nightingale."

CHAPTER 11
WITNESS FOR THE EXECUTION

"We return now to our panel and will hear from William Nightingale, a free-lance reporter that has attended the execution of a death row inmate in this state," announced Dr. Riggs. "Mr. Nightingale, the floor is yours."

"Thank you Dr. Riggs. Listening to Mr. Perry and Mr. Summers, I will address two areas. The first will be to report on my personal observation of an execution with background on the crimes committed that led to the execution, including the time line between conviction and execution. The second area will review some cases in which the death penalty was not carried out or not imposed.

"I can say that it is disturbing to drive to a place where someone's death has been scheduled for a precise time. On this day, the weather seemed pre-ordained for such an event – a heavy rain, ominous black sky, a driving wind.

"I had learned that the State handles executions in a precise and professional way. After I arrived at the correctional center where the judgment would be carried out, I was able to observe the demeanor of the serial killer. He too seemed to have his own version of a professional attitude. He had the same impassive expression. The same he held during his trials. He showed no remorse, no regret for his murders and hence none for their families and loved ones. As he was escorted into the chamber, he was accompanied by two officers, a clergy man and other witnesses. He was asked if he had any final statement and he turned and looked at the one-way glass window on the other side of which I stood with other observers. His voice came over the audio system, cold and monotone. 'Thanks to those who supported staying this.' Then he turned to the guard on his right and said,

'Now get this over with.'

"The guards obliged. The serial murderer entered the death chamber at 9:45 p.m., on a Tuesday and he was dead at 10:12 p.m. The crowd of witnesses had watched intently, those in the chamber, those, like me, peering through the one-way glass, including family members and friends. Then there were others in attendance – lawyers, correction officials and other reporters. What I think we all observed was the painless death of a man who brutally killed eleven people. Devastating eleven families.

"I turned to the man standing next to me after it was over. He was the prosecutor who had sought and won the death penalty. He saw my press badge and volunteered. 'I thought he died a much easier death than any of his victims,' he said. 'He passed quietly after the injection. Just went to sleep. I've witnessed family and friends suffer until the last heartbeat of their loved ones when found hopelessly clinging to life. I've seen the faces of unimaginable grief, sorrow, despair. This monster's death was so much easier and faster than those women who died begging for their lives.'

"The woman standing just behind us turned out to be the sister of one of the victims. Almost to herself, she said, 'This is so macabre. It's been 15 years since he was sentenced to die. After all this time, what could he possibly think. Did he seek forgiveness for his crimes while sitting all those years on death row? I saw no emotion in him just now. So I guess not. I saw a blank stare, like the eyes of a shark. It is disturbing because his expressionless face is the last thing my sister saw.'

"She did not expect any show of remorse, no apology, no request for forgiveness. She turned and walked away. As she did, I thought about the contrast between the process of lethal injection and the horror that had caused its use. I thought that the clinical precision of administering the lethal injunction was society's compromise between public hangings and those who wanted to abolish the death penalty. I didn't feel at the time that either of these two opposing views found satisfaction."

"Thank you Mr. Nightingale. You have other comments I believe," Dr. Riggs said.

"Yes. I debated with myself whether I would bring these matters up after being asked to join this panel. But having listened to Mr. Summers, I think the record has to include some of the following history about when the death penalty has not applied or been enforced."

"Please continue then, Mr. Nightingale."

"The question it seems to me is whether the overall result of abolishing capital punishment, rather than commuting a death sentence in a particular case would be to place public safety in jeopardy. Let me provide some samples why this is a concern. One Demetry Smirnov, in 2011, killed his ex-girlfriend. In the investigation of the case, prosecutors discovered that before deciding to go ahead with the murder, Smirnov had researched the law on the internet to determine if the state had the death penalty. He determined that in his state the death penalty had been abolished. Such circumstances warrant the conclusion that had the penalty not been abolished, the woman would not have been murdered.

"Another issue. Where the death penalty has been abolished for rape and life sentences imposed in its stead, rapists are incented to kill their victims to prevent them from testifying. This suggests that abolition of the penalty has a cascading effect down the criminal justice system that places public welfare at risk. In Britain, which abolished capital punishment some years ago, has gone from one of the most rigorous sentencing systems to one of the most lenient. The result is that there are frequent and wide-spread demands to reintroduce hanging.

"When life without parole is substituted for death, there is no guarantee that the sentence will be fully carried out. In 1966, Kenneth McDuff was sentenced to death for killing two teenage boys and the brutal rape and murder of their female companion. When the Supreme Court ruled the death penalty unconstitutional in *Furman v. Georgia* in 1972, McDuff's sentence was commuted to life imprisonment. Under pressure due to overcrowding in Texas prisons, he was released in 1989. Within three days he had killed again. Over the next three years he killed at least five more women before being caught. There are countless other examples of killers released or escaped who have gone on to kill again, or who even have killed while in prison. The argument these facts make is that it is morally repugnant for the state to privilege the life of a violent criminal over the safety of an entire population.

"And one final example that I'm sure defies credulity, at least for me, is this. It's a different system than ours of course, but on a basic level it still is disturbing. It was recently reported that a district court in Oslo, Norway had ruled that officials had violated the rights of mass killer Anders Behring Breivik. This guy killed 77 people in a bomb and gun massacre in 2011. The court ruled that imprisoning him in isolation violated the European Convention on Human Rights. His 'isolation' was in a three-cell complex where he can play video games, watch TV and exercise. And with all that he has to serve only 17 years. The government has appealed the ruling. But, really? Seventy-seven victims killed randomly and this guy's rights are violated by 'solitary" confinement with TV, video games?

"I will end here. I, and I'm sure all of us and the audience, would like to hear from Mr. Knight."

"Thank you Mr. Nightingale. Once again, we will take a short break. When we come back, we will here from Mr. Knight," Dr. Riggs announced.

CHAPTER 12
CRUELEST OF PUNISHMENTS

"Once again, we are back," Dr. Riggs said. "Our last speaker is Christopher Knight. He is a lawyer whose practice recently has focused on constitutional rights and guarantees. He is well acquainted with this State's Supreme Court's decision overturning capital punishment. Mr. Knight, the floor is yours," Dr. Riggs nodded as the camera swung to Chris.

"Thank you, Dr. Riggs. Let me briefly review Supreme Court's decision to set the stage if I may. The decision came in the case of the defendant who was facing the possibility of lethal injection for a 2000 murder-for-hire killing. The decision overturned his sentence and commuted his sentence to life without parole. However, the Court went further. It ruled that an earlier enacted state law abolishing capital punishment for future crimes must be applied to all those who were then on death row facing execution for killings committed before that law took effect.

Putting aside for the moment the legal arguments pro and con of the decision and precedents relied on in the majority opinion, I want to focus on the ramifications of the decision under the Eighth Amendment to the U.S. Constitution.

"As I'm sure most know, the Eighth Amendment bans cruel and unusual punishment.

To set the focus of my remarks more accurately, I quote, 'Excessive bail shall not be required, nor excessive fines imposed, nor cruel and unusual punishment inflicted.' The common and accepted meaning of these terms is that the ban on inflicting cruel and unusual punishments applies only to those who deserve punishment.

"When the Eighth Amendment was ratified on December 15, 1791, the death penalty existed. The conclusion? It was not considered cruel or unusual punishment. The argument that the late Justice Antonin Scalia would make is that the Founding Fathers not having considered the death penalty cruel or unusual, it cannot be found to violate that Amendment today. The recent decision by the State Supreme Court however is based on their view of present day societal values, at least as the majority of justices in that decision defined such values. For purposes of this discussion it is not necessary to debate whether Justice Scalia's approach to the interpretation of the Constitution or that of the majority of Justices in the recent decision is the correct one. More importantly, let's focus on the State Court's decision outlawing capital punishment in this way.

"It has been argued that the greatness of our Constitution and America itself is dependent on how the Constitution is interpreted to ensure that *all* people are treated equally and fairly and have the same opportunity to exercise the rights to life, liberty, and the pursuit of happiness. The State Court's majority decision in part relies on its views that our notions of fairness, equality, and justice have evolved. And therefore so too must our interpretation of the Constitution. A fair argument. But we need to look closely and be sure to fairly include all factors that shade or color this argument.

"Some take this argument to mean that no provision of the Constitution enshrines its principles more clearly than the Eighth Amendment. And by that they mean that our notions of fairness, equality, and justice demand an end to capital punishment. In my opinion the argument is over stated. First, there are still 31 states that have retained the death penalty. The brutal crimes and the impact they have on the surviving members of the victims raises the question in my mind has never been asked in this debate. Who is actually being subjected to cruel and unusual punishment?

"Let's think for a minute. Let's substitute 'suffering' for punishment. Who is being subjected to cruel and unusual suffering, suffering not of their own making? There is no provision in the Constitution that prohibits cruel and unusual suffering. But there are provisions guaranteeing equal protection of the law. Provisions that guarantee the right to life, liberty and happiness. Amendment IX provides – 'The enumeration in the Constitution of certain rights shall not be construed to deny or disparage others retained by the people.

"As a society, as Americans, we have to ask what these other provisions mean in relation to the Eighth Amendment. Here's an argument. The first principle of legal interpretation of our laws and constitutions is that all provisions of a law or constitution must be read in such a way that any one reading does not make ineffective or ignore any other provision. Most simply, this means that the rights to be free of cruel and unusual punishment must be read in light of the rights to equal protection, the right to life, liberty and happiness. This does not mean that to protect these other rights, someone can be punished in cruel and unusual ways. What it means in my opinion is that we have first to better determine what today is cruel and unusual. In 31 states capital punishment is not cruel and unusual. How might other states address this issue?

"Let's start with the fact that if someone breaks the law, society has the right to take away his or her freedom. Society has the right to impose monetary penalties as long as they are not excessive. When someone murders someone, he or she can be said to have risked forfeiting their own lives. Now pause. There are degrees of murder. Manslaughter is a lower degree. Someone has been killed, but circumstances are such that the killing was not premeditated, not planned and not cruel or unusual. There are murders that result from jealous outrage, from being high on drugs or inebriated when one's emotions are out of control.

"Then there are murders that are abhorrent to a civilized society, inhuman, arising from an evil, sadistic cruelty that has destroyed any civilized restraints. There are murders that are directed at the destruction of society and societal values and needs. There are murders that occur in the commission of other felonies. You can be found guilty of murder by doing nothing. Depraved indifference is a crime if one knows that someone is certain to be killed and does nothing to stop it. And of course there are acts of terror that result in multiple slayings. And there is the shooting of police, judges, jurors that threaten the foundation of a society of law and order.

"Statistics show that the death penalty is rarely imposed. Still there are concerns that its imposition could still cause an innocent person to be put to death. Clearly that is a tragedy. But concerns to avoid such miscarriages of justice do not in my mind support the wholesale repeal of the death penalty.

"Time grows short I see," Chris observed. "So in the last few minutes, let me address some of the points Mr. Perry of CHASE made. First, let me say CHASE's concerns are troubling and need to be addressed. A more balanced approach however in my mind can address those concerns without abandoning the death penalty. For certain heinous crimes, dehumanized perpetrators, for society's protection and the preservation of law and order and for the rights of victims and the cruel and unusual suffering inflicted on their survivors, the death penalty must be retained. What must be addressed are the weaknesses in the process. With today's technology those weaknesses can be addressed more effectively.

"Just a few ideas. DNA. The first bit of evidence in any murder or rape or killing that should be obtained is DNA. DNA has been used to free those wrongfully convicted. For any death penalty case, the state should have DNA evidence to link the accused to the scene of the crime. This was recently done in a case in which a father, mother and young son were murdered after being held captive and tortured. The suspect's DNA was found on a pizza box delivered while they were being held captive.

"Now, quickly. To Mr. Perry's other points. Mr. Nightingale has provided cases that undercut the idea that life without parole is a better alternative. My idea of DNA evidence answers in part the concern about innocent people being tried for crimes they did not commit. But as important, the people wrongfully convicted were not sentenced for heinous crimes.

Societies inability to do better on the race issue affecting this, should be taken into account. But if the death penalty is limited to heinous crimes, race should play a lesser role.

I have long wondered about the cost of lifetime incarceration versus the death penalty. I think this needs further study. But it seems a weak point. For example, are the costs higher because inmates are left on death row for decades? Moreover, citing higher costs as a reason to excuse brutal murders seems callous, particularly when weighed against the sufferings of the survivors.

"As a lawyer, ineffective assistance of counsel should be obvious during trial and the presiding judge certainly has the knowledge and authority to see that no case is given to a jury where counsel has failed to do an adequate job. Next, I must agree with Mr. Summers. No penalties are adequate to deter crime. People who decide to commit crime have motivations that no threat of punishment will dissuade them or is even thought of, except in the case we heard about where the lack of punishment induced a killing. I think that is all I have to add. Mr. Summers provided thorough comments that need no elaboration. Thank you."

"For this station, I want to thank all the panelists for a thorough discussion of one of our society's most serious problems," said Dr. Riggs. "I am anxious to see what our viewers think and hope we will hear from many of them. If so, we may need to have another presentation that picks up where this one ended. Thank you all again and thank you our viewers for tuning in. Good night!"

Oscar Royce turned off his television and dialed. "Hello?" came the response.

"Did you see the show?" Royce asked.

"Yes."

"Did it meet your expectations?"

"Perfectly. I assume you are near the station and know what to do?"

"Yes. As planned. Should be a cake walk," Royce responded.

"Your certain you're a double?"

"Yes. I'm certain."

"Good luck. Let me know when it's over. Goodbye."

CHAPTER 13
BAD THINGS COME IN THREES

The broadcast over, Chris approached Ed Perry. "Mr. Perry, I hope you understand my comments were purely academic theorizing. I hope they weren't upsetting."

"No. We get a lot of push back at CHASE. We're used to it."

"I see. Can I drop you somewhere? My car is outside. It's raining heavily. We'll need our coats."

"No thanks. I took the Metro. It's the shortest and fastest way home. But thanks anyway. I'll be off now."

"Goodnight then. Stay dry," Chris said.

Chris trotted to his car. As he pulled out of the lot, he thought he saw Mr. Summers walking in the same direction as Mr. Perry. It was hard to tell. His shoulders were hunched up and his hat was pulled down against the rain. Perry had his umbrella but was having some difficulty with it because of wind gusts. He saw both men get on the escalator to enter the Metro stop. Then drove away.

It was late, so there weren't any passengers on the platform when Perry arrived. He entered the turn style and proceeded to the center of the platform. He had stopped wondering where the attendants were. They never seemed to be around at the late hours. He looked at the schedule for the arrival of the next train. Ten minutes. He opened his brief case and took out that day's paper. May as well kill some time waiting. He noticed a man at the far end of the platform, a man in a raincoat and a hat. He thought he looked like Summers. But he shrugged and returned to his paper. When he looked up at the arrival time, it was now only a minute away. Perry folded his paper and placed it in his briefcase and snapped it shut. With his back turned, Perry hadn't notice that the man at the far end of the platform had moved closer to him.

With the roar of train as it approached he stepped closer to the lip of the platform not knowing he was standing on the yellow warning line. As the A2 cab car rapidly entered the station, the man behind Perry shoved him off the platform into the oncoming car and then walked to the escalator and left the station.

The engineer in the cab car immediately radioed in that someone had fallen in front of his car. The few passengers on the late night train were told over the intercom that there had been an accident and that the train would not be continuing on. He announced the Metro authorities were notified and would soon be on the scene to assist. He apologized for the inconvenience.

Metro authorities arrived within the half hour. After some preliminary investigation, the police were notified. It had become routine to bring in the police whenever someone fell on the tracks and was run down.

Several hours later, the authorities had found what was thought to be the victim's briefcase. It had been thrown or knocked several hundred feet down the track by the impact. In it, business cards were found that listed an Edmond G. Perry, vice president of Compton Enterprises and a second card that identified him as a Board Member of CHASE. When the officer on the scene saw that the victim was connected to an organization opposed to the death penalty, he called into Detective Edwards. Edwards had circulated a notice that he was to be notified if anyone came across any incident that involved or seemed to involve something related to the death penalty.

"What have you got Sargent?" Edwards asked

"We have a body. What's left of it anyway after being hit by the Metro. We found a briefcase down the tracks from where he was hit. In it were business cards. The cards are for an Edmond Perry and one lists him as a member of that anti-death penalty group, CHASE."

"Okay. Thanks Sargent," Edwards said. He called in Gaines and Whitman.

"What's up?" Gaines asked.

"Ever hear the expression, 'bad things come in threes?'"

"Sure," Whitman said.

"Well, a third one just occurred. An Edmund Perry, Board Member of Concerned Humanitarians Against State Executions, just did a swan dive before a Metro train. That makes three. Justice Baker, the attorney Richards and now this guy Perry. I think the "coincidence" theory about Justice Baker's and Richards' deaths just got debunked, big time."

"Maybe. Have to admit, coincidence stretches the imagination. But stranger circumstances have occurred," Whitman offered.

"Yes, I admit that," Edwards responded. "But until we track this down and prove its just coincidence, I'm convinced these deaths are connected and that they all three were murdered."

"Clever assassin if so," Gaines commented. "Gun shot in the mouth. Anthrax poisoning. Now, swan dive in your local Metro station."

"Yes. But each of these victims have a common connection. Opposition to the death penalty. Let's rely for now on Arthur Conan Doyle's theory that when you have eliminated the impossible, whatever remains, however improbable, must be the truth. I watched the discussion on the death penalty on TV the other night. This guy Perry was on that show. That same night, presumably taking the Metro home, he's run over by it. I also watched Jed Summers who was on the panel. He tore into Perry's defense of outlawing the death penalty. And he has plenty reason to. One of the convicts whose death sentence was commuted by Baker's decision was the one who murdered his wife and daughter. For me, it's enough of a motive to make Summers a person of interest. Let's start checking on him."

"Where do you want to start?" asked Whitman.

"Good question. Let's take this slowly. Summers is obviously a sympathetic figure. All the more so after his appearance on that TV panel. We don't want some hue and cry from the public about police harassment. So let's start with the survivors of the victims of the others on death row that had their sentences commuted. Start by checking out where they were on the night of Justice Baker's murder," advised Edwards.

"That's an obvious starting point, but that might be seen as harassment," Gaines observed.

"You're right. So to start let's eliminate those who do not live in this state. For those that do live here, narrow it to those who live closest to Justice Baker's house. Then check and see who possesses a firearm and check for any recent sales of silencers. Before asking any of the survivors directly where they were that night, talk to their friends and relatives. Since the murder was in the early morning hours it's not likely any of the survivors were at work."

"The first inquiries won't raise any alarms. But asking others about the whereabouts of the survivors may still raise some eyebrows. And won't they contact the survivors directly as soon as they have been interviewed?" Whitman asked.

"I see your point," Edwards responded. "So what introduction can be used to justify the inquiry?"

After a few minutes of silence, Edwards admitted, "Scrap the inquiry on where the survivors were the night of the murder. Let's eliminate as many as we can through the other inquiries – their locations, gun ownership, etcetera. Let's hope that narrows the field of the number of survivors as possible suspects."

"Are we overlooking some other angles?" Gaines asked.

"What do you have in mind?" Edwards asked.

"Well, could we ask them if they knew the attorney, Richards."

"And why would we do that?" Whitman asked.

"We could say that we are interviewing anyone who had been in contact with the attorney about the case."

"Again, why would we do that? I keep forgetting, each of the three victims opposed the death penalty. They would have no motivation to be in contact with any of the murder victims. In fact, any motive to murder these three would arise only after the decision was handed down.

What this tells me is this. We agree we need to tread softly in investigating our suspicions that one or more of the survivors killed Justice Baker and perhaps the attorney and now Perry. But, one of the survivors is at the top of my list of suspects."

"Who?" asked Gaines.

"Jed Summers," was Edwards's instant reply.

"So we focus on him?" asked Whitman.

"Ultimately. But let's be thorough. Check out the others as I first described. My hunch is that the only one that won't be eliminated because of location, possession of a firearm, and so forth will be Summers. If we eliminate the others, then we can decide how to proceed against Summers."

CHAPTER 14
FOLLOW UP

Kelly had watched the broadcast of the panel on the death penalty. She had three good reasons – her profession, her husband and her patient. A few days after the broadcast, she called Jed Summers and asked him if he'd like to discuss the program and the status of his therapy.

Summers was reluctant at first, but decided it might be a good idea after all. Four days after Kelly called, he walked into her office.

"Come in Mr. Summers. Good to see you again," Kelly welcomed him.

"Thanks, doctor," he said and shook hands.

"Please have a seat. I wanted to see you to ask how the clinical therapy sessions were going, how you were doing and, to be honest, how you are after your appearance on TV."

["I see doctor.]-consider removing – doesn't sound like a statement used by a patient in therapy Thanks for being concerned. To answer your questions in order, the therapy sessions have been helpful. They were the reason I agreed to be on that program. Because of the sessions, I'm doing better controlling some symptoms of my PTSD, but my anger is still there. But it's shifted."

"How so?"

"I seem to have redirected my anger to the advocates against the death penalty."

"I see. What was your reaction about the murder of Justice Baker?"

"To be honest, I shed no tears. I have to admit. I took some comfort in it."

"Want to discuss that?"

"Not much to discuss. I was made to live through hell for years, After the murders of my wife and daughter, the time that passed until the fiend was caught, reliving the horror of the trial. Awaiting the verdict. Then its rendered. Then awaiting the sentencing recommendation. The feeling of some vindication when the verdict of death was pronounced. Realizing that same night that the death penalty did not alleviate my sorrow, my loss, my frustration. Then trying to adjust by reminding myself that the fiend was imprisoned and sitting on death row. Then realizing that he would be sitting on death row, alive, for God knows how long. Trying my best to refocus my attention on job, other aspects of my life, despite how crippled they had become. After all these years, the decision comes down and I'm made to relive the entire horror. But now it's worse. Now, the justice, no matter how imperfect it really was, how it would not bring back my wife and daughter back, has been overturned. I have now been denied the little solace the death sentence had given me. If I seem bitter, I make no apologies."

"The TV show, how did that affect you?" Kelly asked.

"At first I refused to take part. As I thought it over, I said why not. Then when I sat there and listened to the drivel that CHASE member spouted, I knew I had been right to join the program."

"You gave a good account of yourself and your position. What about the presentations made by Mr. Nightingale and Mr. Knight?"

"I was gratified that they both seem to support my positions and not Perry's."

"Taken together, the therapy, its results and the program, where are you in your life?"

"I'm not sure I understand, doctor."

"These were three major developments in your life and affecting your loss. Can you say you moved on a little, a lot, or stayed the same?"

"I can't answer those directly. Let me put it this way. I'm beginning to realize that my wife and daughter can never be brought back. That perhaps I'd be cheating them if I let all this defeat me. It will take more time, but I think about the future now which I couldn't before. And I'm looking for something that might help me move on, to do something that might honor their memory, maybe to prevent someone else from having to go through the horror I and others have had to suffer."

"Do you think about advocating for the death penalty?"

"I guess I'd say advocating against abolishing the death penalty."

"Do you have ideas about how you would go about that?"

"Now that you ask, I can tell you I was most impressed with your husband's comments on the program. I think it provides legal and constitutional arguments a non-lawyer like me can't articulate. But his insights and analysis can be a platform to support the fight against abolishing the death penalty."

"Well, I'm sure Chris, Mr. Knight, would be flattered by your comments."

"I don't see it as flattery. I think it simply recognizes the reality of the need for the death penalty for certain crimes."

"I see. What's in the near term future for you?"

"I don't know exactly doctor. It's too soon to be definitive. But, I do think I've made a start."

"You'll continue your therapy sessions then?"

"Yes."

"That's very good. I'll call you in several weeks to check back in if that's alright?"

"I'm flattered. That's fine."

Summers rose shook hands and left.

Chris came in and asked, "How did it go?"

"Well, you, Mr. Attorney, have a new fan, supporter."

"Really?"

"Yes. He liked your comments and insights on the panel the other night. He has an idea of using them, maybe with your help, to launch an effort against abolishing the death penalty."

"Hmm, I see. How do you feel about all this?"

"Somewhat surprised since you asked. As a psychologist, I'm going to consider the mental state of any person who commits a crime. I want to be sure that that state is not the factor that so controls a person as to eliminate culpability for his or her actions. That being said, that program, Summers' tragic experience, Mr. Nightingale's review of how the lack of enforcing the death penalty has inflicted further heinous crimes on society, the lack of consideration for what some victims and survivors suffer, it seems incontrovertible that the death penalty has a place in civilized society. My take is that it isn't the death penalty. It's how it's used, how it's administered. I think that was the point you were making in your comments."

"Well my beautiful wife and most perceptive psychologist, we seem to be on the same page. That's most comforting."

Kelly laughed and they embraced and kissed. Hand in hand they retreated to the bedroom. Working at home has its advantages.

CHAPTER 15
PERSON OF INTEREST

The phone beeped. His finger slid across the screen and the call connected. The screen on the other end flashed and the number calling was recognized.

"Listen. My sources indicate the bait has been taken. It's time to "salt the mines" to use an ancient metaphor. Once salted, confirm."

"Will do."

Edwards read the reports his team's investigation had produced.

The first positive clue came from reviewing the records of trials of each of the inmates on death row that had their sentences commuted by Justice Baker's decision. No survivors were found for a mother and her son who were murdered by one of the inmates. While there were some survivors of victims murdered by other inmates, they were eliminated as suspects by a number of factors. Some were now too old. Others had moved away. Still others were unlikely to have the knowledge or nerve to acquire a hand gun as sophisticated as the one used to kill Justice Baker. In the rest of the cases examined, there were either no indications of the existence of a survivor of the murdered and brutalized victims or that any of such survivors possessed the ability and nerve to kill anyone, much less a Supreme Court Justice in execution style. There was one exception. The records revealed that the husband of a murdered wife and daughter had actually been accused by the murderers of participating in the home invasion that led to the murders and rapes of his wife and daughter – Jed Summers. It was quickly shown that the accusations were made in an attempt to create a basis for reasonable doubt as to who actually did the killings.

"This information on the Summers murders, would you agree it supports the suspicion that a survivor could be responsible for Justice Baker's murder?" Edwards asked.

"It is supportive," Whitman answered.

"But it's hardly conclusive," Gaines said.

"I agree," Edwards responded. "But we also know that Summers still lives in town. So he has opportunity as well as motive. His being accused by the actual murderers of participating in the deaths of his wife and daughter had to have an even greater effect on his psychic condition when he learned that the death penalty had been thrown out. Obviously, he couldn't get to the murderers in prison. So who better to seek revenge against than the man responsible for letting his family's killers off the hook? So let's continue. We have a strong theoretical case establishing motive and opportunity. We need to establish that Summers had the means as well. Let's check and see if there are any records of gun purchases by Summers."

"We can run the records of gun stores in the area. But it will take some time. There are a lot of them."

"I know. But knowing that the weapon was a 38 caliber Glock 42 should help. Let's get started," Edwards finished. "In the meantime, I'll check with the District Attorney and see if we have enough to get a search warrant of Summers' home, and his place of work. I'll get Sherry down the hall to check on whether Summers has any other property like a vacation cabin, boat, whatever."

"If he did shoot Justice Baker, he's not likely to leave the gun lying around in any place connected with him," Gaines warned.

"I know. If we find he did purchase the gun that was used or already owned one, we'll deal with having to find it later. First things, first," Edwards concluded. "I'll be seeing the DA on how close we are to getting a search warrant."

Janet Newberg was re-elected to another four-year term as District Attorney last November. She first joined the office in 1997 and was promoted to Assistant DA in 2002, then Executive Assistant DA in 2005. Newberg had a solid track record of successful prosecutions including capital murder, violent sexual assaults, domestic violence and drunk driving. As DA, she supervised a staff of assistant DAs, victim/witness specialists and support staff who handle a broad range of felonies and misdemeanors in both adult and juvenile court. Newberg grew up on Chicago's South Side. She was all business. Edwards knew he had to have his ducks in a row.

Newberg's secretary opened her office door and announced that Detective Edwards had arrived to see her.

"Come in Dan. What brings you here this time?" she asked.

"I'm here about the Justice Baker murder case."

"Really! What about it?"

"We're working the case in an unusual way."

"Go on."

Edwards continued. "We... I... decided that there was a need to think about who was responsible in a different way. We have been pursuing that theory and believe we have a good lead on a suspect. We have evidence of opportunity and motive and are now searching to link means to the suspect."

"I see. Who's the suspect? Does he or she have name?"

"Yes. Jed Summers."

Newberg looked at Edwards and remained silent. Then she asked, "Let me be sure I'm following. If memory serves, Summers' wife and daughter were murdered during a home invasion. The murderers tried to implicate him and failed. Why is he a suspect in Justice Baker's murder?"

Edwards explained his suspicions and what the investigation had produced thus far.

"I see. So why are you here exactly?" Newberg asked.

"We need a search warrant?"

"To search whom and where?"

"Summers and his home, place of work, other haunts if there are any. We're checking gun sale and ownership records now. I was hoping we had enough to get a warrant now to search his home…"

Newberg cut him short. "No you don't detective. Surely you realize that issuing a warrant to search the home of a survivor of victims of brutal murders on the suspicion he murdered a Chief Justice of our Supreme Court will be a field day for the press. The public reaction will not be good for this office or the police department. You'll need more than your novel theory and what you think you've discovered thus far."

"Now that you've heard it, what do you think of the theory? I mean that a survivor could be the murderer?"

"I've been in this office long enough to know that no theory can be rejected out of hand. In this case, your theory isn't as far-fetched as others I've had to deal with."

"You think so. Why?" asked Edwards.

"It has not escaped me that we have had two deaths of others who are connected to the death penalty. The attorney who won the appeal that led to Justice Baker's decision and a prominent member of an organization that opposes the death penalty. Both of these deaths, as you know, are also under investigation. So far as I know now, we know one death is due to bizarre causes. The other is suspicious but accident or suicide haven't yet been ruled out. Nonetheless, we don't have enough to be charging around pointing fingers at those whose losses make them highly sympathetic figures to the public. Your target is even more in that realm after his appearance on that TV panel show. To get and keep this job, prosecutions have to be successful. They also have to be limited in number. We don't have an unlimited budget and successful prosecutions are expensive. So, no! As I said, you don't have enough for a search warrant as of now. And I have to say, you may never have unless you come up with stronger links than you currently have."

"Okay. I understand. I was afraid that would be the case. But I am glad you don't think the theory is bonkers."

"Well, you made some progress then. Get back to work and come see me when you have something concrete to support your suspicions on opportunity and motive."

Edwards nodded, turned and left the DA's office.

CHAPTER 16
MATERIAL WITNESS

Edwards left Newburg's office disappointed. Not that he didn't get the search warrant. He knew that wasn't likely. He was disappointed because he had forgotten about the other investigations of the deaths of that attorney Richards and the member of CHASE. If he could establish any kind of link between their deaths and Justice Baker's murder, well…

He would start with Richards. He recalled that his death was due to anthrax poisoning. He called the office of the police department's Chief Medical Examiner and made an appointment.

The next day Edwards met with Doctor Milton Levine.

"Detective Edwards. Our paths have not crossed for a while. All is good?"

"As good as anything can be in this job, doctor. But thanks for asking. I have a question for you. To become a pharmacist does one have to take chemistry courses?"

"Now that's a strange question detective. But I'm sure you have a very good reason for asking it. The answer is yes."

"You worked on the autopsy of Fleming Richards, the attorney who died of anthrax poisoning?"

"Not directly. But I was kept informed, so I do know about it. Do you have a question about that?"

"If someone wanted to poison someone using anthrax, he'd have to be very careful so he didn't poison himself?"

"Yes. But Richards died from inhaling the anthrax from an object – a Zebra skin African shield I was told."

"Yes. I just checked on that before coming to see you. Could someone have added the anthrax to the shield?"

"Well it's possible. But I know of other cases in which people have inhaled anthrax from African drums. My understanding was that the anthrax spores were naturally present in the skins that were used to make the drums. Not that they added the spores to the skins."

"But for arguments sake, if someone wanted to add the spores, it could be done by someone who would know of the danger and would be able to do so without infecting himself?"

"A reasonable assumption."

"Would a chemist or a pharmacist have the knowledge necessary to do so?"

"I would say yes. Even assuming that that person was not an expert microbiologist he could research the subject and would understand what it meant and use it to avoid infecting himself. He might even arrange to be inoculated against it."

"That's what I thought. Thanks Doc, you've been a big help."

"You think someone deliberately infested the Zebra skin Richards had in his office with anthrax?"

"Yes. At least it's a theory I'm working on."

"I see. Good luck."

Edwards left the ME's office and went back to his computer and logged on to the Internet. He typed in Jed Summers name and a menu of articles appeared. He had to click on only one and found what he was looking for. Summers was a pharmacist. Another brick in the wall of his theory that Summers was responsible for Justice Baker's murder motivated by anger and revenge for his part in commuting the death penalty of the murderers of his wife and daughter. Edwards realized that if Richards poisoning was deliberate, it was not obvious that it had a connection with Baker's murder. But a motive of revenge could be broad and Summers could have decided to punish all who were responsible for overturning the death penalty. Richards appeal was certainly a major factor. Edwards called in Gaines and Whitmore and told them of his theory and his meeting with Doctor Levine.

"Well, I'll admit it has some logic. But are you then going to try and connect Summers to Ed Perry's death?" asked Gaines.

"I've been thinking about that after I spoke with Doctor Levine. Assume that Justice Baker was murdered because he overturned the death penalty. That a survivor of one of the victims was forced to relive the horror of the crime that led to conviction and sentencing of the murderers and decided to seek revenge. His emotions snapped. Then assume his vendetta grew and he decided that others needed to pay for their part in overturning the death sentences. After Justice Baker, who is the next logical target? The attorney that filed and won the appeal."

Whitmore chimed in at this point. "It's logical. But Summers doesn't seem the type to commit premediated murder even once, let alone twice."

"How about three times?" Edwards proposed.

"Three times? Who else?" asked Gaines.

"Ed Perry of CHASE," Edwards answered.

"Perry. He fell off a Metro platform."

"Or was pushed?" Edwards countered.

"Well pushing folks in front of oncoming trains is a common enough modus operandi," Gaines said. "But what do you have to link Summers to Perry's fall?"

"Remember that TV panel show that Perry and Summers were on?' asked Edwards. "Remember how Summers lit into Perry's justifications for getting rid of the death penalty? Then recall the comments of that reporter and the lawyer on the panel. They not only supported Summers, but added fuel to the fire."

"Yeah! I remember," said Whitmore.

"Right. Now after the program ends, the panel leaves the studio. It's raining so they all have hats and coats on. Perry heads to the close by Metro station. According to the station manager with whom I checked, he refused a ride from that lawyer, Knight. The manager can't recall when Summers left. According to him in his words, 'He sort of disappeared.' He was also able to account for that reporter's departure because he remembers chatting with him for a few minutes about whether the program would be rerun. So, where did Summers go off to so quickly? The station's parking lot is not far from the Metro station. So Summers could have gone to the station and waited for Perry to come along. No one is around. That was confirmed by the Metro employee the police interviewed after being called to the scene. The employee explained he had left his booth to take a piss. When he came back all hell had broken loose but there still was no one around."

"So you're suggesting that Summers gets to the station before Perry. Keeps out of sight. Waits. When Perry arrives and as the train approaches steps toward the track. Summers bides his time and just as the train is pulling in, still at a good rate of speed, comes from behind and pushes Perry onto the tracks where he is struck and killed, then disappears," Gaines proposes.

"Yes. It has not escaped my attention that the escalator to the floor of the station above was close by. Even if someone was at the station at the time, someone could have dodged up the escalator before being seen," Edwards added.

"Nice and neat. Can we prove it?" Whitmore asked.

"I think in Perry's death, we have grounds to establish motive, opportunity and means. Summers motive is the same, anger and revenge against an anti-death penalty advocate. Opportunity? He was in the area at the time of the incident. Means? The train was his weapon and to 'fire" it, he only had to push. While we're waiting to get the records of any possible gun ownership, we can bring him is as a material witness in Perry's death and grill him about where he was and what he did when he left the station and why he left in such a hurry."

"Makes sense Dan," Gaines said to Edwards.

"In addition, I established that Summers' training and profession would make it possible for him to handle anthrax. We can question him about that as well."

"When you ask him about that, he'll lawyer up," Whitmore stated. "He's not a material witness in the Richards death."

"Probably. But we all know that people forget their right to an attorney at first. We should be able to play to his ego about his training and skills to admit he could handle anthrax before he realizes why he's being asked about that when he has been questioned only in connection with Perry and the program they were on together," Edwards responded.

"Could work. When do you propose to call him in?" Gaines asked

"Soon. First I want to know where we are in our search of gun registrations or purchases. If we can link a gun to Summers, all the better."

"But even if there are records, they would have to be for the Glock 42 used to kill Justice Baker. Any old gun won't incriminate Summers." Whitman observed.

"I know. First things first. We'll start with calling Summers in as a material witness in connection with Perry's death."

CHAPTER 17
A CASE IN POINT

"Your honor, the defense objects to the prosecutions intent to show the jury photographs of the victim. It would be unduly prejudicial."

"Your honor, the prosecution has a right to present its case using all the credible evidence it has. The jury has the right to see that evidence in order to make its determination based on a complete presentation of the facts as they exist. This is a murder case in which the victim was killed in a brutal manner. Those are the facts. Are they prejudicial? Yes! Properly so. The defendant chose the method of killing and he should be prejudiced by that choice, but such prejudice is not undue. It is of the defendant's own making."

"Objection overruled. There are times photographs must be admitted when they relate to the brutality of crime. The prosecution may proceed."

"Thank you your Honor," said the district attorney.

"Exception, your Honor," countered the defense attorney.

The prosecuting attorney addressed the jury. "Let me summarize what the evidence for the prosecution has shown so far. In November 2015, the defendant, armed with a butcher knife twelve inches in length, arrived at the victim's townhouse and found him in the kitchen. There, the defendant stabbed him and slashed the victim 89 times. Apparently not content with such mutilation…"

"Objection your honor. Speculation," the defense attorney interposed.

"Sustained," ruled the judge.

Resuming, the prosecutor stated, "The defendant used the knife to saw on the body of the victim," pointing to a large image of the body lying on its back. "Then, the defendant reached in with his bare hands and pulled out the victim's liver and left it on the victim's chest, for display, whatever."

Several jurors turned their heads and grimaced. Those who didn't had blank stares on their faces. Despite their revulsion, it was nothing like that of the victim's relatives who were in the courtroom. Some sobbed. Others shook their heads in disbelief.

The prosecutor continued. "The attack started on the victim's back. Moved to his head and chest. Attacking different parts of the body indicates the defendant could have halted his attack much earlier. Because he didn't, it shows his intent, his premeditation, to commit this atrocious murder, to do so as cruelly as he could."

When the prosecutor finished his summation, the defense presented its.

"These photos are gruesome and sickening. But I have to ask you to control their emotional impact. For all their blood and gore, the photographs do not show what may have been the cause of the attack. They do not show who made the attack. Apparently, someone, some people were out to get the victim. But, it wasn't the defendant."

It was a game attempt by the defense, but the weight of evidence showed that the defendant knew the victim, had called the victim before going to his house and was let in. At some point, the two went down to the basement. The victim's sister found the body, called 911. The records showed that investigators found a bloody hand print and bloody shoe prints which were later matched to the defendant. When police went to the defendant's house he had on white Nikes that made prints that matched the bloody print found at the scene. His cell phone showed numerous calls to the victim. There were no additional calls after the victim had been killed. Most incriminating, the police found a butcher knife with defendant's DNA on it.

Then there were the photos of the Medical examiner's autopsy. Six in all. They were admitted based on their being probative of intent. The jury reached its verdict a few days later, finding that the defendant was the killer and that he acted willfully and with premeditation. Because of the recent ruling that found the death penalty unconstitutional under state law, the sentence imposed was life without parole.

One juror summed up his reactions to the photos.

"They were shocking. They put me in a daze. The mutilated body of the victim seemed like I was looking at a horror movie or one of those medical mystery TV shows. But this was real. This was a human being. I'm no lawyer or judge, but I can't understand why the life of a person like this who committed a monstrous crime should be spared and then supported by the state. It's one thing to kill in a fit of rage or emotional upheaval where one can act without thinking. But to knowingly seek to inflict fear and the most gruesome types of pain and then pull out the victim's organ, that's inhuman. If a dog or a bear attacked and tore someone apart like this, it would be shot. This guy's supposedly a human being, not an animal. But you won't convince me of that."

CHAPTER 18
MATERIAL WITNESS

Detective Edwards went back to see District Attorney Janet Newberry confident he had what he needed to bring Jed Summers in for questioning as a material witness.

"Well detective, what is it this time?" Newberry asked.

"I want to bring Jed Summers in for questioning. I am convinced he knows things we need to know to start solving these murders."

"What murders?"

"The murders of Justice Baker, the attorney Richards and Perry of that organization CHASE."

"Quite a haul. And you have evidence that links these deaths. Note, I didn't say murders because the only murder we have is Justice Baker's. There's nothing I know of that indicates that Richards and Perry were murdered. Just unlucky. So what have you got? I should say, what do you think you have that supports your belief Richards and Perry were murdered?"

"I've been in homicide for over twenty years. You get vibes after all that time. Hunches. Hunches that won't go away. That push me in a direction."

"These hunches ever pay off, detective?"

"More often, than not."

"Share your hunches with me, detective."

"First, all these 'deaths' occurred after the court decision outlawing the death penalty. The three victims have a common connection. The Justice rendered the decision overturning the death penalty. Richards was the attorney who won the decision overturning the death penalty. Perry is a prominent figure in an organization that opposes the death penalty."

"That it, detective?" DA Newberry asked.

"No. Jed Summers."

"Jed Summers, again!"

"His wife and daughter were murdered by one of the convicts whose death sentence was commuted."

"So?"

"He's the only survivor of murder victims whose killers had their death sentences commuted who lives in the area. He's the only one of the survivors of the victims of the murderers whose death penalties were commuted with the physical opportunity to be involved in the deaths of the Justice, the attorney and the death penalty opponent. We checked on all the others and we eliminated them because they are not living in this area or have infirmities or characteristics that eliminate the possibility of their having the physical, emotional or mentality to commit a crime of any nature, much less murdering a Supreme Court Justice. On the other hand, Summers went on a televised panel show on the pros and cons of the death penalty. His opposition to getting rid of the death penalty was visceral. But not just the decision, but those who were responsible for the decision. Watch the show, you'll see what I'm talking about."

"Motive. From Summers comments on the TV panel, his motive is obvious. Revenge. Revenge against those responsible for denying the justice he had won when the death penalty was imposed. I don't know what demons rose in him when he learned of this. But after twenty years, I know people kill for far less reasons."

"This leaves means. To get evidence of that, we have to question Summers. We need to search his premises."

"Ah, but therein lies the rub," Newberry said. "Summers is a victim that has suffered another grievous loss. If you prove his involvement, fine. If not, we'll have one hell of a public relations problem."

"I've taken that into consideration. That's why I want to bring him in as a material witness."

"A material witness? To what? There's nothing to link him to Baker's murder. Nor Richards's."

"Aha! But there is to Ed Perry from CHASE. They were on the TV panel. They left the station about the same time. They both went to the Metro station. So, we need to question him about what he saw or may have seen after he left the TV station and went to the Metro station."

"Hmm! Could work. I mean, the approach that he's a material witness. But where do you go with that?"

"My experience says that someone like Summers, never in trouble with the law before. Clean as a whistle. Chances are if he is involved he'll crack. If he doesn't, but we can get a search warrant, we can discover incriminating evidence against him."

"All in all, your plan has positives and negatives. I'm not completely sure."

"Ms. Newberry, you're in an elected office. The public won't keep quiet for long if there is no progress on Baker's murder or the deaths of Richards and Perry given the anti-death penalty connection. What alternatives do we have?"

"You mean. What alternatives do I have?"

"It's your call Madam DA."

"Don't patronize me, detective. Okay. I'll get a court order designating Summers as a material witness. When you bring him in, keep me well advised and up to date. I don't want any nasty surprises."

"Understood. Will do," Edwards affirmed and smiled.

CHAPTER 19
PRESSURES

Three days after his meeting with Newberry, Edwards had his warrant to bring Jed Summers in for questioning as a material witness. As he was preparing to serve the warrant, his phone rang.

"Hello! Detective Edwards, here," he responded.

"Detective Edwards, this is Oscar Royce. I'm on the board of CHASE, Concerned Humanitarians Against State Executions. It's my understanding that you are investigating the death of our fellow board member, Edward Perry."

"Yes Mr. Royce. I am. May I ask why you're calling. I cannot discuss any details about an on-going investigation."

"I understand detective. My call isn't seeking information. On the contrary, I have some information you may find useful."

"I see. What might that be, er... Mr. Royce?"

"Did you happen to see the panel discussion on the death penalty on TV, the one in which Jed Summers participated?"

"Yes. We reviewed a tape of the discussion as a matter of routine given the subject matter and the its relevance to certain matters being investigated."

"Very good. As I'm sure you can understand, Mr. Perry's death and the manner in which it occurred is most disturbing to our organization and, in particular, its board members."

"Yes. I can see that."

"The reason I called is that some of our members are concerned that there may be a link between Mr. Perry's death that occurred just after the conclusion of that TV program and a member of the panel."

"Go on. I'm listening." Edwards said guardedly.

"None of us wish to rush to any conclusions. But, one has to admit that the opposition to Mr. Perry's presentation on why the death penalty is wrong and that the recent decision abolishing it in this state was quite vehement by one member of the panel."

"Some may have thought so," Edwards acknowledged.

"Not to take up too much of your time, I will tell you that the comments of Mr. Summers got our members' attention. While we realize he suffered a terrible tragedy, the juxtaposition of his appearance on the panel, his denunciation of Mr. Perry's presentation against the death penalty and Mr. Perry's death following so close to the airing of the show, raised some suspicions. One of our board members knows the producer of the show and made an inquiry."

"What kind of inquiry, Mr. Royce?"

"The question was about whether Mr. Summers and Mr. Perry had any words, talked to each other, after the program ended. The concern was whether Mr. Summers might have continued his attack, might even have threatened Mr. Perry."

"Did your board member learn anything?" Edwards asked.

"Yes and no. That is, Mr. Summers did not speak to Mr. Perry. He left shortly after the show ended. But, as he was leaving, the producer asked if he needed a ride and that the station would be glad to have one of their cars drive him. The producer said he refused, saying he was going home and would take the Metro. We know Mr. Perry also took the Metro that night. Looking up Mr. Summers' address in the phone book, it was determined that Mr. Summers and Mr. Perry would have gone to the same Metro station. That being the case, Mr. Summers could have been on the same platform as Mr. Perry that night."

"Perhaps so, Mr. Royce. There's a logic to what you say. But it hardly points to Mr. Summers being involved with Mr. Perry's accident."

"Accident? Have the police determined that Mr. Perry's death was an accident?"

"I didn't say that. His death is still under investigation. I can't really get into any more detail at this point."

"I understand detective. One last comment. Under the circumstances, would Mr. Summers qualify as a 'person of interest'?"

"I can't respond to that, Mr. Royce."

"I see. But detective, our organization and others who oppose the death penalty are quite concerned with the events following the court decision outlawing the death penalty. There have been three deaths. One was a murder. The other two deaths were of persons also opposed to the death penalty. The coincidences are unsettling to say the least. The longer it goes without finding a suspect for Justice Baker's murder and whether the deaths of Mr. Richards and Mr. Perry are connected, we at CHASE and the public will remain concerned. They need the police to make some progress."

"I'm well aware of that, Mr. Royce. Thanks for your information. Goodbye."

After Edwards hung up, he slammed his fist on his desk. "Time to get Summers in here," he said to himself.

With Royce's information, Edwards felt his hunch about Summers was playing out. At least now he had narrowed the field to one primary suspect and the District Attorney got the warrant to bring Summers in as a material witness. The warrant issued, Edwards gathered his team and served the warrant at Summer's home.

CHAPTER 20
DETAINED

Bert Keene of Channel 10 news was bird dogging the investigations of Justice Baker's murder and the odd coincidences of the deaths of Richards and Perry. When his producer told him about the inquiry Oscar Royce of CHASE had made about Summers and Perry after the broadcast, he decided it was time to grill the homicide squad on where its investigation stood.

Several days passed since the court issued the order designating Summers as a material witness but it had not yet been served.

Keene walked into the homicide squad's bull pen and went straight to Edwards desk.

"Hello Dan! he said.

Edwards looked up and said, "My, my, look what the cat dragged in."

"You know you're dating yourself with that expression," Keene rejoined.

"Like I care. What do you want Bert?"

Edwards didn't like the press snooping around his investigations. But it was a necessary evil. Keene, like other reporters covering the crime scene, proved they could be helpful at times.

"Ed, I need some update on the Baker case. There must be something I can tell my viewers."

"I wish I had something for you. But the truth is, I don't. We're working the case. But so far, nothing's turned up."

What about the deaths of Richards, that attorney and Perry that guy with CHASE?"

"Both under investigation."

"That I know. There's got to be more."

"These cases have led down blind alleys so far. We have an outright murder of a Chief Justice, shot to death in his bedroom as you know. You also know, that that attorney Richards contracted anthrax poisoning. Then you have this Perry who takes a dive before a Metro rain. The causes of death give no map to a common MO."

"I know that. But there is a common thread. Baker and Richards overturned the death penalty. Perry was a board member of an organization opposed to the death penalty. It can't be coincidence, or if it is, it's a lulu of one."

"Now who's dating themselves?" Edwards asked.

"Yeah, yeah! I know enough about you detective to know you don't believe in coincidences, particularly when they relate to three deaths. If I were a betting man, I bet you're working the case using the anti-death penalty positions of the three deceased."

"Look. I can't go out on any limbs here. I don't look kindly to walking a beat."

"I understand, detective. But whatever update I can get will not be attributable. I can use the standard 'since the matters are under investigation, the following information is from an unnamed, but reliable source.'"

Edwards thought for a few minutes. Then he said, "You didn't hear this from me or anyone in the Department. Agreed?"

"Agreed."

"We obtained a warrant to bring in someone as a material witness. Our focus is that by being able to question this witness we can start tying up some of these loose ends, get some leads to further the investigations of all three deaths."

"Who is it?"

"I won't tell you now. When we serve the warrant, I'll call and tell you. Deal?"

"Deal."

The next day, Edwards and two uniforms arrived at Summers residence at 7 a.m., rang the doorbell and waited.

Summers opened his front door in his robe and pajamas.

"Yes."

Edwards flashed his badge.

"I'm detective Daniel Edwards, Homicide Squad. I'm here to serve this warrant."

"Warrant? Homicide? What is all this?" Summers stammered.

"We are taking you in as a material witness. We want to talk to you about the night you were on a panel with Ed Perry of CHASE and what you did and saw after you left the TV station."

"What? I don't know anything about Perry's death if that is what you're interested in."

"We'll determine that, Mr. Summers. You will need some time to arrange for the fact that you will be with us for a time."

"How long?"

"Can't say. Depends on what we learn from you."

"Can I refuse?"

"No sir. You cannot."

Summers looked at Edwards expression and then at the two uniforms standing behind him. He knew he had no choice but to cooperate.

"I see detective. I have to get dressed of course and as you say make some arrangements due to my absence. I'll have to make some calls. Okay?"

"You can get dressed and make some calls. My men will be out front and in back while you do so. You're an intelligent man and realize any attempt to leave would be foolish on many levels."

"Yes. Yes, of course. I'll get started. May I close the door?"

"Yes, of course."

With that, Summers closed the door and went up to his bedroom to change. Then he called the pharmacy where he worked. When his call was answered, he said, "Marlo, this is Jed. Look something has come up unexpectedly. I won't be in… No I don't know when I will be. But as soon as I know more, I'll call and let everyone know… Thanks."

After he had gotten dressed, he packed some things for a short duration stay not really knowing how long he would be away. Then he made another call.

"Doctor Young. This is Jed Summers."

"Hello, Mr. Summers. How are you doing?" Kelly asked.

"I'm… I'm not sure."

"What's the problem? May I help?"

"My problem is not in your area, doctor. May I talk to your husband?"

"Hold on, Mr. Summers. I'll have him pick up in his office."

"Thanks."

Summers heard Kelly call out, "Chris, Mr. Summers is on the phone. You remember, don't you?"

After a moment, Chris answered, "Yes, yes, I do," and picked up the receiver in his office.

"This is Chris Knight."

CHAPTER 21
INTERROGATION

Summers was led into an interior room at the police precinct. He was made to empty his pockets and turn over his personal possessions – keys, wallet, watch, phone and his overnight bag. All were checked into the Property Room and he was given a receipt. He was then led down a hallway to a room with a table and three chairs. Three walls were bare, but one had a glass panel several feet wide and high. He was told to take the single chair by the table and Edwards sat on the other side and introduced detective Gaines who sat down next to Edwards.

"May I ask why I'm here, detective?"

"I told you this morning. You're here because we have reason to believe you may have information concerning the death of Edward Perry. You know, the CHASE representative that appeared with you on that TV panel and who was killed later that same night."

"I don't understand. I have no information about Mr. Perry or his death? I only met him that night of the broadcast."

Ignoring Summers' assertion, Edwards started the interrogation.

"This interrogation is being recorded. Present are detective Daniel Edwards, detective Louis Gaines and a male Caucasian who is being interrogated as a material witness, Mr. Jed Summers. Mr. Summers, please state your full name and address for the record.

Summers did so.

"How long have you lived at your present address?

Summers said, "Fifteen years."

"Where do you work?"

"I'm a pharmacist at the Best Care Pharmacy."

"How long have you been a pharmacist?"

"Twenty years."

"How long have you worked at Best Care Pharmacy?"

"Twelve years."

"Before that?"

"I was at the pharmacy at General Foods Supermarket."

"Before that?"

"That's where I started."

"Do you own a gun?"

"No."

"You've never owned a gun?"

"No. I mean I did own a gun. I got rid of it."

"How long ago was that?"

"It…it was after… after the… the murders."

"What murders, Mr. Summers?"

"The murders of my wife and daughter."

"Why did you get rid of the gun at that time?"

"I saw it was useless to have one."

"Why was that?"

"Why are you asking these questions?

"Mr. Summers, we ask the questions here. This will go much quicker if you just answer the questions."

"It was a terrible reminder."

"A reminder of what?"

"That it didn't stop the murders of my wife and daughter."

"What did you do with the gun?"

"I don't recall."

"Did you sell it?"

"No. I… I don't recall. I probably just threw it away."

"Did you have a license for the gun?"

"Yes."

"Didn't you know that you should have turned the gun over to the police?"

"Back then… back then I wasn't thinking about such things. I just wanted to get rid of the gun because it was a reminder that I failed to protect my wife and daughter."

"But your wife and daughter were not attacked in your home. And you were nowhere around at that time. So the weapon wasn't available to use."

"Look! It made no difference. I purchased the gun believing it would let me protect my family. It didn't. Maybe it makes no sense now. But at the time, as I told you, it was a reminder that I failed. So I got rid of it."

"The man who murdered your family was convicted and sentence to death, correct?"

"Yes."

"But the court commuted his sentence. You know that?"

"Yes."

"How did that court decision affect you?"

"How do you think?"

"Just answer the question, please."

"I was upset."

"How upset?"

"I was angry. I was shocked. That decision made me relive the horror all over again."

"Did your anger focus on the court or its judges?"

"I don't recall exactly."

"Did you think about revenge?"

"Of course."

"Against whom?"

"I'm not sure. I don't know much about courts, the law or sentencing. I suppose I was just angry at the whole system."

"Did you read or hear about the murder of Justice Baker?"

"Yes."

"How did that make you feel?"

"Detective. I thought I was brought here because of the death of that Mr. Perry. I don't see the relevance of these questions about guns and the courts and Justice Baker."

"Again, Mr. Summers, we're the judge of what is relevant when investigating a death. Just answer the questions."

"Alright."

"Again. What was your reaction to the news of Justice Baker's murder?"

"I was surprised. I guess I thought when I first heard that it seemed like, like maybe he deserved it. But that only lasted a short while. I realized that his death wouldn't bring back my family."

"Do you think the decision to eliminate the death penalty is right?"

"No."

"You favor the death penalty?"

"In certain cases, yes."

"Do you oppose those who support eliminating the death penalty?"

"How do you mean?"

"Do you think that organizations like CHASE should not exist?"

"There are a lot of organizations that I can think of that society would be better off if they didn't exist."

"Let's stay with CHASE. You appeared on a TV panel on which Mr. Perry of CHASE also appeared. We've reviewed the tape of that broadcast. Your opposition to Mr. Perry's defense of eliminating the death penalty was quite vehement. Would you agree?"

"My opposition was based on the facts that Mr. Perry's 'excuses' were just that, 'excuses.' Excuses that ignored the pain and suffering, the cruelty that those who were sentenced to death had caused to the victims' families and loved ones. I couldn't sit there and abide his arguments. They were one sided in favor of criminals, criminals that committed heinous, inhuman crimes. I said what I had to say. I could not do otherwise."

"Did you ever think that Mr. Perry should be made to experience what you and other survivors suffered?"

"I thought that if he experienced what I and other survivors experienced he wouldn't be against the death penalty. He wouldn't be sitting on CHASE's Board of Directors."

"After you left the TV station that night, where did you go. It's reported you left the station in a hurry."

"I left because I was upset and I didn't want to risk losing my temper."

"Losing your temper. Against whom or what?"

"Perry."

"When you left the station, where did you go?"

"I went to the Metro station to take the train home."

"Did you see anyone?"

"No. It was late and raining. Well, actually, when I got to the station, the man on duty was leaving his kiosk."

"Did he see you?"

"No. His back was turned to me when he left the kiosk."

"You saw no one else."

"How long did you wait for your train?"

"The schedule board indicated there would be a delay in the arrival of my train. So it was twenty minutes, perhaps more."

"While you were waiting, did you see anyone?"

"At the far end of the platform, I saw a man. I didn't recognize him. He was far away. With the storm, the platform lighting was poor. I don't know who he was."

"Did another train arrive at the platform before yours that was delayed?"

"I didn't see any. While I was waiting I went to the rest room. I heard a train arrive or at least it sounded like one arriving."

"At any time while you were in the station, in the rest room, did you see anyone other than the man you couldn't identify?"

"No."

Where were you when Mr. Perry fell off the platform?"

"I was coming out of the restroom. It was getting close to the time my train was supposed to arrive."

"Were you aware that someone had fallen off the platform.?"

"Not really. My schedule board indicated my train was arriving. It was going in the opposite direction. So my back was turned as I waited for it to arrive which it did about a minute after I left the restroom. When it arrived, I boarded and sat down. Because of the glare on the windows, I couldn't see out so I had no idea of what was going on on the other side of the platform."

"So to summarize. You arrived at the Metro station. You saw no one except the station man, but he did not see you. Then you did see a man at the other end of the platform but didn't recognize him. You went to the restroom but saw no one and when you came out, did you still see the man at the other end of the platform?"

"I didn't look. I was looking at the schedule board to see when my train would arrive."

"Can you estimate the amount of time between when you heard the train when you were in the restroom and when your train arrived?"

"Couple of minutes, I guess."

"Okay, let's change the subject. You're a pharmacist, correct and have been for twenty years, correct?"

"Yes."

"In your studies, you would learn about bacterias. Different kinds of bacteria. Is that correct?"

"Yes."

"Would those studies include anthrax?"

"Yes."

"As a pharmacist have you been called on to prepare an antidote for someone who has come in contact with anthrax?"

"No. It's very rare for someone to be infected by the anthrax bacteria. At least in this country."

"Rare, perhaps. But if someone did become infected with it, you would know what to prescribe to treat it?"

"I wouldn't be prescribing. I would be fulfilling the prescription from the attending physician."

"Understood. But you would know to do that?"

"Yes. There are antibiotics available to treat such infections. But the person infected needs to get these as soon as possible. If one doesn't, it can lead to a very quick and nasty death."

"I see," Edwards said. "Let's move on to another topic. Where were you on the night of October 26th?"

"I'm not sure. Is this day special somehow that I would remember?"

"It was the night Justice Baker was murdered."

"What's that got to do with me?"

"Do you recall where you were the night of October 26 and the early morning of October 27th?"

"Off the top of my head, no."

"You live alone now?"

"Yes."

"Back around that time, do you recall going out. Meeting some friends? Going to a movie or play? Anything like that?"

"I rarely go out like that anymore. But in answer to your specific question, I have to say I do not recall anything about being out at night or early morning around that time."

"Would you say that odds are you were at home alone?"

"Without checking for some possible notes, or like that, I have to say I was at home alone."

"Can anyone verify that?"

"I just said I was home alone. How could there be anyone?"

"Someone could have called you, dropped by, sent you an email or you sent an email to someone. Perhaps you purchased a movie to watch."

I can check my emails, but I haven't purchased a movie and have no recollection of anyone phoning me or dropping by around this time. Of course I could be wrong. It's been a while and there's nothing special about those two dates that reminds me of anything specific."

"Mr. Summers, would you consent to a search of you home and surroundings?"

"Whoa! Just a minute. What's this really all about? Do you suspect me of something?"

"It's routine. We need to check all possible avenues to find facts that will help in our investigations."

"It may be routine to you. But it isn't to me. I want to call my lawyer."

CHAPTER 22
BUILDING THE CASE

"Has there been any progress?"

"Yes."

"Enlighten me."

"Interrogation has established that the target has knowledge of bacteria. It has established that the target has no corroboration for his whereabouts. Prior possession of a gun has been established, and there is no record of what happened to it. Motive has been developed. The Metro platform scene has been constructed in an incriminating way. All in all, the potential tie ins are incriminating. My contacts indicate that Detective Edwards is all the more convinced that Summers is a suspect as to Perry's death."

"Does he intend to charge him then?"

"No. Not at present."

"Why?"

"As a material witness, Summers can be held almost indefinitely. I was given a few examples. One material witness was incarcerated for thirty-six days in the county jail. Another was held for eighty-four days and his diet was mostly beans. Still another was in jail for fifty-two days and one guy spent 158 days in the state penitentiary."

"The cops can get away with this?"

"Well, let's put it this way. They do, but not always."

"Meaning?"

"Summers can demand a hearing before a judge and has a right to retain counsel. He can also post bond and be let go."

"Do you know if Summers has or will take these actions."

"So far, I've been told he's only asked for counsel."

"Do we know who that is?"

"His name is Chris Knight. He appeared on that TV panel with Summers and Perry."

"Yes. I remember that now. But there's something else about him. What is it? Oh yes, he's the attorney that got under the skin of the gun advocates. Filed a suit to limit the right to bear arms under the Second Amendment."

"I think you're right. Does it matter?"

"It could. This guy Knight's a crusader. He'll go to the wall for his clients. He could cause trouble. But worrying about Knight can wait. What about the other 'evidence?'"

"With Summers in custody, it will be no problem getting into his house."

"You sure? What about a security system?"

"Some months after the murderer was convicted and sentenced to die, he had it disconnected."

"Hmm... And if traces of a powder were found, it could provide a link to Richards."

"Right!"

"What about Baker?"

"Summers admitted to the cops that he owned a gun. He claimed he threw it away after he lost his family. A local gun dealer cooperated and supplied an old registration statement. It has Summers name on it, but the information on the make of gun has been obliterated."

"Meaning?"

"It establishes that Summers had a gun. He can't account for his whereabouts on the night Baker was shot. By linking him as a suspect in Perry's death, then Richards, there is enough circumstantial evidence with the registration statement to link him as a suspect in the Baker shooting."

"Seems thin to me."

"I agree if you look at each death separately. But looking at all three as connected and given Summers' PTSD symptoms, his diatribe against Perry and anti-death penalty advocates, the prosecution has motive, means and opportunity. Besides, nothing has turned up to suggest another party or parties were involved. Edwards is adamant that his 'hunch' is right. The only logical conclusion is that three deaths of people that are against the death penalty, all relatively close in time were caused by one perpetrator. That perpetrator owned a gun, is a pharmacist and admits he was on the Metro platform when Perry was there."

"Well. It is neat. Perhaps too neat. On the other hand, it looks like the police aren't looking for any other suspects at this time. Even if Summers is arrested, tried and acquitted, no one will be looking for other suspects tied to these deaths until that verdict is rendered. It could end in a hung jury too. And that would require a retrial and more time will pass. Keep me informed."

"Of course!

CHAPTER 23
FOR THE DEFENSE

Chris Knight arrived at the precinct at 10 A.M. Walked up to the duty officer and said, "I'm Christopher Knight. I'm here to see my client, Jed Summers."

The desk sergeant responded, "Mr. Knight. Good morning. Please empty your pockets and put your belongings in that tray by the scanner. Do you have a cell phone?"

"Yes."

"You'll have to leave that here. You can put it into one of those cubicles over there. Shut the door and lock it and take the key with you. You can retrieve it when you leave."

"After you clear security, an officer will come and escort you to one of our interrogation rooms. Mr. Summers will be brought in to see you."

"Thank you Sargent."

Chris turned and proceeded through security. On the other side, he picked up his belongings and brief case and was led down a hallway to a door that opened into a windowless room with a metal table surrounded by metal chairs. He sat down and waited. Several minutes later Jed Summers was brought in. He looked tired, fearful and upset.

"Hello Mr. Summers. I'm Chris Knight. Please sit down. Not exactly a comfortable setting."

Summers nodded and sat down on the opposite side of the metal table.

Chris pulled out his notebook. "I'll be taking notes on this. Do you have any objections?"

Summers didn't answer, just nodded.

"Since you called me and asked me to come down to meet with you, am I correct that you intend to retain me as your counsel?"

"Yes."

"Have you had occasion to hire an attorney in the past?"

"For something like this?"

"No for any reason?"

"No."

"Then let me set some ground rules. I have a right to decline to represent you. Our meeting today will determine whether I will or not. You have the right to change your mind and not retain me for whatever reason. You have a right to an attorney. If you can't afford one, one can be appointed one at government expense. If you decide to retain my services, I will provide you with a retainer letter that details the terms and conditions of my representation. You are free to review it, ask questions, accept its terms or reject some or all of them. If I agree to change any terms, then my representation will be provided according to those revised terms we agree to. Is all this understood so far?"

"Yes," Summers said.

"Good! Now most importantly. What you tell me now, today, even if I choose not to represent you or you decide you want someone else to, is strictly confidential. It's only between you and me. I am bound by the canons of legal ethics not to disclose anything we discuss, any facts about anything connected with your case. And the police cannot make me or you reveal what we discuss or what you disclose to me in connection with your being held as a material witness in connection with the Perry death. All of our communications is protected by the attorney-client privilege. Do you understand?"

"Yes."

"Do you believe our communications are not subject to disclosure and will not be disclosed? Before you answer, let me explain why our discussions are privileged and confidential. As your lawyer, I need to know everything about your case. You need to disclose everything completely. You are not to make your own judgments about what you think may or may not be relevant or important. Every detail that comes to mind, what you know, what you suspect, what you guess at, you have to tell me. I will be the judge whether what you disclose is important, useful or not. Is that clear?"

"Yes."

"Any questions?"

"No."

"Fine. Let me tell you why your agreement and understanding of these terms is important to your rights and legal representation. Every lawyer at one time or another has clients that fail to disclose fully. Sometimes it's due to oversight, sometimes thinking some fact or incident is unimportant. And sometimes because the client believes the disclosure will hurt his case. Regardless of the reason, anything but full disclosure is more likely to harm a client's case than help it. An attorney without full knowledge can be hamstrung in his or her representation. The party that gets hurt however is the client that failed to disclose. Do you understand and accept this?"

"Yes. Yes, I do."

"Do you want to proceed?"

"Yes."

"How long have you been here, Mr. Summers?"

Summers looked at Chris with blood shot eyes and said, "Since early yesterday."

"Tell me what happened?"

Summers described the police arriving at his house, advising him they were there to take him in as a material witness, gave him time to collect some belongings and contact his work.

"Then they brought me here. Once here, I was questioned by two detectives."

"For what are you considered to be a material witness?"

"They say it's in connection with the death of that man from CHASE. You remember I think. He was on that death-penalty TV panel we both were on."

"You mean Ed Perry?"

"Yes."

"He was killed at a Metro station, the same night as the TV panel was broadcast."

"Yes."

"Why do the police think you would know anything about his death?"

"I don't know anything about it. But I was at the same Metro station that night. And it seems that's enough for them to bring me in here."

"Do you know anything that might be helpful to the police?"

"No. And I told them everything that happened."

"Tell me what you told them. And if there is anything you did not tell them, for any reason, tell me now. Understood?"

"Yes."

Summers than retold what he had told Detective Edwards.

"Okay. Is what happened that night the only thing you were questioned about?"

"No. And that's why I called you."

"Explain."

Summers then told Chris about being questioned about his being a pharmacist, what he knew about antidotes for anthrax, where he was the night Justice Baker was murdered and did he have anyone who could corroborate his whereabouts that night. Whether he owned a gun.

"You were right to call for an attorney."

"Why are the police asking me these things? Do you have any idea Mr. Knight?"

"It's too soon to draw any solid conclusions. The questions can be seen as routine. The police are being careful not to overlook any potential leads or facts that may help determine who is responsible, if anyone, for the death of Mr. Perry, whether his death is somehow linked to the death of that attorney Richards and whether those two deaths are linked with the murder of Justice Baker."

"I guess I can see that Mr. Knight. But, why me? What motive would I have to do harm to any of those people?"

"I agree, in general. But there is a common factor here."

"What?"

"The three people who died were all against the death penalty. You are a survivor of the victims whose murders incurred the death penalty that was

commuted by the court due to the efforts of Richards, and a result supported by Mr. Perry's organization. You made no bones about your position on
the death-penalty and did so on public television. Then your proximity to
the death of Perry, your knowledge about anthrax, and your ownership of
a gun at one time, taken together, and in the absence of other leads, pretty
much explains why you have been brought in as a material witness."

"But, I was told I was a material witness only about Perry's death. But
it seems the police think I'm somehow involved in the other two deaths."

"I agree. So, let's start with you telling me everything about your knowledge of anthrax, your ownership of a gun, and where you were on the night
Justice Baker was murdered. I also want you to tell me about your PTSD and
therapy sessions you agreed to undertake after seeing Dr. Young.

"Are you taking my case? Will you represent me?"

"Yes. I will."

CHAPTER 24
EQUALLY DIVIDED

Chester Gibbons, CEO of Universal Energy and his corporate counsel, Don McCallum arrived at Powell and Morley's law offices at 10 A.M. sharp. They took the elevator to the twenty-fifth floor where they were greeted by the receptionist and taken into the ornate conference room where coffee, juices and bottled water stood in an array on the side board next to an enormous conference table. McCallum poured himself and Gibbons cups of coffee and sat down at the far end of the table. A few minutes later Leon Powell, senior partner and founder of Powell and Morley, joined them.

"Good morning gentlemen," Powell said as he entered and shook hands with his clients.

"Have a seat and let's get started. I have some news about the court appointment to replace Justice Baker."

"Good or bad?" Gibbons asked.

"I'd say you'll think it's good," Powell responded.

"Great! Let's hear it."

"The Judiciary Committee members are squabbling over whether to schedule a hearing on whomever the Governor decides to nominate to take Baker's seat."

"Why is that?" McCallum asked.

"Part of the Committee members want to first consider proposals to reinstate the death penalty before considering a nominee. Their position is that any nominee should be questioned about his or her position on over-turning the death penalty or reinstating it through new legislation. Their opponents argue that the Court needs a complete panel so that decisions on which the vote is evenly split are not passed over or decided in effect by defaulting to the decision made by a lower court."

McCallum asked, "How does this play on our issue?"

"First, while the committee members wrangle, the court will remain of even number. If they don't settle their differences, then for an indefinite period, any lower court decision that is controversial is likely to be passed over until the beginning of next term," Powell advised.

"Good! exclaimed Gibbons. "I assume there is no dispute that our case is controversial?"

"It's probably the most controversial one on appeal, I should think," said McCallum.

"Agreed," Powell said.

"So, are we overlooking anything here?" asked Gibbons.

"How do you mean?" asked Powell.

"It's helpful that the confirmation of a new justice looks as if it will be delayed. That's a positive. But we still have to worry about who the Governor nominates, because eventually, the committee will hold its confirmation hearings."

"And you're worried about the nominee's position on the death penalty?"

"Not at all. I'm concerned about his or her position on fracking and whether he or she would overturn the lower court's dismissal of the lawsuit against us."

"I see," Powell said. "But that leads me to another subject and this time I think you'll think this isn't so good."

"What?" asked Gibbons.

"We've been advised by counsel that they intend to file a similar suit, but this time as a class action."

"What! Can they do that?"

"The putative class plaintiffs will be the citizens, residents or property owners who live within a yet to be defined radius of where UEC is currently..." Powell paused and picked up a paper he had laid in front of himself..."in the process of gas production, natural gas exploration, extraction, collection, treatment, transmission, including hydraulic fracturing."

"On what grounds?" McCallum wanted to know.

"The overall claim is that throughout the process of fracturing and the collection, treatment and transmission of shale gas, the process causes the migration of caustic, carcinogenic and flammable chemicals and compounds such as methane and hydrogen sulfide that contaminate the soil, ground-water, lakes, other water sources, etcetera, if located within three miles of where UEC is drilling," Powell explained.

"That sounds pretty much like the claims of the farmer who first complained and had his suit against us dismissed," McCallum said. "Yes. But that is on appeal before our Supreme Court. Apparently counsel believes that by suing on behalf of all those living within three miles of where UEC is drilling he's increasing the chance that the dismissal of the original plaintiff's suit will be overturned. And even if it isn't, there's a new suit of broader proportions – strength in numbers, one might say."

Gibbons looked at McCallum and asked, "We had that farmer's well water tested, didn't we?"

"We conducted four well-water tests on his well-testing for different variations of bacteria. All four tests showed that the farmer's well-water was not harmed and suitable for use. But then he got a private company and the results of its tests claimed that there was a high quantity of Alpha Methylstyrene present, a flammable and poisonous chemical allegedly a known component of fracking fluid."

Gibbons turned to Powel. "When did you hear about this class action?"

"Shortly after our meeting when we discussed what Justice Baker's death meant in terms of the appeal of the dismissal of that farmer's suit. After that meeting, I decided to call the farmer's counsel and see if he had changed his mind about settling. With Justice Baker gone, the chances that he'd win the appeal changed as we discussed. Unfortunately, he hit on a new strategy, the class action. This is the first time we've met since I found out about the class action gambit."

"Damn! I thought..." Gibbons started to say. Then stopped.

"You thought what, Chester?" asked Powell.

"Oh! Nothing! Nothing! Anyway, this class action doesn't affect our timing, does it? I mean there will still be a delay before the court takes up the farmer's appeal because of Baker's death. And it will take time for the class action to be tried. And it appears the legislature won't soon be confirming a replacement for Baker. So we still have time as we discussed last time, Gibbons stated.

"Yes, that's true," Powell agreed.

"Leon, I want you to keep tabs on all this. When the Governor might nominate Baker's replacement, who he intends to and the background on whomever it is. Also on the stalemate in the Judiciary Committee. We all know that a delay works in UE's favor. If we learn of something that may shorten the delay, we'll have to be ready."

"Ready for what, Chester?" Powell asked.

"Ready to support or oppose the Governor's nominee. Ready to lobby those on the Judiciary Committee in regard to refusing to hold hearings on the nominee or to lobby for or against the nominee depending on where he or she stands on the death penalty and fracking," Chester answered.

"That's a surprise," Powell reacted.

"What's a surprise?" Gibbons rejoined.

"Of course we need to know where the nominee is on fracking, but the death penalty?"

"They're linked, right Chester?" McCallum volunteered.

"Yes," Gibbons confirmed. "But that's all for now. We have another meeting we're running late for. Thanks Leon. Be sure you stay on top of things for us."

"Will do," Powell affirmed.

CHAPTER 25
SEARCHING

After Knight's meeting with Summers, he needed to talk to Kelly. He needed her assessment of his client's psychological make-up. Stated simply, was Jed Summers capable of murder?

Stated more pointedly, was he capable of three murders? Was he that clever and what...? Deranged? So evil that he could not only kill three people, but do so three different ways – shooting, bacteria, shoving into an ongoing train. Was his PTSD, resurrected by the commutation of the death penalty for the murderer of his family, the tipping point that changed a human being into a murderous avenger? After talking to Summers, Knight didn't think he revealed a psychological profile that suggested the possibility that an educated man, husband, father with a professional career could be turned into a murderous psychopath, the only psychological type Knight could think of for the person, or person responsible for three deaths. Then he remembered a squib in the news, searched through some old newspapers and found "Manhunt continues 40 years after deaths in Bethesda."

The article reported that despite the passage of 40 years, the FBI was still engaged in a worldwide search for William Bradford Bishop Jr., in connection with the bludgeoning of his wife, their three sons and the man's own mother. It was believed that after the killings, Bishop or whomever, coolly drove the mutilated bodies to a rural area some hundreds of miles South and set them on fire. During all this time, Bishop has been charged with unlawful flight to avoid prosecution. But after chasing down over 650 leads over 40 years, he is still at large somewhere. If he is still alive.

Chris put down the article and mused, "I guess one must be very careful in drawing conclusions about what a person is capable of doing. Still..." he thought to himself, put down the paper and walked into the kitchen where Kelly was preparing dinner.

"Honey, can I ask you a question?"

"Sure.

"Well it isn't exactly one that fits when you're cooking."

"Go ahead. If I don't like the question, you can take over making supper."

"Hey! Let's not get nasty!" They laughed.

Kelly said, "So ask already!"

"It's about Jed Summers."

"What about him? I know you've taken him as a client."

"I know your practice is more focused on victim counseling, but I wonder if you could give me some insight into someone's personality?"

"I think I can with some degree of confidence. It's a subject I have to deal with."

"Great! In talking to Summers, he just doesn't give one the impression of being violent or so cold blooded he could sneak into someone's bedroom and shoot him at point blank range. Or create a lethal concoction of anthrax bacteria that would result in an agonizing death. And then, shove a person into an oncoming train."

"Wait! I'm not following. I thought he was only being held as a material witness in connection with the man who fell in front of the Metro train."

"That's what the police say. But when I talked with Summers, he told me when the police questioned him, he got the impression they suspected he was connected to all three deaths."

"How does that make any sense?"

"From what he told me about his interrogation, the police focused on his knowledge as a pharmacist of antidotes for bacteria, including anthrax. They asked him if he owned a gun. When he admitted he had, they asked him where it was and he answered that he got rid of it after his family was murdered. Then he was asked about his whereabouts on the night Justice Baker was murdered. Of course, living alone, he could not prove he wasn't anywhere near the Justice's home. Then the police focused on his appearance on that TV panel on the death penalty. His criticism of the organization opposed to the death penalty and Ed Perry, its representative. Perry was killed by the train, falling off the same platform Summers was on to take the Metro home after the broadcast."

"Your question again?"

"Do you think Summers has the personality to commit murder? Do you think he could murder three people? Do you think the PTSD he suffered, suffers, as the survivor of his wife and daughter who were murdered, would turn him into someone who could plan and carry out three murders by three different means?"

"No."

"That was quick. Why are you so sure?"

"I'm not sure, 'sure.' But I can say this. While it's possible and often happens that traumatic events involving the worst kind of personal loss, like the violent deaths of loved ones, can and often does alter a person's personality, without more, a lot more, that that alteration would turn someone into a person capable of committing multiple murders is a psychological stretch. If asked, and I had to give my opinion, like testifying in court or before a panel evaluating a patient, I'd say no way."

"Okay. If I act on your opinion, then I have to search for others who committed these crimes. That means someone else had to have a reason to kill these three."

"You mean you now think the other two deaths were murders, not accidents?"

"I have to go on that assumption. First, the police seem to be working on that basis. If they do come up with circumstantial evidence incriminating Summers, my job is to raise reasonable doubt. To do that, I have to point to others who would have a motive to murder these three men."

"You think there was one person responsible for all three deaths?"

"I have to work on that premise until proven otherwise."

"Any idea where to start?"

"Hmm. You know? I think I do."

"Care to share?" Kelly asked.

"It's very rare that a judge is murdered. When it does happen, it's usually by someone he or she sentenced. Revenge is the motive. In Justice Baker's case, it's unlikely it was someone whom he ruled against. He's been on the State Supreme Court for a lot of years and hasn't been involved in any sentencing decisions in that time, other than the one that overturned the death penalty. All those sentenced would applaud his decision. I need to contact his law clerk and see what other controversial decisions he may have been involved in."

"Sounds like a good idea," Kelly said. "But I wonder…"

"What?"

"Suppose you find out Justice Baker was somehow involved with a decision and that decision might suggest a revenge motive for his murder. How does that tie into the other two deaths?"

"Good point. It may not. Except that it just seems unrealistic that these deaths are wholly unrelated. They have the common element of each victim being against the death penalty."

"Okay! Well enough for now! Dinner's ready! Get out the wine and let's eat," Kelly ordered.

CHAPTER 26
THE BEST LAID PLANS...

So far the plans had worked to near perfection. But with Summers having hired Knight to represent him, there was cause for concern. At any rate, it was time to consider what next steps might be necessary. It would be only a matter of time before Knight arranged for the release of Summers from his detention as a material witness. Then there was the Governor's reported consideration of at least two possible nominees to replace Justice Baker. With the release of the nominees' names, research had begun on their positions on certain legal issues and their personal legal philosophies.

At the same time, a close watch was kept on the jockeying for position of the members of the Judiciary Committee. When the Governor decided which of the two to actually nominate, focus would shift to picking the strategy to follow, if any, in lobbying the various members.

Crunch time came sooner than expected.

Word had arrived that Knight had insisted on Summers' release or that he be charged in the death of Perry. The police resisted, but Knight was preparing a habeas corpus motion and would get Summers released and soon. So it was time to provide the police with additional information lest the success so far achieved would be undone. The best laid plans...

Detective Edwards received an anonymous tip from someone claiming to see a man fitting the description of Summers by the lake near the cabin he owned in the foothills that surrounded the city. The man threw something, heaved it, into the lake. From the splash it seemed to be relatively heavy. Edwards ordered divers to search the area. They found a gun.

It was the same type listed in the registration papers found in Summers home. When confronted with this, Summers didn't remember throwing anything into the lake but admitted as he had before that he had disposed of the gun after the deaths of his family. Under questioning, he couldn't remember when he had gotten rid of the gun. Whether it was before or after Justice Baker's murder.

When the ballistics report came in, it showed that the gun thrown in the lake was not the one used to kill Justice Baker. Summers thought that would be enough to convince the police he had nothing to do with Justice Baker's murder. But Edwards wasn't buying. He came up with the theory that Summers throwing the gun into the lake in broad daylight was a ruse. He had planned to be seen and knew that when the gun was found, it would be evidence that it wasn't the gun used to kill the Justice. Edwards realized he might be seen playing for time, but he was convinced there was no other possible suspect than Summers.

Then Edwards got lucky again, or so it seemed. He was paid a visit by Oscar Royce from CHASE. Royce informed Edwards that the Board had decided to do something about Ed Perry's death. At first, they had no idea of how to do so. Then decided to hire a private detective. He went to Metro and got access to the tapes of the video cameras at the station where Perry was killed. The tape recording of the area of the platform contained a blurred image of a figure in a hat and coat moving toward the escalator on the other side of the platform from where Perry fell. When Royce was asked how the private investigator was able to get the tape from Metro, Royce said he was told that no one had asked to see it before. The death being viewed as an accident, the Metro police didn't ask about it, or if they did, after viewing it, didn't think it was important. The city police didn't get involved.

Edwards knew the grainy image on the tape didn't prove Summers was the person being caught on camera. But it was another piece in his puzzle. After Royce left, he pulled out his file and went over what he had. He started his review with the conviction that the only plausible suspect was still Summers. He reviewed what he had to support that theory and knew it was thin. But now he had a possible tie in with Perry's death and the bogus gun toss. What he needed was to look closer at the death of the attorney, Fleming Richards. Summers was a pharmacist and knowledgeable about bacteria and their antidotes, including anthrax. But he had to place Summers at Richards office, or had to find something connected with the packaging and delivery of that infected Zebra shield.

The receptionist at Richards office didn't pay much attention to the person who delivered the package. She was away from her desk filing some papers and when the person came in, she just nodded towards Richards' door for him to enter, saying only, "He's in." Not much help but it did establish that it was a man who delivered the package. Then she had a recall. She told Edwards that the man wore gloves. She noticed because it was summer.

Edwards thanked her and concentrated on the fact that there had to be some paper work connected to that package and its shipping. Edwards went online and started to search for African artifacts. He narrowed it to African war memorabilia and soon found what he was looking for. He called the company, explained who he was and was put through to the head of shipping. He learned that the package was sent to the post office serving Richards postal code with instructions it be held for pickup. The addressee was listed as AAA Importers.

Edwards signed off and went to the post office. No one there recalled the package or who picked it up. Too much mail, too many people coming and going. Whoever picked it up showed some I.D. or the package wouldn't have been released. No one recalled what kind of I.D. was shown but indicated that any kind would be accepted – a business card would do. They did guess it was a man who picked it up given its size.

"So what did he have," Edwards asked himself. Nothing concrete but enough to make some reasonable assumptions. He could organize these and use them to outline to Summers how he caused the deaths of the three anti-death penalty advocates. He saw Summers as emotionally vulnerable. He had gotten confessions from others like Summers before with the right kind of incessant questioning, mixed with sympathy for what the accused was suffering, then shifting again to agreeing that the victims got what they deserved. Whatever worked.

To get maximum effect, he first thought he had to grill Summers before Knight got him released. Then he changed his mind. It would be more effective if Summers was released. It would give him a false sense of security. Then hauling him back in would be discouraging and weaken his resistance to Edwards. onslaught questioning. His approach set, he called in Detectives Gaines and Whitmore to go over the plan. Being grilled by more than one increased the pressure on the suspect. He was even ready to handle what would be Knight's objections. The reality Edwards knew was not that Summers would agree with what Edwards questions were suggesting or admit anything. He wanted Summers to sweat. He wanted to watch his eyes and body language as Edwards laid out his theories of the facts that showed Summers was responsible for the three deaths. A confession would overcome the absence of hard evidence of the facts Edwards was sure existed as he surmised. It was a good plan, a well laid plan and Edwards was confident it would work.

The next day, Edwards briefed Gaines and Whitmore on his plan. They both were veterans playing at "good cop, bad cop." Then Edwards called Knight. He told him they were going to release Summers, but that his status now had changed to a "person of interest." Knight thanked Edwards for the information. He then drove to the precinct and took Summers to his home. Summers remained quiet on the drive there. When there, he got out of the car, then turned, and said, "Thank you." With that he walked off and went into his house. Chris decided to give his client some time before taking steps to address his new status as a person of interest and what that might mean.

CHAPTER 27
JUSTICE BAKER

With his client released from police custody, Chris had time to focus on his own investigation. He was sure that Edwards wasn't finished with Summers and his belief that Summers was responsible for the deaths of three people. Chris called Sheldon Morris, Justice Baker's law clerk. They met in the Justice's chambers which were still draped in black bunting.

"Thanks for seeing me Mr. Morris."

"I understand you are representing Mr. Summers. The husband whose wife and daughter were murdered and whose murderer's death sentence was commuted by Justice Baker's decision."

"That's right. Let me get something straight right away. I am not here to pass judgment on Justice Baker, the death penalty or the decision that outlawed it in this state. I am here in defense of my client."

"I appreciate your candor. So how can being here, help your defense?"

"Fair question. My wife is a psychologist – deals mostly in counseling victims of traumatic events. She was contacted by my client, Jed Summers. She advised him in general that PTSD is an unfortunate result of such trauma as the murder of one's loved ones. Not just military combat. When the police detained him as a material witness, after he was questioned in that capacity, he believed the police thought him responsible for at least one of the deaths. He decided he needed legal counsel and I agreed to represent him."

"I see. What has this to do with Justice Baker. I assume you are here about his murder."

"Correct! Indulge me a moment. Neither I nor my wife believe Mr. Summers is capable of harming anyone, much less committing murder. The police believe that the only logic is that a survivor of victims is responsible for the death of Justice Baker, the defense attorney and the advocate to abolish the death penalty. Based on the belief that Mr. Summers is not capable of such actions, despite his burden, I have to look at other possible suspects. That is what brings me here."

"Go on."

"My first theory is that a judge is murdered for revenge, for sentencing someone who holds a grudge until released and then seeks revenge against the judge that sentenced him. I don't think that applies to Justice Baker's murder."

"Agreed. He hasn't sentenced anyone in years."

"That leads to my theory that, if Summers or another survivor of the murder victims is not responsible, who would be? What I come up with is that there may be a pending appeal that has serious ramifications depending on how it's decided. If one of the party's interests might be seriously harmed depending on the decision made by the court, it could provide a motive. If that interest is worth millions or billions of dollars or some other interest equally transcending in value, and a justice's view on the issue is known, it could lead to drastic action to prevent that view from becoming the prevailing view. That is, become the law that would damage that interest. The only way to stop this is to make sure such an adverse decision is not rendered."

"I see your point. You want to know what cases were coming before the court that would involve a decision that could have consequences for what you described as having transcending value to interests that would be affected by that decision."

"Yes."

Morris, said, "Wait a minute." He went to the office next door and returned with a file.

"This file contains a list of matters on appeal yet to be decided. Where would you like to start?"

Thinking a moment, Chris said, "If my theory has any merit, I'd say criminal case appeals would not be relevant. So, let's review civil action appeals."

Of the twenty pages listing the legal issues in cases on appeal, Chris selected three. One was his own declaratory ruling on the Second Amendment's right to bear arms. Another concern was whether a manufacturer's failure to disclose risk information which inflated the price of a medication supported plausible RICO claims. The third concerned whether towns and cities are allowed to pass bans on oil and gas drilling and fracking.

"Mr. Knight, I think I understand your selections, but enlighten me to see if we are on the same page."

"Of all the civil cases on appeal, these three cases involve companies worth hundreds of millions or billions of dollars – gun manufacturers and merchants, drug companies and oil or energy companies. I have to ask you, as law clerk to Justice Baker, do you have an opinion on where he stood on the issues these cases raise?"

"I have to preface my replies with some caveats. First, the press, the public and politicians generally view Justice Baker leaning to the left on many issues. Certainly, his decision to overturn the death penalty places him in that category. However, he always took his time in formulating his opinion. One case at a time. Once he decided the direction he wanted to go, he'd outline his position and then discuss it with me, sometimes with the other justices. But that was usually after he had thought out his position. When he did inform other justices of where he was coming out on a case, it was to see if they might have a point or analysis he overlooked or hadn't fully thought through. Then he would instruct me to do the research and gather the facts to support where he was going with his decision."

"Sounds most judicious. No pun intended," Chris said. "So can you tell me or do you have any understanding where Justice Baker was on these three cases?"

"The first one, your appeal, too new. He didn't have the time to get into it. The medical RICO, he was always doubtful about the ethics of drug manufacturers, but he knew proving a RICO case was a high mountain to climb."

"I see,' Chris said. "And the case of cities banning oil and gas drilling and fracking?"

"On that one, I can be a little more certain. Justice Baker was expected by the press and other court observers to come down on the side of the municipalities who sought to ban fracking. The oil companies had argued that the state's oil, gas and mining law took precedence over local zoning laws. Their position was upheld in the lower court. Four of the court's justices agreed with the lower court's decision. Four of the justices disagreed. Chief Justice Baker's decision would break that tie."

"And where did Justice Baker come out on the issue?" Chris asked.

"At Justice Baker's direction, I was well into drafting the decision that local governments have the authority to decide how land is used, including whether or not fracking and drilling should be allowed on public lands."

"Had Justice Baker lived until after the decision was rendered what would have been the result overall?"

"The five to four ruling in favor of the municipalities would have meant that other municipalities in the state could pass laws that ban fracking and drilling. At the time, it was known that over 150 towns and cities in the state had passed fracking bans or imposed moratoria. The decision would have upheld those bans."

"So, the oil and gas industry are facing hard times. The decision would have made it even tougher on the industry. And conversely, no decision or a delay in issuing a decision gave the industry a much needed reprieve. Do you agree?" Chris asked.

"Yes," said Morris.

"Do you think the Court will act on the appeal before a replacement for Justice Baker is seated on the court?"

"Hard to say. If I had to guess, I'd say no. Based on the logic that with the eight justices equally divided on the issue, a split decision would uphold the lower court's ruling and allow fracking to continue. So unless one of the justices that supports allowing municipalities to control fracking changes his or her mind, the appeal will remain pending. "

"And that allows fracking to continue in any event."

"Yes it does."

"Do you think one of the justices that supports the industry would change his mind and rule in favor of the municipalities?"

"No, I don't."

"So it looks like the issues depend on the Governor's nominee to replace Justice Baker and the legislature confirming that nominee's appointment?"

"Yes. And it is not known who the nominee will be or what his or her position is on this fracking issue. I'm sure whoever it is, he or she will be grilled by the Judiciary Committee on the issue as well as many others."

"Well, Mr. Morris, I've taken up a lot of your time. Thank you."

"Has this been helpful to you?"

"Yes. I think very helpful. But to just what extent remains to be seen. I've got work to do, but I think I have a path that I can pursue with greater confidence. Thanks again."

Chris arrived home and Kelly came to greet him.

"How did it go with Justice Baker's law clerk?"

"I think it helped." He told her of his discussions with Sheldon Morris. That he was able to narrow his focus on three possible appeals that might have the kind of financial impact, depending on how they were decided, to cause some powerful interests to be worried.

"In my own mind, I've settled on just one of the three pending appeals whose outcome would have been decided by Justice Baker adversely to some very powerful interests."

"Can you prove anything? I mean, what you have is theory. Perhaps the right theory, but that isn't proof of anything is it?" Kelly asked.

"No. It isn't. But my job as Summers' attorney doesn't require me prove my theory. Of course if I could, that would be the best. But, all I have to do is find another plausible reason for Justice Baker's murder other than a survivor's revenge for overturning the death penalty."

"You lost me. Mr. Summers hasn't been charged with murder. He was detained only as a material witness about that Mr. Perry's death, not Justice Baker's. And you told me they have let Mr. Summers go."

"Yes. You're right. But I don't think this is over for Mr. Summers. I think the police are playing a game. A gamble that Summers, let go, will relax and get careless."

"So you think the police still think Summers is involved not only in the Perry death, but Justice Baker's murder?"

"Yes. And my reasoning is that the police are fixated on their theory that a survivor decided to take revenge against those responsible for letting murderers off the hook. Right now, they don't have evidence to prove their theory, but on the other hand, they have no other theory. That means they aren't looking at any other possible suspects, any other possible motives. And that tells me they are lying in wait for Summers to trip himself up."

"But if he didn't do it as you believe, how could he trip himself up?"

"Good point. I'm sure the police don't know how he could do so. They just believe he could and can wait until he does. They have no other suspects or leads. In these circumstances, the tactic is to give their prime suspect enough room to do something that will prove their theory. It's something you would fully understand."

"You mean their playing a psychological war game.?" Kelly surmised.

"Yes. Look! They know Summers is distraught. They saw his rant on that TV show. They know his psychological makeup is far from 'cold blooded.' On the other hand, they are relying on his psychological makeup to snap. And if they're right, and he does, they'll have the proof, the confession if you will, they need to convict. That's why I need another plausible suspect or suspects to undermine their case if they are successful. I also need it to bolster Summers. He needs to know there are other possibilities for who committed these murders before he starts believing he did regardless of the plain fact that he didn't."

"You're right. People under such stress can believe they are guilty. It's a release in a way. The emotional and psychological pressure of being 'suspected' can be eased by admitting they are responsible – guilty. If for no other reason than to stop the suspicions, stop the accusations, stop the pressure of being under the spot light."

"Your analysis is spot on, doctor," Chris said with a smile. "And that is why I have to work on developing a suspect or suspects that have the motive, means and opportunity to have been involved in these deaths. These murders."

"Looks as if the team is back on the field," Kelly said with a smile.

"And what a team it is," Chris said.

CHAPTER 28
THE NEXT PHASE

It was Monday morning, Raining. Raining for the fourth day. The gray sky, ominous, depressing. It was 9 A.M. Edwards walked into the office of the Chief of Police, Sharon Wilcox.

"Good morning Chief."

"What's good about it detective? Anyway, yes! What is it?"

"Summers got an attorney. We decided not to hold him any longer as a material witness. We released him Friday."

"His lawyer responsible?"

"No. His showing up did have an effect however."

"How so?"

"It gave me the idea that releasing Summers may actually help our investigations."

"Explain."

"While in custody, Summers was nervous, suspicious and fearful. After he was interrogated, he called for a lawyer. We think he was catching on that he might be a suspect and not a witness. If he talked with his lawyer about his fear, we'd be told to charge him or release him. We could have charged him. But I thought of a better approach."

"Go on."

"We are building a case that he was involved in the death of that anti-death penalty advocate, Perry. But my suspicions have grown that he was responsible for all three deaths. But, we don't have enough yet to go down that road."

"You think that releasing Summers will help uncover some links to all three deaths?"

"Yes."

"How?"

"Being released, Summers will relax. If he is involved in all three deaths, he'll feel safe, that he's fooled us. And then he may get careless."

"That's a long shot detective."

"Maybe so. But having him sit in lock up won't do us any good. And if he was released because he was charged, he'd stay on his guard. But being released voluntarily, he would think differently. In any event, I came to see you to get authorization to do a stake out on Summers."

"That's expensive as you know."

"Yes. That's why I'm asking. You know the media wants to know if we're making progress in our investigations. Truthfully, we're not. What we do have points only to Summers. So, we have to concentrate on him."

"What do you hope to find by watching him?

"There are several things. He did have a gun. He said he got rid of it after the murders of his wife and daughter. We discovered that was right. A witness saw him throw something into the lake next to his vacation cabin. We fished it out only to find it was not the gun used to murder Justice Baker. We were disappointed. But then it occurred to me that he knew if we found his gun and it wasn't the one that killed the Justice, he'd be in the clear. He could have gotten another gun, the one used to kill the Justice. He wouldn't repeat throwing it into the lake. Too obvious. So we think he may still have it hidden somewhere. If he thinks he's in the clear and he still has the gun, he'll make a move to ditch it. If we have him under surveillance, we have a chance to catch him in the act."

"And if he's already disposed of the gun?"

"We missed out. But the gun is not the only focus."

"What else?"

"Summers is a pharmacist. He knows bacteria, including anthrax. He goes back to work. If there are any spores in his lab, he'll get rid of them."

"Same question. If he's already gotten rid of them?"

"Same answer."

"So, it's likely you get nothing incriminating in either case."

"I know. But hear me out. Summers is not the criminal type. If he's responsible for the three deaths, his actions arose from extreme emotional distress. That kind of distress can make a person nervous and paranoid. The state, the legal system seemed to have worked properly in avenging the murders of his family. Then that closure is undone by the state and the legal system. Back to being paranoid. That paranoia turns an everyday person into his own avenger.

We know Summers suffered PTSD when his family was murdered. When their killer was saved from death, the PTSD returned, probably with equal or more vehemence. He feels he and his family were betrayed. Those who were involved on the betrayal have to pay for it."

"Your theory is plausible. And say you're right. Summers defense is that he was not in his right mind and he's not convicted due to mental deficiency – not knowing the difference between right and wrong."

"My job is not to try him. My job is to present the evidence that he is the killer. Once tried, it's up to a judge and jury to decide what his sentence should be."

"When do you want to start the stake out?"

"As soon as possible."

"It's worth a try. But something has to develop. I'll want reports. If nothing develops after a reasonable period of time, I'll close it down.

"Fair enough."

Edwards left Wilcox's office and headed down to the homicide unit. He gathered his team and informed them that they would begin staking out Summers' residence and would contact the management of the pharmacy where he worked. Gaines and Whitmore groaned. Both hated stake outs – boring, tiring from "doing nothing,' for hours on end.

Gaines asked, "How are we going to do this? There's no place around his house or where he works where we could observe him without his knowing."

"Not a problem," Edwards responded. "I want him to know he's being watched."

"Really? Then how…"

"There are two ways a stake out can work. The obvious one is that the suspect is caught doing something incriminating. The other, and one I think applies here, is pressure. Summers exhibited a lot of discomfort, nerves, when we had him in here, particularly under questioning.

When he sees he's being watched, he'll have to try and get rid of any evidence he may still have - somewhere. Or, he may just snap and we get a confession. In addition, we're still investigating and hopefully we'll turn up something that will increase the heat on him – get something that will support a search warrant of his home, job site, whatever."

"Okay. But we can't watch is home day and night," Whitmore protested.

"Right," Edwards admitted. "In setting this up, I canvased the surrounding neighbors. I persuaded enough of them to keep watch when we're not there."

"And they agreed? Over Summers who lost his wife and daughter?" Gaines asked.

"I told them we were concerned about him. That he might be depressed. I told them he was a material witness and while our investigation was on-going, we wanted to be sure he wasn't bothered."

"They all bought that?"

"Six out of seven."

"And these neighbors, volunteers, they know we'll be watching too."

"Yes. They only have to observe when we're not there. And with six volunteers, I assured them they didn't have to interrupt the usual routines."

"And where exactly are these six stake outs located?" Gaines asked.

"Three are across the street in front of his house. The next door neighbor to his left where there's a side entrance is another. And there are two behind his house. So when he leaves and returns, all sides are covered," Edwards replied.

"If Summers is aware he's being watched at home. How do we handle this when he's at work?" Whitmore asked.

"Same way. I've spoke to the store manager. Gave him the same story about Summers being a material witness and we wanted him safe, but would not be able to be around all the time. Plus, he didn't want cops hanging around. Bad for business. He got the message and agreed to report any actions out of the ordinary when he's on the job, let us know when he leaves the premises, when he returns, and if they know, where he went."

Edwards looked around at the officers, then said, "Anymore questions?"

Gaines said, "Yes. Who's first up"?"

"Since you asked Lou, that would be you and Whitmore."

"Thanks Lou, you, nitwit," Whitmore complained.

"Let's get rolling," Edwards ended the meeting.

The next morning, Gaines and Whitmore rolled up in their unmarked car at six a.m. They parked on the other side of the street facing the front of Summers' house and the garage. Each had their donut and coffee.

"I really hate these stake outs," Whitmore said.

"Relax Jim. I'm no fan either, but it's the job. Look on the bright side. We're sitting down most all of the time. We can take turns napping. We get food and drink the city pays for and we get relief after eight hours and sixteen hours off. With our seniority, we can avoid most night time surveillance. Plus, with the volunteers Edwards arranged for, I don't see us being here every day. In fact, he told me, it would add pressure if we skipped a day or two."

"Yeah. Why?"

"Summers notices us. Sees our car. Sees us sitting here. We don't move for hours. On the days he leaves for work, we let him get ahead, then fall in behind him and follow him. He knows he's being watched. Followed. Right? Then the next day, we're not here. He relaxes, right? Then the following day, or even two days later, we're back. So his relief is destroyed. He's back to being irritated, angry, upset, whatever. Mind games. He starts asking himself what is going on. He gets concerned. He thinks we're on to him. He'll think it's only a matter of time until we turn up the gun that killed the Justice or some anthrax spores. He starts thinking that he has to do something to be sure we don't find the gun or spores, so he has to risk taking some action to be sure the gun and the anthrax aren't found. He makes his move, and we grab him."

"You been watching too many cop shows on TV," Whitmore said

"It sounds like a script. I agree. But, it's only part of Edwards plan. Don't forget the mind games. Assume Summers has already gotten rid of the gun and the anthrax so they can't be traced to him. They're possibilities Edwards recognizes. That's where the mind games come in. Summers isn't a hardened criminal. He didn't have anything to gain by killing those three people but revenge. Okay, so now, he's had his revenge and he knows now it didn't really change anything. It didn't bring back his wife and daughter. He feels remorse and guilt. Knowing what he's done, he can't move on. He can't establish any close relationships. Can't consider loving someone else. He's trapped in a never ending nightmare of his own making. The mental and emotional pressure becomes unbearable. He snaps. He confesses."

"Now you've been watching too many doctor shows," Whitmore rejoined.

"I don't know. We both know that the solutions to some murders have rested on equally far-fetched scenarios. Anyway, Edwards knows that pressure is growing to solve these murders, and we've got nothing to lead us in other directions."

"Wait!" Whitmore said and grabbed Gaines arm. "The garage door is opening."

Summers came out a side door to the garage and walked around the front of his car to get in. Stopped. Look across at the car and Whitmore and Gaines. He recognized them from his interrogation as a material witness. He was about to walk over to them, then stopped. Got in his car, pulled out, pressed the remote and shut the garage door, turned left out of his driveway and proceeded down the street. Gaines waited until Summers was a block ahead, then pulled out and followed Summers, keeping a full block back. Gaines wasn't worried he'd lose him. He had to be going to work. Of course, if he was wrong, that would be hard to explain.

CHAPTER 29
STORM CLOUDS

"Hello? You have news?"

"Yes," the voice on the other end of the line responded.

"Good or bad?"

"It's a mix bag perhaps. You have to decide."

"Damn! Okay, go ahead."

"First. The police are more convinced that Summers is guilty."

"Good. But how do you know?"

"They put him under surveillance – basically around the clock."

"That helps?"

"They think it will unnerve him. Force him to make a mistake."

"What kind of mistake?"

"Panic. If he does, they think he would try to get rid of anything that connects him the three deaths or at least one them."

"But, he hasn't got anything to get rid of."

"No that's right. But they realize that possibility. So their fall back is to make him so unnerved he confesses."

"You think that's possible?"

"I'm no psychologist. Don't know. I suppose it could work."

"We wait this out? For how long?"

"No way of knowing."

"That it?"

"No. There's this lawyer. Summers lawyer. He's poking around. He's convinced Summers didn't kill anyone."

"What's he done?"

"He met with Justice Baker's law clerk."

"So?"

"According to Baker's clerk, he went over the roster of cases pending before the court. He was looking for a case that depending on how it was decided could have huge financial consequences for someone."

"Did he find any?"

"Yes."

"I don't like your tone. What did he find?"

"The appeal of the cities' and counties' rights to ban gas and oil exploration and fracking."

"This lawyer? We know him don't we?"

"Yes. As we talked before, his name is Christopher Knight. Does corporate work, but started a suit concerning the right to bear arms. He's what you might describe as a 'crusader.'"

'In other words, he's trouble."

"Could be."

"What options do we have?"

"Well it depends on timing."

"How so?"

"How much time it takes for the police stake out to panic Summers. If he does panic. Even if he does, he won't lead the cops to some place where he's hid anything incriminating because there isn't anything. That leads to his being panicked enough to confess."

"How realistic is that?"

"It's realistic. Just can't tell how long it would take. In the meantime, this guy Knight will continue his search for other suspects."

"Suggestions?"

"Waiting around for Summers to confess has the most uncertainty."

"But he won't be caught trying to get rid of any incriminating evidence because there is none."

"Yes. But that can be corrected?"

"Corrected? I don't follow."

"Summers has a cabin near the lake. He doesn't go there, so no one's around. It will be easy to get in the cabin and leave some things for the police to find."

"But haven't the police already searched that cabin?"

"No. They haven't had enough to get a search warrant."

"So, what's it going to take to get enough to get that search warrant?"

"First things first. The 'evidence' has to be placed on the premises. Once that's done, Summers has to visit the cabin. The police will be watching."

"So what? They see him go to the cabin, assuming there's a way to get him to go there. Just going there isn't incriminating. It won't support a search warrant."

"You're right. But suppose someone reports some strange looking bags in the back of the property with white powder in them and calls the county concerned that they be poisonous. It's a bit of a stretch, but given the news reports about Richards's death, Summers' appearance on that TV panel, and that he is a pharmacist, it will be checked out. When it is, the bags will be found to contain anthrax spores. It's reported to the cops. They get their warrant to search the cabin. When they do, they find a Glock 42 hidden under a floor board."

"Do you think this will work?"

"I think so. Is it worth the risk? Probably not. Except for this guy Knight. He'll keep snooping around and could stumble on to something that won't be good for us."

"I don't know. Mistakes could be made that would backfire. Summers may snap if the cops keep up the pressure. What can be done to interfere with Knight?"

"Not much directly. But his crusade for better gun control may be useful."

"How so?"

"His case on the Second Amendment is pending before the state Supreme Court. During argument before the appeals court, he was challenged to draft legislation that would implement the holdings on the limitations of the Second Amendment if he won his case. The Judiciary Committee is soon going to have the Governor's nominee to replace Baker. We have good relations with Senator Mitchell who is on the Committee."

"Yes. Go on."

"Senator Mitchell contacts Knight and asks him to draft his legislation assuming he wins his case before the Supreme Court. He tells Knight that his proposed legislation is needed now more than ever. Knight is curious, but hesitant. He's a practical guy and he knows drafting such legislation is no easy cakewalk. At this point, Mitchell plays his trump cards."

"His trump cards?"

"The first one is the recent press reports on the rapidly growing so-called 'patriot' groups. The federal government sees these groups as anti-government extremists, even domestic terrorists. Their members are all armed to the teeth, AK-47s, AR-15s, and all manner of other military weapons. The second is the unexpected result of the Governor's sponsoring and wining legislation to restore voting rights for several hundred thousand felons. The restoration of those rights will mean fewer hurdles for these felons to get guns. Then he delivers the clincher."

"Which is what?"

"Given these developments, Knight is told the Committee should ask the nominee about his or her position on gun control legislation and specifically about Knight's proposed draft."

"It might work. But how does it keep Knight from further snooping around on Summers?"

"It's no easy thing to draft legislation, particularly this kind of legislation. Moreover, when some of these groups hear about the proposed legislation, Knight may find himself a target of some of the more extreme gun advocates. And we don't need him distracted for a long time. We just need him thrown off the track until things are set up for Summers' arrest."

"How soon can you set this up, assuming you'll be successful."

"I'll call Senator Mitchell tomorrow and set up a meet. I'll tell him I want to drop by to inform him of a contribution to his PAC and to bring up an issue on the upcoming hearings on Baker's replacement."

"How much?"

"For the PAC, $10,000 should do it for now."

"Get started and keep me informed."

CHAPTER 30
FIXING THINGS

It was early morning when the Toyota Camry pulled away from the driveway, slowly as if to minimize any sound of its leaving.

Two hours later, the car pulled off the deserted highway about fifty yards from the driveway for Summers' cabin by the lake. A man got out of the car, retrieving a small black bag. The sky was overcast and a slight rain was falling. No moon. No stars. Dressed in a black jump suit with hood and wearing black sneakers, his face darkened, he was invisible. After a few minutes, he was at the cabin's back door. All was quiet. He took out his hook pick and was soon inside the cabin. It was pitch black inside so he had to risk using a pen light to find his way.

He found the bedroom. It was on the other side of the cabin away from the cabin next door. He would be able to work without concern that his movements would be seen. He pushed the king size bed to the side and took a small crow bar from the bag he carried. He gently inserted the thin blade of the bar where the floor boards met and pried one board up. He did so slowly keeping the sound to a minimum. He took a package from his bag that was wrapped in bubble warp and placed it into the space beneath the board. Then he lowered the board and gently tapped the exposed nails back in to place. Finished, he pushed the bed back into place and returned to the back door by which he had entered. He exited and quietly closed the door and heard the latch click into place. He stood straight for a moment and listened. No sound came to him.

He stepped off the porch and walked to the propane gas tank at the right rear of the cabin. He reached into the bag he was carrying and pulled out a trowel and two small packets. He dug into the soft earth near the rear of the tank. Making a hole of about six inches, he placed the packets in the hole and covered it up. He replaced the trowel into the bag, stood up and once again listened. No sound. He went back down the driveway, got in his car and drove slowly away.

The following morning, the homicide division received a call from one of the volunteers staking out Summers house.

"Hello, this is Corwin Bromley."

"Yes, Mr. Bromley, this is Detective Edwards, what can I do for you?"

"I volunteered to watch Mr. Summers' residence."

"Yes, I remember. Have you something to report?"

"Yes, maybe. I don't know. But I was instructed to report anything I thought unusual. So here it is. I stayed up late last night to catch the NBA game between Oklahoma City and Golden State. They were playing on the west coast so it ended about 2 A.M. When I walked into my bedroom I decided to take a quick look at Mr. Summers' house which is right across the street from me. I saw his car, at least I think it was his car, pull out of the drive way and turn to my left, his right. I watched a few minutes and he headed straight out. Then he drove out of my sight."

"That's it?"

"Yes. I was told to report…"

"You did just right. Thanks for the report. We'll follow up."

"Will you let me know if this helped you?"

"I can't say Mr. Bromley. But you did what we asked and we're grateful. Thank you."

Edwards hung up. "Now where would he be going at 2 A.M. in the morning," he thought. He called Gaines and Whitmore. They left their desks and came over to his.

"What?" they asked in unison.

"One of our volunteers saw Summers leaving his house at 2 A.M."

"Okay. What do we do?"

"First, Whitmore, get over to the other volunteers. See if any of them noticed when he returned. Gaines, where do you think Summers went at 2 A.M.?"

"Right! Like I would know."

"Humor me. Pretend your Sherlock. Do some deduction."

Gaines stared for a moment. He could see Edwards was serious. He wanted him to speculate. Then he said, "Really? Okay. Here goes. He could be going to his work to take care of something he forgot to do and it was important. Or he could just have needed some medication for himself."

"Go on. Where else?"

"He could have gone to some lady?"

"Get real!"

"Yeah, as soon as I said it, I knew — no way."

"Where else?"

"Liquor store?"

"Could be, but if so, he would have returned shortly after he left. Whitmore is checking on when he returned. If he learns he came back after a short time, that hunch might be right. But let's go on and assume he didn't get back after a short time."

"Then he had a mission to accomplish. A mission he didn't want anyone to know about because he undertook it under cover of darkness at a time when everyone should be asleep."

"Right! And what might that secret mission be?"

"Well, he's suspected of murder. So, logically it has something to do with his being a suspect."

"Right again! And where might he go on such a mission?"

"The only place logic suggests is some place under his control where he would feel it was safe."

"Safe for what?"

"Safe to conceal anything that might incriminate him in a murder."

"Right again! And where might that place be?"

"It could be anywhere."

"Come on! You can do better than that."

"Someplace he controlled. Someplace he had privacy."

"And where might you think that would be?"

"The only place other than his home and his office would be is cabin by the lake."

"Bingo! Let's go!"

Edwards and Gaines went to the police garage, picked up an unmarked car and headed out. They arrived at Summers' cabin. Parked. Edwards told Gaines to go around back and look for anything out of place, anything that might be suspicious. Edwards went to the cabin next door, knocked and waited. The door opened and an elderly lady asked, "What?"

"Sorry to disturb you, ma'am. I'm detective Edwards." He showed her his badge.

"Yes. What do you want with me, young man?"

"What's your name... please?"

"Bertha, Bertha Schlapp."

"When was the last time you noticed Mr. Summers was here at his cabin?"

"Don't recall. I don't spy on my neighbors."

"Of course not. Just thought you might have heard or seen something recently. We have reason to believe Mr. Summers might have come here last night."

"I go to bed early. Sleep like a log. If he was here I wouldn't know."

"Would you know of anyone around here that might know if he was here or not?"

"No. But, look, when he does come here, he always makes coffee, takes a cup and sits on the back porch."

"Would he do that late at night, early morning, the wee hours of the morning?"

"I wouldn't know. But if you're all that concerned, go look."

"What do you mean?"

"If he was here at the times you mentioned, if he followed his usual habits, he would have made coffee and sat on the back porch. Check his kitchen."

"We don't have a way of doing that."

"Of course you do!"

"We do?"

"There's a key under the mat in front of the back porch door. Mr. Summers was very friendly and trusting. He wanted me and few others to know we could enter if we had a reason to. Go retrieve it and take a look."

"Thank you, ma'am. You have been most helpful. I'd like to ask you if you could help some more."

"What do you mean?"

"You indicated Mr. Summers wanted his neighbors to be able to enter his cabin if they thought there was a reason. We believe there is something in the cabin that may be relevant to our investigation of events in which Mr. Summers may be involved. As government officials, we are restricted from entering private property without consent or authority. But, if a neighbor, you, someone Mr. Summers invited to enter his cabin if they thought there was a reason to do so, then that would be consistent with his wishes."

"Look young man, make sense! Why would Mr. Summers want me to enter his cabin because the police want to do so?"

"He's recently been released as a material witness in the death of an anti-death penalty advocate. It's routine for us to check out all aspects of a material witnesses' background. It may provide leads that help with our investigation of the death. Part of that investigation would include his whereabouts, habits, where he lives. His cabin here is part of his background. Knowing if there is anything there he may have forgot to tell us may help our investigation and to understand whether Mr. Summers has information as a material witness that we need to know. He's been questioned and as a result what he uses his cabin for and what may be in there may help clear him from further involvement.

"Really! Don't see how. Goodbye!" And with that she attempted to slam the door.

Edwards blocked the door with his foot.

"Ms. Schlapp, I'm sorry, but this is a murder investigation. We need to be sure our investigation is thorough and complete. I must insist."

"Oh! Alright! Let me put some shoes on."

The old lady returned to her front door and pushed open the screen door and started for Summers' cabin, Edwards right behind her. She walked up the steps on Summers' back deck, bent down and lifted the mat. She picked up the key, inserted it into the lock and pushed the door open and stood back. Edwards saw Gaines looking around and called to him. "Gaines, come here."

Schlapp had descended the stairs and headed back to her cabin.

"What's going on? How did you get in?"

"Never mind. We're in. Start looking around."

"Edwards! If we find some evidence, Summers' lawyers will have it excluded because we don't have a warrant."

"Let me worry about that. Start searching."

Gaines shrugged and did as he was told.

The third room Edwards searched was the bedroom. When he entered he saw nothing unusual. He paused and slowly gazed around the room. Then his eye caught something. He saw scrape marks on the floor underneath the bed. He pushed the bed along the track of the marks. Then he closely examined the floor under the bed. He noticed marks on the floor boards.

"Gaines, get me something to pry up these floor boards."

It took a few minutes, but Gaines came back with the tire iron from the car.

Edwards jammed the tongue into the boards where he saw the scars on the wood. He pried them up and found the bubble wrapped package. Carefully he opened it and found a Glock 42, the type of gun used to kill Justice Baker. Ballistics would confirm it was the gun used to murder Justice Baker. But he couldn't take it just yet. No matter that Edwards was convinced that this was the gun that killed Justice Baker, it would not be admitted in evidence. The gun had to be found as a result of a valid search warrant. Edwards carefully replaced it. Nailed the floor slat back into place and pushed the bed back into place.

"Gaines, come here."

Gaines came in the room. "What?"

"Have you found anything outside?"

"Nothing. Other than it looks like someone was doing a little digging at the back of the propane tank."

"Show me," Edwards commanded.

Gaines led Edwards to the spot by the propane tank. It was evident that the earth had been recently disturbed. Edwards went back into the kitchen, retrieved a large spoon and started digging. After a few spoonful's he hit the cloth sacks. He backed off. Then he used the spoon to lift the sacks out of the small hole and laid them on the concrete footing of the propane tank. He replaced the sacks, covered them over again and handed the spoon to Gaines and said, "Rinse this off and put it back in the utensil drawer in the kitchen. Close the door and lock it. Put the key back under the mat." When Gaines finished, Edwards said, "Okay, let's get back. I have enough to get a warrant. And with a warrant I've got Summers for these murders."

CHAPTER 31
ARRAIGNMENT

Edwards convinced District Attorney Newberry to seek a warrant to search Summers' cabin relying on his theories that since nothing had been found in Summers' residence, if there were any helpful evidence it had to be at his cabin. Based on the continued surveillance of his home, the only place he went to other than work was his cabin. He argued that if the search didn't uncover anything incriminating, they could end his surveillance and redirect the investigation. Executing the warrant, Edwards retrieved the Glock 42 and the cloth sacks. Ballistics confirmed that the gun was the one used to kill Justice Baker and the lab confirmed that the sacks had residue of anthrax spores. Summers was arrested and charged with the murders of Justice Baker and Richard Flemings. The direct evidence linking him to the murders of Baker and Flemings when linked to his presence at the Metro platform where Perry was killed following his appearance on the death penalty TV panel provided sufficient circumstantial evidence that he was also responsible for Perry's death. Summers was arrested and charged with first degree murder in the deaths of all three victims.

At his arraignment, he pleaded not guilty. Chris Knight argued that he be released on his own recognizance. Given the prosecutions possession of the gun that killed Justice Baker and the cloth sacks, the judge rejected Knight's argument and set bail at one million dollars. Unable to post bond in that amount, Summers was returned to his cell to await trial.

"You read this morning's paper?"

"You mean about Summers being charged with having murdered all three involved with overturning the death penalty? Yes. I saw the report. Good work! What are the chances for conviction?"

"One would have to say good. But, the prosecution has to prove the case beyond a reasonable doubt."

"Can there be reasonable doubt here? The paper says the cops found the gun hidden in his cabin and the sacks buried behind it."

"True. Very incriminating. But his lawyer, Knight, is sharp. He'll mount a defense."

"Based on what?"

"I'm no criminal defense attorney, but he could argue Summers is being framed. That the gun and sacks were planted at his cabin. He'll also likely argue that Summers has no history of violence and that he's been a solid citizen. He may also argue that as he is suffering from PTSD as a survivor of the murders of his wife and daughter, he wasn't capable of such cold blooded actions."

"That could be a two-edged sword. It shows motive."

"Yes. My guess is that if the prosecution's case is well-presented, Knight may be forced to bring his emotional state into the trial. If the gun, the sacks, his presence at the Metro seem to be persuading the jury, Knight could be forced to bring in a psychologist to testify about Summers mental and emotional state."

"Knight's wife is a psychologist, isn't she?"

"Yes. But I don't think he'd call her because she is."

"But she could assist outside the trial. Picking another psychologist and advising Knight on how to build a defense that Summers isn't capable of such killings."

"Yes. But it might do no good. Summers could be held responsible, but due to diminished capacity, he can't be found guilty of premeditated murder. If he is found not guilty by reason of his diminished capacity, the verdict is still that he killed the three and the cases are closed."

"So, we still win. Either way?"

"That's right."

"That good news is as good as the news that oil barrel prices are rising again. If they keep doing so, it proves getting the time we've gained from Baker's death was the right play.

"Appears so."

Chris Knight and Kelly sat in the interview room, waiting for Summers to be brought in.

When he arrived, Summers was pale, gaunt and nervous. His eyes had dark rings and seemed sunken. It was only 48 hours since his arraignment. Chris rose and held out his hand. Summers was looking down and didn't see it at first. Then said, "Oh. Sorry," and weakly shook Chris' hand.

"Sit over here, Mr. Summers. You remember Kelly."

Summers slumped into a chair and said, "Yes. Of course," without looking at her.

"Mr. Summers it's important we go over your case if you're up to it."

"I... I don't know."

"Well, let me start with some preliminaries. Doctor Young is here as a consultant to the firm... me, as defense counsel. As such the attorney-client privilege covers our conversation with her present. Anything we discuss cannot and will not be disclosed. So please speak freely and tell us all you know about what the police claim to have found at your cabin."

Summers bowed his head and remained silent for a minute.

"I have no idea how those things got there. I never saw a gun like the one they say killed that Justice. And I haven't been near any anthrax sources for years."

"When was the last time you were at your cabin?" Chris asked.

"I don't recall. Couple of weeks?"

"What about the floor beneath the bed in the main bedroom?"

"What about it?"

"Did you know there was a floor board that could be pulled up?"

"No."

"No? You never hid or had reason to hide anything underneath the board?"

"Hide?" Like what? Why would I?"

"You know. Valuables. Money, jewelry, drugs?"

"No."

"Was your cabin ever broken into?"

"No. Not that I'm aware of."

"Is it true you left a key under the mat on the back porch?"

"Yes."

"And you told your neighbors it was there?"

"Yes."

"Can you recall where you were the morning Justice Baker was shot?"

"Like I told the police, I was home. Alone. At that hour I would have been in bed asleep."

"You don't have any way of verifying that? Is that correct?"

"Yes. How could I?"

"You might have received a phone call. If so, phone records may establish that."

"I don't recall any phone calls."

"What about hearing a noise outside the house? It might have awakened you. If there was and it could be traced to a car accident or some other incident that might have been reported to the police …"

"Look Mr. Knight, I know what you're trying to do. But I have no way of proving I was at home in bed."

"Can you think of anyone who would think you might have been involved with these deaths?"

"What? Other than the police?"

"Yes."

"No."

"Would you have any idea of anyone who would want to throw suspicion on you for these deaths?"

"No. Mr. Knight, I'm sorry. I'm not following your line of questions."

"Mr. Summers, I think somebody may be trying to frame you. Make you the fall guy to keep from being found out."

"Frame me? How? Why?

"The police think you have motive. Revenge for the court's overturning the death penalty. Since you have no alibi for the night Justice Baker was murdered and live in the area, you had opportunity. And now that they found the gun that killed Justice Baker in your cabin, you had the means. Same for that Mr. Richards. You are a pharmacist and have knowledge and experience with anthrax and anthrax killed the murderer's defense counsel. And finally, you were at the Metro station when Perry of the CHASE organization was killed."

"I can't explain the gun or those sacks being at my cabin. I didn't push Mr. Perry. I was nowhere near him at the station."

Kelly broke in.

"Mr. Summers, I'd like to ask you a few questions. I don't want you to be offended. I think they are necessary to understand how these terrible events have been laid at your doorstep."

"You think I'm lying?"

"No. Not at all. While my opinion of you is not based on a detailed analysis, I am comfortable that I know enough about you to ask my questions. You can stop me at any time if you get uncomfortable."

Summers looked at his hands he had clasped before him. After a minute, he said, "Okay. Let's try, I guess."

For an hour, Kelly spoke softly and posed questions seeking answers that were intended to reveal Summers mental and emotional state at the time of his wife's and daughter's murders, the arrest and indictment of their murderer, his trial, conviction and sentencing and his life afterward. She then focused on his reaction to the overturning of the death penalty, the murder of Justice Baker, and the lawyer representing the man convicted of his family's murder. She pressed him, gently, on his participation on the TV panel on the death penalty along with Ed Perry of CHASE and his reaction to news of his death at the Metro station where Summers himself had been present at about the same time. She concluded her interview with questions about the psycho-therapy sessions for his PTSD.

Summers' body language and answers varied throughout the interview. At times he was withdrawn, tortured by his memories, indifferent, frustrated and scared. He clearly did not understand why he was being accused of causing the deaths of three people and had no idea of who would want him blamed for their deaths. Deaths he denied causing without emotion, instead displaying resignation and hopelessness.

The interview over, Chris and Kelly assured him they would do all they could to clear him of the charges against him. Summers nodded, stood, gave a weak smile. The guard was summoned and he was led back to his cell.

When they got to their car for the drive home, Chris asked, "What did you learn?"

Kelly was silent for a moment before she answered. Then, "He's depressed, but you don't have to be a psychologist to know that. What is strange, or perhaps concerning, is that he seems to be resigned. Not caring about his situation."

"I got that impression. What does it indicate to you?"

"Indicate?"

"Sorry, about his guilt or innocence."

"No matter how many years in practice, how many patients one counsels, a psychologist can never be fully certain of their diagnosis of any patient. Dealing with an individual's psyche is not an exact science. On the one hand, Mr. Summers can be convinced, is convinced, he was not involved in the deaths of three people. On the other hand, he could have simply erased the events from his mind. His psyche rejects the horror of those deaths. Or he could be a cold blooded liar considering his acts as justifiable revenge against those who brought back all the pain of his losses made worse by the frustration of knowing that the man responsible for everything would not live knowing he was eventually going to die and knowing that he, Summers, could not do anything himself to change that. In such a case, one's resentment and anger could turn to hate of those he considered responsible for his having to relive old and live anew the agonies that had been receding."

"So, you think he is guilty?"

"No. I don't think he is a person capable of such actions."

"But you just said…

"I gave you my opinion… my experience on the difficulty of drawing conclusions from psychoanalysis with absolute certainty. Despite that fact, I do not believe Mr. Summers capable of killing three people in cold blood."

"I'm glad to hear that," Chris responded. "It agrees with my experience. He isn't a murderer."

"So, what now?" Kelly asked.

"We prepare for trial. We build a case of reasonable doubt."

"And how do we do that?"

"I have to follow up on my hunch that someone else is behind all this."

"Any candidates?"

"Yes. The problem is finding some evidence to prove my hunch has a basis in fact."

"You have to prove someone else did these murders?"

"That would be ideal. But no. I only have to have enough to create an alternative. To convince the jury that someone else could have the motive, opportunity and means to commit these murders. If I can raise a doubt in at least one juror's mind, I get a hung jury."

"What good does that really do? Won't they try Summers again?"

"Yes. But that takes time. With time, maybe we can find proof that someone else is responsible. And, if in preparing for this trial, I was really lucky and found evidence that someone else is responsible or might be, the jury can acquit."

"I hate to mention this, but could you prepare a defense based on mental deficiency?"

"I can. If it comes to that, it's only slightly better than a verdict of guilty."

"Why? He's incarcerated in an institution for the criminally insane. Sounds stupid I suppose, but wouldn't he be better off in prison?"

"That's one way to look at it. But there are concerns."

"Yes. What are they?"

"Well, he could be imprisoned with the murderer of his family. Assuming the prison system wouldn't make that mistake, there's a possibility he could be sentenced to death."

"What? That's been outlawed."

"I know. But this trial and appeals will take time. A new justice will be appointed. There's a movement to create a referendum to reinstate the death penalty. We've haven't heard the last of this."

"What a mess!" Kelly expressed her exasperation.

CHAPTER 32
BEYOND DOUBT

After Chris and Kelly's discussion, Chris' belief in Summers innocence increased to a near certainty. But his work was cut out for him. Where to begin building Summers' defense.

The prosecution had the facts that the gun that shot Justice Baker and the cloths with anthrax spores were found at Summers' cabin. But Summers' finger prints were not found on either. Nor was his DNA. The timing of the death of Perry at the Metro was complicated. It was probably the weakest link in the prosecution's case against Summers, but that mattered little. The prosecution only had to convince a jury that Summers killed either Justice Baker and/or Richards or both and Summers would spend the rest of his life in prison.

Knight had little to go on. The facts that the gun and cloths did not bear Summers' prints or DNA suggested they were both planted to frame him. But who would want to do that and why. He had to start with the only theory he had been working on - the pending decision on banning fracking. His research of companies that would be affected by the ban turned up several, but only one was headquartered in the state. It would be easy enough for a company with resources to get the Glock 42 and hire an operative. The bizarre nature of Richards's death from anthrax was a puzzle at first. But it occurred to Knight that Summers' knowledge of the poison was not only incriminating in regard to Richards's death, but served as a link the prosecution would rely on to incriminate him in Justice Baker's death, both would support the prosecution's case that Summers was motivated by revenge.

Then, as required, the prosecution turned over to Knight the evidence they intended to use against Summers. There were few surprises. But there was one. The notes, written in code, that had been found at the Baker and Richards crime scenes. When asked, the prosecution told Knight it hadn't as yet cracked the codes, but were working on it. They would let him know once the codes were deciphered.

Knight decided not to wait for the prosecution. He called a friend he served with in the Army National Guard who now worked for the Department of Home Land Security, Neal Hurley.

"Neal, this is Chris Knight. It's been awhile."

"Gosh! I'll say it has. How long?"

"Too long. How are you doing, Neal"

"I'm doing well. You? Er… Sorry. I forgot about your…"

"That's okay Neal. Time does heal and it's been a long time and with some help, I've been able to move on. Still…"

Embarrassed, Hurley asked, "Well it is good to hear from you. To what do I owe the pleasure?"

"I need your 'spook' talents. Still got them?" Chris asked.

"My 'spook' talents! Now that isn't something I expected! What's up?"

"I'm defending someone suspected of being involved with the deaths of Justice Baker and two others. I just learned from the prosecution that it has some writings it found at the crime scenes of two of the victims. They're in some sort of code or cipher. The prosecution claims it hasn't decoded them yet but when it does it has to provide those to me as defense counsel. I'd rather not wait and was wondering if you could help me out?"

"Well, I haven't had much decoding work here. But sure! Can't promise I'll be able to crack the codes, but I'll try."

"Thanks Neal. They're short. I can email them to you."

"That will work."

After confirming Neal knew that the codes and deciphering them were confidential, Chris emailed the two codes - BRYPDHHIEEGGHFLWLRQISUZLLFKXKLWLVTCBFCFN.

Then, GHDWKZLOOEHFHUWDLQDQGDJRQLCLCQJ, and asked Neal to confirm he received them. Neal replied, "I have the codes.

Can't be sure right off the bat. It's been a while since I did this kind of stuff. But, I'll get started tonight after work.

"Good, Neal! Really appreciate you helping me out on this."

"No problem. Hope I can actually be of help. I'll get back to you as soon as I think I have the key to cracking these."

"Look forward to your report."

Hurly got home, had supper, told his wife he'd be in the den working on something for Chris Knight. When she asked what it was, he told her he couldn't say. It was confidential. She was used to this answer and said, "Got it. Okay."

After several hours, Hurley called Chris and told him he thought he deciphered the two codes and could email him what he thought he found and asked if Chris wanted information on how he had done it. Chris said he did. He needed to know how to be able to compare whatever the prosecution might come up when it deciphered the codes.

Hurley emailed Chris.

These are classical ciphers, a type used historically but not used very much today. Classical ciphers operate using the letters of the alphabet. Today, they're not very reliable. That is, can usually be deciphered. Modern schemes use computer or other technology using bits and bytes.

These two are substitution ciphers. Letters or groups of letters are replaced with other letters or groups of letters. A well-known example is known as the Caesar cipher. Julius Caesar created his own scheme. So did Napoleon. Then they were used by the general populous who needed to communicate in confidence.

Using this type, each letter forming the actual message is replaced by letters that are three positions later in the alphabet, e.g., A becomes D, B becomes E, C is F, and so on. Caesar used the three letter rotation, but any number of rotations works. On these, I first tried the 3 letter rotation. It didn't work. Neither did other "wholesale" rotations, e.g., four positions later, then five. When they didn't work out I tried a combination of mixed letter rotations. With some trial and error, it worked.

When I rotated every third letter of what seemed to be a word suggested by the three letter rotation one more rotation. A four letter rotation. So this cipher's pattern uses a three letter rotation, then switches to a four letter rotation for each third letter in the deciphered word. The results are-

BRYPDHHIEEGGHFLWLRQISUZLLFKXKLWLVTCBFCFN deciphered means –YOUMADEABAD DECISIONFORWHICH-THISIS PAYBACK

GHDWKZLOOEHFHUWDLQDQGDJRQLCLCQJ deciphered means –DEATHWILLBECERTAINANDAGONIZING.

I can make some guesses about what the intent was behind these messages, but I'll leave that up to you Chris. You obviously know a lot more than I do about all this. Anyway, hope this is some help.

Best regards, Neal.

When Chris finished reading the email, he called to Kelly. "Read this email."

"What's it about?"

"The prosecution found two notes at the crime scenes. One at Baker's. One at Richards.

They were in code. I just had an old friend decipher them. He did so in this email to me."

Kelly sat down in Chris' desk chair and read. Then she looked at Chris and asked, "The first one is Justice Baker?"

"Yes."

"Then the second is Richards?"

"Yes."

"Your conclusions about these?"

"Whoever left these ciphers was after revenge. The obvious thing these two victims had in common was the elimination of the death penalty. The obvious person who would want revenge against these two is our client, Summers."

Kelly sat back in Chris's chair and stayed silent. Then she said, "Do you think that these notes are part of the scheme to frame Summers? I mean, finding the gun and the anthrax spores on his property and now these coded notes? They all fit neatly with the case against Summers. Perhaps too neatly?"

"I agree," said Chris. "The problem is that that conclusion lacks supporting evidence. Right now, it's just our suspicions."

"Well, suppose Summers has no knowledge of codes or ciphers?"

"He probably doesn't. But it's only his word."

"Let me check something," Kelly said. She went online and typed Ciphers in the browser. A slew of sites was listed in seconds. She checked a few. After several minutes, she turned to Chris, "This isn't good I'm afraid. Even if Summers had no knowledge of ciphers, with the Internet he certainly could become familiar enough to create his own."

"You're right, but... It's all too pat. I have to find someone or some organization with a motive to cause these deaths."

"But who or what entity would have a motive other than revenge for overturning the death penalty?" Kelly asked. "I mean that's the common link and it seems especially strong."

"I agree. But that's because we are looking at all three murders as being tied together. What if we approached this a different way?"

"And what way would that be?"

"The murder of Justice Baker was the only one that was 'necessary.'"

"Necessary? What do you mean?"

"Other than revenge for overturning the death penalty, the murder of a justice could be to prevent his ruling on some case."

"Chris, you've said this before, haven't you?"

"Yes. I suppose I have."

"And you interviewed Justice Baker's clerk"

"Yes. And I narrowed it down to the pending case on the right of local governments to outlaw fracking. So follow me on this. Justice Baker was the swing vote on the issue and it was widely predicted he would cast his vote upholding the authority to ban fracking. So he has to be eliminated. When he authors the decision to overturn the death-penalty, the opportunity presents itself."

"What opportunity?"

"The opportunity to silence him. Prevent his vote to uphold the authority to ban fracking.

"I'm not sure I follow."

"If you were going to risk murdering a Justice of the State Supreme Court, you want to provide a motive for the police as far away from the real motive as possible. The publicity on the decision to over-turn the death penalty provided the means to lead the police to look for suspects seeking revenge for that decision. But that theory might not, probably wouldn't work, if only Justice Baker was killed. So, to be sure the police focused on the motive of revenge, Richards, and then Perry had to be killed. Their direct and indirect involvement with the death penalty issue made revenge the most likely motive. If revenge for that decision is believed to be the motive, then focus falls on the survivors of victims whose murderers were convicted and sentenced to death. They are the only logical suspects."

"The police soon enough narrow their search to those survivors with the greater opportunity to commit the crimes – those who live in this area. Now they have motive and opportunity and these point to only one suspect – Summers. The suspicion that Summers is guilty is aided by his appearance on that TV panel, his knowledge of anthrax, and his presence at the Metro station. But the police still needed to find evidence that Summers possessed the means to commit the murders. This was handed to them when they found the gun and anthrax spores at Summers' cabin."

"Unfortunately Chris, your analysis is very convincing… convincing your client is guilty."

"I agree, except that, as I think you agree, it's all too neat and goes against our agreement that Summers is not the calculating murderer of three people."

"What's next then?"

"I talked with Justice Baker's clerk. There's no one really to talk to about Richards. This leaves members of CHASE and representatives of companies opposing the banning of fracking."

CHAPTER 33
CONCERNED HUMANITARIANS

Chris looked up the contact information for CHASE online. He called its Chairperson, Caitlin Madison.

"Hello, Ms. Madison. My name is Christopher Knight. I'm an attorney and I'm representing Jed Summers who has been accused of being involved with the three deaths that appear linked by the victims' positions on the death penalty."

"Okay, Mr. Knight? Why call me… us?"

"I would like to interview some members of your organization. More specifically, those who knew Mr. Perry."

"To what purpose?"

"I must be candid. I'm not sure. But given the importance of the matter for my client, I have to look into anyone related in any way to what has happened. As you know, Mr. Summers and Mr. Perry were on that panel on the death penalty."

"Yes. I saw the program. As I recall, Mr. Summers was quite strident in his opinions."

"That's correct."

"I don't see how any of us can assist you or perhaps would want to."

"I can understand that. But consider this. I don't think Mr. Summers is capable of murder. I don't think his understandable emotional reaction to his family's murderer receiving leniency makes him capable of murder and surely not three murders. Your organization is dedicated to protecting the rights of convicted felons against what it believes is overly severe punishment. All I'm asking is that it, its members, use their dedication to see if they can render any assistance in defense of someone who is most likely innocent of any offense and who has suffered the worst loss a human being can — the loss of his loved ones."

"Well, our regular monthly meeting is tonight at 7 P.M. Perhaps you could start by joining us and after our discussions, I can turn the floor over to you to address the members. I would ask that it not be for a long period of time."

"Fair enough. I will be there tonight at seven."

Chris arrived a few minutes before seven. He took his seat at the end of the conference table farthest from the Chairperson at its head.

Madison opened the meeting. "Ladies and gentlemen. Mr. Christopher Knight was invited to join us for reasons he will explain after we have our regular meeting. Let us begin."

The first to speak was Anna Vernon.

"A jury in Cleveland, Ohio recommended death by lethal injection for a 38-year old man convicted of multiple counts of aggravated murder and kidnapping. The jury disregarded expert testimony that the man suffered from post-traumatic stress disorder from being physically abused as a child by his drug-addicted mother, his mother's boyfriends and other family members. While the judge could have sentenced him to life without parole, she imposed the death penalty."

"Any other particulars?" Madison asked.

"Yes. He was convicted of the rape and murders of three women — one 18-years-old, another 28-years-old and a third 38-years-old. There were photos presented to the jury of the women's mangled and mutilated bodies that were found decomposing in trash bags around the murderer's apartment complex. Police detectives and forensics experts described how the victims were choked, beaten and in at least one case raped.

"The press reported their killer smirked as the father of his final victim took the podium to read a statement about his daughter's life and her gruesome death. He then turned toward the defendant just as he sprouted a grin. The father then bolted from the podium and lunged across the hardwood table where the serial killer, as he was described, was seated.

"Experts in corrections testified that he could be safely held in the state's prison system for the rest of his life. It was the only other sentence the judge could have granted. The judge was not persuaded. In rendering her verdict, she is quoted –

In coming to my decision today, I am struck by the sheer inhumanity of what one human being can do to not one, but three human beings. It is incomprehensible, People who commit the kind of crimes that you have committed must be punished, and must be punished as severely as the law allows. It is absolutely necessary."

Continuing, Vernon reported, "Executions are on hold right now as the Ohio Department of Corrections is trying to find the drugs they need to carry out lethal injections. And although the County Prosecutor had campaigned on a promise to reduce the number of cases in which the death penalty is sought, he reportedly said that death was the only fitting punishment in this case. He called the man evil, a personification of it. And while admitting that the sentence wouldn't bring back the victims, the prosecutor warned other cold-blooded criminals will know that death is in the equation for them. He stated his belief there is some value in capital punishment and that this is one of those cases."

"Have we been in contact with defense counsel about assisting in the appeal?" Madison asked.

"Yes."

"Thank you Anne. Todd?"

"Yes Caitlin, thanks," said Todd Webb as he was given the floor to report. "My report is more encouraging than Anne's," he began. Continuing, he stated, "A Pew poll reports 40 percent of Democrats support capital punishment, down from 71 percent in 1996. The same poll showed Republican support dropped from 87 percent to 77 percent. Even so, Republican lawmakers in Nebraska, Utah, Missouri, Kentucky, Kansas, Ohio, Wyoming, Montana, South Dakota and New Hampshire have sponsored legislation to repeal the death penalty.

"On the Federal level, the U.S. Supreme Court has announced it will review two cases brought by African Americans on death row in Texas. Both cases come from Houston. In Harris County, Texas where about half of African American prisoners on Texas's death row are from. And since 2004, all of the new death sentences in this County were for Hispanics and Blacks. And, as we all know, Texas has carried out six executions most recently, almost half of the most recent 14 executions nationwide."

Chris raised his hand.

"Yes, Mr. Knight?" asked the Chair.

"Sorry. I don't want to interrupt, but I'm familiar with the circumstances of one of those cases and thought they would be of interest."

"Please proceed then, Mr. Knight."

"In one of the cases the defense attorney at trial is said to have presented testimony from a so-called defense expert that the defendant was more likely to be dangerous in the future simply because he was black. In Texas, testimony must be taken about a defendant's 'future dangerousness' in order to impose the death penalty."

"Do you draw any conclusions based on what you have just reported?"

"This may not be consistent with the goals of this organization. But I think it does show that the courts do try and be sure that the death penalty is not imposed in such highly questionable circumstances as are involved in this one case the Supreme Court will review."

"Thank you Mr. Knight. Let's move on. Mr. Royce?"

Oscar Royce cleared his throat, shuffled some papers and began.

"There are recent developments in what many would call a Midwestern conservative state – Nebraska. The legislature there has outlawed the death penalty, but the Governor is pouring his own financial resources into getting it reinstated and claims that two-thirds of Nebraskans back the death penalty. Some in the press say that a growing number of religious conservatives have turned Nebraska into a test lab for opposing the death penalty from the right. It's anybody's guess how this will turn out.

"In Los Angeles, a jury decided that a serial killer should be sentenced to death for murdering nine women and a teenage girl over more than two decades ago in South Los Angeles. The murders had a pattern it's reported. The women were shot, choked or both, and their bodies dumped in alleys and trash bins in the area where the killer worked as a trash collector.

Survivors of the victims and others in the area had complained that the killings weren't being investigated because the victims were poor and black and some were prostitutes and cocaine addicts. The killer was finally unearthed when a task force reexamined the cold case files, and eventually found the killer's DNA that connected him to evidence found on some of the victims."

"Is that all, Oscar?" Madison asked.

"No. I have some more. But I think we should use up our remaining time to hear from Mr. Knight."

"I'll take that as a motion. Seconds?

"I second."

"Thank you. All in favor say aye. Those opposed, no. The ayes have it. You have the floor Mr. Knight."

"Thank you. And thanks to all of you for your generosity in letting me attend your meeting. I will be as brief as possible. First, how many saw the TV panel on the death penalty that your Mr. Perry was on?"

A show of hands indicated all had.

"Then you know my client, Jed Summers. The sole survivor of his family who were murdered?"

Nods indicated they knew Summers.

"You all know this is a difficult issue. Highly emotional. As we heard here tonight, opinions are changing in some places across the country. I was surprised to hear the reports on some recent decisions imposing the death penalty. Not so much the fact that the sentences were being imposed, but that the details of the crimes were included. Listening to those details, does it affect any of you? That is, does it affect your opposition to the death penalty? Like it did that county prosecutor who campaigned on getting rid of the death penalty, but in that one case supported the judge's decision to impose it."

Chairperson Madison, said, "Let me answer that Mr. Knight. All of us are equally as horrified about what some humans can do to other humans. We allow the details of the crimes to be included in the reports for several reasons. One is to test our commitment to ending the death penalty. That commitment is based in part on not punishing one horrible killing by committing another. To us that is revenge, not justice. The state should not be in the job of exacting revenge."

"Sorry to interrupt, but the 'state' that you refer to, isn't that actually you and me? The state are officials elected by a majority of us and so the state can be said to be us. Acting for us, the state acts through judges, prosecutors who are elected, at least many are, and juries. Juries again are 'us.' You see no disconnect involved?"

"The 'State' as you say is us. And the 'us' part of the state is trying to get all of 'us' on the same page in regard to capital punishment. You agree that we all have a right to petition the government?"

"Yes. And if you succeed in getting the state to agree with you, and capital punishment is abolished, then you will have succeeded in getting the State out of the business of exacting 'revenge' as you put it. But is it revenge? The laws passed by elected officials are laws that a majority of us support. The laws imposing capital punishment for certain well defined offences reflect the decision of us all. If a majority of elected officials sense the will of the people is to do away with capital punishment, then they will take that law off the books."

"Are you agreeing with us then Mr. Knight?"

"Not exactly. And that brings me to the reasons I asked to attend and to speak with some of you. My client is being accused of the murders of Justice Baker and the lawyer, Richards and perhaps your Mr. Perry. The prosecution claims his motive was revenge. Revenge for letting the murderer of his family escape the fate he visited on my client's family. That escape resulted not from a change in the position of the people on capital punishment as if expressed by elected officials passing a new law, but by the opinion of one judge who was able to garner four votes to support his opinion. So, the first question, was the court's decision an action of the State? I would say no, because the State composed of elected officials did not repeal capital punishment – five unelected judges did."

"Aha, Mr. Knight! But the judges were appointed and confirmed by elected officials," Oscar Royce interrupted.

"Yes. And when appointed and sworn in they swore to uphold the law. The laws that were on the books when they were sworn in. And those laws authorized capital punishment."

Chairperson Madison broke in. "All this is very interesting. But is there a point to be made?"

"My apologies, Madam Chair. Yes, there is. Given the discussion… debate just now, given all of your backgrounds and understandings on the issue of capital punishment, I have a few questions for you all. In all of your activities, involvement, study, review of death penalty decisions, observations of executions, has the heinous nature of any killings ever shaken your faith in your opposition to the death penalty? Secondly, have you ever encountered the fact or a suspicion that a survivor of victims whose murders resulted in the death penalty has sought to harm any of you or other advocates of abolishing the death penalty?"

"I think I speak for all of us here," Chairperson Madison said. "The answer to your first question is no. As to the second question, each have to answer for themselves."

"In answering no to the first question, have any of you ever interfaced at any time, during trial, after a verdict, after sentencing, at the execution with the family members or loved ones of the victims of the crimes for which the death penalty was imposed?"

Silence answered the question.

"What about the second question?"

Oscar Royce stood up, his face contorted in anger.

"That's that. I've heard enough. Good night Mr. Knight." And with that he turned on his heel and stormed out of the meeting room.

Knight smiled, shrugged his shoulders and said, "I didn't think that was a question that would have had such an effect on any of you. But of those who remain may I get an answer?"

The remaining members looked at each other and they gave a group shaking of their heads side to side indicating a negative response.

"As I thought. Would any of you, or several of you, be willing to testify to that fact?

Silence.

Chris continued, "I fear that most human reactions in these circumstances is — 'I don't want to be involved.' But a man's guilt or innocence is at stake. You are all fearless in defending the right to live of those convicted of viciously taking the lives of innocent people who had a right to their lives, a right not to be viciously attacked and not to have their basic dignities denied. All that is being asked is that you, experts in vicious crimes, advocates of the rights of vicious criminals testify to what you know. That is, that never have you encountered a survivor who sought revenge against anyone that advocated, worked for the abolishing the death penalty, or actually abolished the death penalty."

Silence.

"Mr. Knight, your request is a fair one. But give us some time. May we get back to you later?"

"Of course. Thanks again for your time and look forward to hearing from you. Good night."

CHAPTER 34
WARNINGS

After Royce walked out on CHASE's Board meeting with Knight, he drove to City Central Park, pulled into a spot at the far end of the parking lot tapped a number into his cell phone, waited to hear two beeps, hung up and waited. Fifteen minutes passed. At the other end of the lot a car pulled in and parked and turned off its headlights. No one got out. After a minute, the headlights flicked on and off two times. Royce opened his door and got out, looked around, punched his key fob to lock the doors and headed for the Fountain of Pegasus.

He sat on the bench opposite the north side of the Fountain. Spotlights illuminated the statute leaving the areas surrounding the circular pool beneath it in shadow. A man, his hat pulled down hiding his face approached the statue from the side opposite from where Royce sat, looked around, then proceeded around the Fountain and motioned for Royce to follow him. Royce rose and followed the man onto a path that led into the wooded area surrounding the Fountain. After he paced twenty yards along the path, Royce and the man stood face to face.

"I hope this is really important. You know I don't want anyone seeing me with you and vice versa."

"It is. You can judge for yourself."

"Okay. But make it quick."

"I just came from a meeting of the Board. Chris Knight, Summers attorney was there. He asked to come and the Chair let him."

"Yes. So what?"

"He came to ask whether one or more members of the Board would testify on behalf of Summers."

"Testify for Summers? About what? None of them even know him."

"That's true. But that's not what Knight asked for."

"Then what?"

"He wants testimony from us that we have never known or heard of any survivor of victims like Summers seeking revenge against anyone involved with doing away with the death penalty or advocating for its being banned."

"That's it?"

"Yes."

"You risked this meeting for that?"

"I thought you should know. And I wasn't comfortable talking over the phone."

"Do you think anyone on the Board will agree to testify?"

"My guess is yes."

"Okay. This gives Summers a 'character' witness. I don't see that as a cause for

much concern."

"Neither do I. But Knight's building a defense based on proving someone else had a motive to kill Justice Baker. I think he has concluded that the other two deaths had nothing to do with seeking revenge for getting rid of the death penalty that let the murderer of Summers' family off the hook."

"Clever guy, this Knight. But what's he got to go on?"

"He's been to see Justice Baker's law clerk."

"How do you know and what difference does that make?"

"I met Baker's clerk, Morris, some time ago. As part of his work for the Justice, he was charged with doing the research on the death penalty and he contacted CHASE to interview its members about what information, records, studies it had on the death penalty and its effects. I met him because of that and stayed in touch with him. After his recent meeting with Knight, he called me and told me that Knight had come to see him. When I asked why, he told me he was looking for the cases that were pending before Baker. Specifically, he was looking for cases that might have an impact on powerful interests and that were surrounded by controversy."

"And…"

"And Morris said Knight narrowed it down to the appeal on the ban on fracking. Morris also said Knight sought to confirm that Baker would uphold the ban."

"Did this clerk confirm that"

"He didn't come right out and say so. But he said Knight seemed to think he was right."

"Right about what?"

"Right about there being a different motive for Baker's murder. It wasn't a survivor seeking revenge."

The man with Royce remained silent for a few minutes. He was thinking. He didn't know that much about Knight. But he knew he was a danger. An alternative motive still has to be proven. Even then, it was only an alternative for the jury to consider. It didn't mean it would be convinced and even if it were, it only meant Summers might get off. But then, if he did get off, the investigation of Justice Baker's murder would have to continue. At that point, looking for other motives would eventually make Knight's theory one to be investigated. Others might be found, but the chances were slim they would provide the same degree of plausibility. He came to a conclusion. Turned back to Royce and said, "Something must be done."

"About what exactly?" Royce asked.

"This lawyer and his theories."

"And you have an idea what must be done?"

"Not fully. But I will. You stay here for five minutes after I leave."

"Okay," said Royce.

With that, the man walked back to his car and left.

Walking back to his car, Royce thought, "What is he thinking. Something must be done, he says. I agree, but what is it and who will do it? That's a question, my 'friend' may not be the only one who needs to find an answer for."

Leaving the meeting with Royce, the man wasted no time in thinking of possible means to keep Knight's theory from undoing all that had been accomplished so far. He thought, but dismissed, trying to interfere with or stop Knight from pursuing his defense of Summers based on reasonable doubt. The answer had to lie elsewhere. Could Summers be made to confess? He knew many times people found confessing to crimes they didn't commit easier at the moment than being continually accused and subjected to interrogations, threats of what would happen if they didn't confess or promises that things would get better if they did. But this was already being tried with Summers, and so far hadn't worked. Still it was early in the game.

Could some other case be found that was pending before Baker that would either benefit or harm powerful interests depending on which way Baker voted? But from what Royce reported from his conversations with Baker's clerk, this was a non-starter. Then he thought to himself, "Royce." Royce was up to his eyeballs in this. Could he be made the scape goat? Royce was vulnerable. Royce wasn't against the death penalty. He joined CHASE to meet those of its members with the interest in and need for his products or because they were venture capitalist with access to funding sources he had need of. His membership was a grand con. Summers' prints were not found on the murder weapon. But no one was looking for other prints. What if... At that moment, he pulled into his driveway. He was home. Time to put this away for now.

When Royce returned home, he opened a bottle of wine poured himself a glass. Read the note his wife left that she was at book club. He flipped on the TV to catch the late news. His cell phone rang. He switched off the TV and answered.

"Can you talk?" the voice asked.

"Yes. Myna is at her book club."

"Good. I want to revisit what we discussed a little while ago."

"You mean about Knight and his plans for a defense of Summers.

"Yes," the voice answered.

"Well! I can assure you I am giving this my full attention. But this lawyer Knight. He's clever and perhaps worse, dedicated. And his wife is a psychologist and she is helping with Summers' case."

"A psychologist you say?"

"Yes. What's her name?"

"Well her married name is Knight of course. But professionally she stills uses her given name, Kelly Young, Dr. Kelly Young."

"Do some research on her. Find out if she is on any boards or charities."

"Why?"

"Just do as I say. And be quick about it. Where does her husband have his firm?"

"Downtown I'd guess. Like most law firms I'm sure its got its own web site."

"You're right. I can look that one up myself. You get working on Dr. Young."

"Will do. That it?"

"For now."

CHAPTER 35
OFFERS

"Is Mr. Knight in?" asked the well-tailored gentlemen. Age 48, graying at the temples, tall and lean.

"Yes."

"Is he free?"

"I'll have to check," said the receptionist. "May I ask who is calling?"

"Yes. Of course. I am Arthur Church, Chief Financial Officer of Chain Link Investment Opportunities, LLC. My card."

"It would help if I could tell Mr. Knight the nature of your visit."

"I wish to speak to Mr. Knight about engaging his services."

"I see. Just a moment please." With that the receptionist pressed the key on the intercom. "Mr. Knight. Sorry to disturb you. There's a Mr. Church, the CFO of ChainLink Investment Opportunities, LLC here to see you. He says it's about engaging your services."

"Hmm… This is strange," Knight thought. "May as well find out what this is all about."

"Give me a few minutes and then show Mr. Church in, Marcy."

"Of course. Mr. Church, please have a seat. Mr. Knight will see you shortly. May I get you coffee, tea, water…?"

"No thank you. I'm fine."

Five minutes passed and Chris decided to go out and greet Church himself.

"Hello, I'm Christ Knight, Mr. Church. Please come back to my office."

Church took a seat in front of Chris's desk. "I'll get right to the point Mr. Knight. My company, think of it as a Carlyle Group that avoids publicity, is looking for an attorney to advise on several credit arrangements it is considering. Our search turned up your name as having experience in this area. Would you be available? Have the time?"

"That depends I suppose. What kind of time table are you working with?"

"It's all-consuming and indefinite."

"That sounds demanding."

"Yes. It is and will be. However, the remuneration will reflect the demand. The credit facility is in the neighborhood of $500,000,000. There will be considerable due diligence required and expertise in negotiating such a large facility. We are looking for a special counsel arrangement precisely because of the demands of the representation."

"And when would this representation have to begin?"

"Immediately. Or almost so."

"I see."

"I should clarify. Given the demands of the representation, it is expected, required really, that you devote full time to the enterprise. This would require your withdrawal from other representations you currently have."

Chris opened his mouth to say something, but Church held up his hand.

"We know that's an onerous demand. But before we go further, you should know the fees we are willing to pay for your exclusive representation until the credit facility is secured."

"Go on," Chris said, more out of curiosity, then true interest.

"We will pay an upfront retainer of $500,000. You do not have to record your time on an hourly basis. Rather, we will pay you $100,000 a month beginning in the third month and then every month thereafter until completion of the representation. This means you make $500,000 upfront simply be taking on the representation, then $100,000 a month thereafter until closing. At closing, you will be paid $1,000,000."

"I don't mean to be disrespectful. But this is an offer you would put in writing?"

"Of course! These terms would be included in your retainer letter which I am, on behalf of the company, prepared to sign today."

Chris drew back in his chair then said, "I would like a few days, Mr.

Church."

"I can understand that. But is it really necessary?"

"First, I would have to know more about the proposed terms and conditions of the credit facility, who the creditors would be. Other facts, as many as possible, to be sure I could provide the representation you need."

"From our perspective, that is unnecessary. We didn't come to you without having done our due diligence and satisfying ourselves that you have the qualifications we are looking for."

"I'm flattered by your confidence. But I would need time to arrange for transferring my other clients. And I would like to talk to my wife as well."

"That's fair. Would 48-hours suffice?"

"Not really. I mean I don't know. I have never had to do something like this before. I appreciate your time constraints. Can I let you know by this time next week?"

"That's a problem we would prefer to avoid. However, we are sincere in our belief you are the lawyer we need. All things considered, you can have your week."

"Thank you, Mr. Church. If I make up my mind sooner, either way, I'll let you know."

"Good. I'll let you get back to work and look forward to hearing your acceptance. Good-day Mr. Knight. I'll show myself out."

Chris went home that evening and shared the unique proposal with Kelly.

"You thinking of accepting?" she asked.

"At first, it was out of the question. Then I looked at our future. With something like making $2,000,000 in a year or two, and more if it took more than that amount of time, our financial needs would be well taken care of. And I could continue to practice and so could you, but with no real financial pressures."

"Well, like the ad says, 'I'm pregnant.'"

"What?" Chris shouted. "Really? When were you going to tell me?"

"First, yes really! Second, I was going to make a fantastic candle light dinner and then break the news. But your news accelerated the disclosure," Kelly said with a smile.

Chris grabbed her and hugged her until she said, "Chris, you'll crush the baby," then laughed.

"Oh! Yes." And released her from his embrace.

They stood for a moment and looked at each other. Then smiles crossed their faces and they embraced again, softly.

"Well! What was I telling you? I've forgot."

"You were telling me you were going to be the next Donald Trump type mogul."

"Huh! Oh! Yes. Do you think this tells me… us, I should take the offer from this Chain Link outfit?"

"No! I mean, we're perfectly fine as we are. Having our baby doesn't change the considerations on whether it's right for you and your practice."

Chris thought a moment and then said, "You're right. Of course. Buy okay, what do you think?"

"I think you need to take your time and think it through now that you know our baby isn't relevant to your decision."

"Yes! I see your point."

"Good! Because I have more news!" Kelly announced.

"Twins?" Chris stammered.

"No! Silly! I received a call myself today. It was from a concern that wanted to fund a study of psychological problems or needs that I chose."

"Really! What's the catch?"

"I have to agree to be in charge and devote full time until the program is up and running."

"What's the offer?"

"A $2,000,000 endowment and depending on results, more."

"You going to accept?"

"Like you, I asked them for time to consider the offer."

"What do you know about the concern?"

"Not much. Just having heard, I haven't had time to research it."

"You intend to?"

"Yes. It's worth some time given the potential good that might be done."

"We both have a lot to think about and not much time to do so. In the meantime, let's go out and have that candle light celebration at that Italian restaurant where we had our first 'date.'"

"I thought you'd never ask!"

CHAPTER 36
DOUBLE JEOPARDIES

The governor made his nomination to replace Chief Justice Baker. But it wasn't only the Judiciary Committee that would want to know about the nominee's qualifications. Those with cases pending before the State Supreme Court were also interested, including Chris Knight and the appeal over the proper interpretation of the Second Amendment. Then there were the oil and gas companies concerned over the appeal on the ban on fracking. But the biggest issue was the nominee's view on capital punishment. The State Attorney General had advised that a rehearing of the decision to end capital punishment in the State would be sought once the new Chief Justice was confirmed. The hearings on the nomination would be a mixed bag for the Committee members. There would be press coverage and that meant publicity – a lot of it. For politicians, publicity is usually a coveted prize, but unless you were a political "newbie" you knew publicity was a two-edged sword. The political jeopardy covered all involved – the governor, the nominee the Committee members, the interests of those whose cases were pending before the State Supreme Court and to a greater or lesser degree, the public.

For those whose fortunes were linked to the ban on fracking, the confirmation or rejection of the nominee hinged solely on that issue. Gas and oil interests, including Gibbons' UEC, retained their lobbyists and did a full court press on the Committee Members. In subtle and non-subtle ways, the members were informed that it was imperative to their districts to learn the nominee's position on fracking given the precarious financial condition of the industry, an industry that provided hundreds, if not thousands of jobs, that would compel consumer spending and increase sales and other taxes to be used to provide improved public services for which voters would show their gratitude by viewing the members favorably. Studies and colorful charts and diagrams were provided showing these and other benefits. These exhortations were supported by promises of generous donations to the members' PACs and/or other political fund raising entities.

It was recognized that the Committee could not be seen as voting for or against the nominee based on how she or he would vote on a single issue. So, Committee members and their staffs were encouraged to meet with the nominee and others with supposed knowledge of the nominee's leanings on the issue. If the nominee sounded out on the right side of this issue, hearings should be held and concluded promptly. If not, then hearings should be delayed as long as possible while work was done to gather enough votes to reject the nominee.

To further cover over the appearance that the fracking issue was controlling the confirmation process, the members were encouraged to examine the nominee on the pending cases on the Second Amendment and overturning the death penalty. The combination of supporting the broadest interpretation of the Second Amendment and the reinstitution of the death penalty was a natural fit to distract the media and the public from the role the fracking issue played in the confirmation process.

While the agents of the oil and gas industries labored to remove the jeopardy of a confirmation of a justice that was anti-fracking, Chris had to deal with his own jeopardy. Choose a secure financial future for Kelly, himself and most of all their son or daughter, at the cost of withdrawing from representing Summers. There were equally qualified criminal defense attorneys, if not better ones. In discussing the issue with Kelly, she advised that Summers' mental and emotional state was already a cause for concern. If Chris did withdraw, she feared it could have adverse repercussions on Summers' stability. After much discussion, she recommended that Chris test the matter at his next conference with Summers. She told Chris he had to be subtle in doing this. He couldn't just come out and tell him he was thinking of withdrawing or make up a story about having to withdraw. There wasn't an easy way to do this.

In the end, the decision was taken out of their hands. Not comfortable with any approach, it was decided that Chris would have to feel his way with Summers. Ask him if he retained confidence in Chris' defense strategy. Tell him he had a right to change counsel if he wasn't able to completely rely on Chris. This at least would raise the issue of a possible change in counsel without any indication Chris might be seeking to withdraw.

Uncertain and uncomfortable with the strategy, Chris scheduled his next conference with Summers. When Summers was led into the interview room, he looked straight at Chris, slumped in his chair and did not respond to Chris… "How are you, Jed?"

Jed sat and stared at Chris. Then looked away.

"Jed. What's wrong? What's happened? Tell me."

Summers turned slowly and looked Chris in the eye. "Is it true?"

"Is what true Jed?"

"Is it true?" Summers shouted this time.

"Jed calm down. I don't know what you're asking about."

"You don't?"

"No."

"You're withdrawing from my case. You think I'm guilty." With that Summers lowered his head to the table and began to sob.

Chris had his answer. "Jed, who told you that?"

"I heard the guard and some other policemen talking. They said they had heard you had been offered a big client that would pay you huge fees, but you had to stop representing all other clients."

"When did you hear this?"

"When I was being taken to have supper the other night."

"Do you know who the guard or the policemen were?"

"I didn't see them. I just heard them talking as I walked by. I did think I recognized one of the voices, but can't be sure. But you haven't answered my question. Is it true?"

"I'll be honest with you Jed. Kelly and I discussed it. Seriously discussed it. Included in those discussions was sincere concern for you."

"Thanks. For nothing!"

"Hold on, Jed. I've never been confronted with such a conflict before.

But with the baby, I had to take some time before I decided."

"So. It's true!"

"It's true I received an offer, a very lucrative offer. It's true I considered if I should take it. It's not true I decided to take the offer."

"Not yet! You mean!"

"No. Jed this meeting was to see if we could determine what effect my withdrawing from your case would have on you."

"We?"

"Kelly and I."

"She thinks I'm unstable?"

"No. She thinks… knows you have been under extreme pressure. Pressure that would unnerve the best of us. The concern we share is about you. Sincerely, about you."

"You still haven't answered my question."

"No. I haven't. But here it is. I'm not taking the offer. I will continue to represent you. That is, after all this, you still want me to."

"You throwing this back on me?"

"I don't understand."

"It's easy. You come in here you say, to see what effect it would have on me if you withdraw from my representation. I know about the possibility. Now you say you won't withdraw. Why shouldn't I believe all this is a set up?"

"Set up? How?"

"It's clever. All this 'nobility!' You condescend to remain on my case expecting me to say I don't believe you. You destroy my confidence in you and your representation so that I discharge you. You leave with a 'clean' conscious to pursue your riches. Result? The same. You quit on me but assuage your conscious by saying I fired you. You didn't quit on me."

"Jed. I didn't count on this as your reaction. I regret I didn't expect this. I should have, perhaps. But that's irrelevant to me. I came here to see what your reaction would be if it were possible I would withdraw. If that reaction was concerning, Kelly and I have already agreed, I would not withdraw. And I am not withdrawing."

"Am I supposed to believe your representation will be as effective now?"

"Yes. I can see why you would question that. But all I can tell you is, none of this will make a difference in my representation. The only change will be in your confidence in that representation. And that is a big change, unfortunately."

Summers looked at Chris for a long minute. Then he turned and yelled, "Guard!"

"Jed! Wait!" and reached out to grab his arm.

Summers tore it away and yelled, "Guard!" again.

The guard came in. Summers got up and walked out of the interview room.

"That was horrible, Kelly! Horrible! I never felt so cheap! So tawdry! I never should have even considered that stupid offer. Why? Why?"

"Because, my shining knight, you are still human."

"What do I do?" Will he talk to me? I can't prepare a defense for a client who distrusts me. I can't be confident he will tell me the truth. Oh! This is the biggest mess in my career. God, how could I let this happen?"

"Calm down, Chris. Beating yourself up won't solve this. Let this rest for now. Arrange another interview in a few days and I'll go with you."

"Damn! Damn!" was all Chris could say.

Meanwhile, the guard in charge of Summers during his interview with his lawyer was asked what he observed.

"I was called. Shouted for actually. Twice."

"How did Summers seem when you went in to take him back to his cell?"

"Upset! Angry!"

"What about his lawyer?"

"Stunned! Sat there staring. Both hands on the table. Mouth open. Then I closed the door."

"Okay. Thanks."

"Time to report," the man talking with the guard thought to himself. The phone was answered on the second ring. "Chain Link Investments."

"I need to speak with Mr. Church."

"I'm afraid he's busy, can I take a message."

"Tell him it's his recent offer to retain legal counsel."

"Oh! Just a moment."

A minute later, "Hello!"

"It appears to have gone as planned. Summers was upset and left the interview angry. Knight was disbelieving and also upset."

"I see. Well, I'll call Mr. Knight and ask if he has other questions and see what response I get. Goodbye."

Church hung up and called Chris' office.

"He's not here. Can I take a message?"

"This is Arthur Church. I think you recall who I am and the important matter I discussed with Mr. Knight. Do you have his mobile number? I'm sure he would want you to let me contact him," Church said with an edge to his voice.

"Yes sir. I understand."

Church took down Knight's mobile number and called.

"Yes? Chris Knight."

"Mr. Knight, Arthur Church. Sorry to disturb you out of the office. But I have to leave for a few days and thought it best to check in before I left to see if you have any additional questions."

"Well, Mr. Church, no I don't. I do have an update."

"Very good!"

"Not really. In the interest of full disclosure, I have decided not to take the offer. However, there is a chance my decision will be reversed."

"I see. Well, I don't see, actually."

"I wouldn't expect you to. No disrespect intended."

"None taken. But can you tell me, are you still considering the offer?"

"The best answer to that, is 'yes,' but with the caveat that I don't really want to take the offer. However, the reasons I don't may disappear and that could change my mind. I need a few days and think I still have those within the time frame we agreed I had to make a decision."

"That is correct, Mr. Knight. But no more questions for me?"

"That's right."

"I can expect to hear from you in a few days then?"

"Yes. I think so."

"Very well, Mr. Knight. Goodbye."

Kelly was standing nearby and heard Chris' comments. "What was that all about?"

"That was Church about the offer."

"I got that. But you didn't turn him down!"

"No. Kelly, it occurred to me that if I have so damaged my relationship with Summers and he either fires me or I decide he needs other counsel because he no longer trusts me, taking the offer is no longer relevant. I mean, why pass up such an opportunity because I failed to see its effect, an effect that has already happened?"

"I don't like that excuse."

"Neither do I. But I can't let my failure deprive us, our baby, of opportunities in the future. No one can predict the future. So for now, I'm keeping options open despite my failures that underpins those options."

"I understand Chris. To some extent. But, I love you. And I trust you. In time you will make the right decision."

"Thanks. I need you and your support. I am so disappointed in myself. I have to recover my belief in myself."

"You're being far too critical. If you expect to deal with this unemotionally, you have to set it down. Leave it go for a while. You're too close now to do a rational versus an emotional analysis. Leave it be. Come with me. I have a new piece of wardrobe I want to wear before little Knight starts to show."

Chris stood with a stern look, but could not resist Kelly's charms.

CHAPTER 37
TWO CAMPS

The day before the expiration of the week Chris was given to consider Chain Link Investment's offer to retain him, he received word that Summers' trial date had been set four weeks hence. When he received notice, his ambivalence left him. When he told Kelly of the date for trial, he also told her he was rejecting the offer and would meet with Summers and tell him he had turned down the offer he had received and would continue to represent him. If Summers showed any hesitancy or doubts, Chris would live with that. He doubted Summers would want other counsel, but even if he did, it wouldn't change his mind. Chris called Arthur Church and thanked him for the offer, but he had decided not to accept. Church offered to give him additional time, but Chris said it wasn't necessary. He had made up his mind and his decision was final. After the call to Church, Chris called the precinct and told the duty officer he want to meet with his client at 10 A.M. the following morning.

For his part, Church called his principal to tell him of Chris's decision to reject the offer.

"I see. Not unexpected I guess. We'll have to have a meeting to discuss this. And there's been another development that will have to be discussed."

"That being?" Church asked.

"The Governor's candidate to replace Baker and her confirmation hearings. I'll round up everybody. We meet tonight at 9 P.M."

Chris got to the precinct where Summers was being held a few minutes before 10 A.M. the next day as planned. He was escorted to the interview room and waited. Twenty minutes passed before Summers was led in. He didn't look at Chris, sat down and lowered his head.

"Good morning, Jed. I am not taking that offer. I'm continuing to represent you. Any objections?"

Summers kept his head down and didn't reply.

"Jed, I understand if you're upset. I can only tell you I've been kicking myself for even considering that offer. If you have any doubts about me, my representing you, you should tell me now. Your trial is scheduled to begin in four weeks. That doesn't give us much time, unless…"

Summers looked up suddenly and asked, "Unless what?"

"Unless you want new counsel. If you do, they have to give you time to find new counsel of your own choice or assign a public defender to represent you. In either case, new counsel will be given as much time as is reasonably necessary to learn about your case."

"How long might that take?"

"Could be several months," Chris responded.

"And I'd be sitting here all that time?"

"Yes."

Summers fell silent and sat there. Looked at Chris, then away. Stood up and paced back and forth. Sat down. Folded his hands on the table in front of him. "I can't take much more of this. Sitting around here. Not being able to work. At least my work kept my mind off things. When I got home from work, I could distract myself with television or go up to my cabin to be alone and think – just get away. Away from everybody and everything. Sitting here day and night, I can't find a way to escape any of this. I either get depressed or angry. Very angry!

I want this over with and I don't care how this ends."

"You want your freedom, Jed. You must! You haven't done anything wrong!"

"You seem to be a party of one that thinks so. Besides, like the song says, 'Freedom is just another way of saying I've got nothing further to lose.'"

"Jed! Am I still representing you?"

Summers looked squarely at Chris for a minute that seemed a lot longer to Chris.

"Yes. Yes, you are, Mr. Knight. I told you! I can't sit around here while I wait to get a new counsel. Besides, I don't believe in miracles. Not anymore. I don't see any lawyer winning my freedom with what I know the prosecution has to convict me."

"I won't argue that point with you Jed. You're entitled to your opinion. What I will do is get us ready for trial. We will go over all the evidence, your whereabouts at all times when these killings took place, the missing pieces in the prosecution's case. We will build a case based on reasonable doubt. The prosecution loses if it fails to prove your guilt beyond a reasonable doubt. And since both Dr. Young and I believe you're not guilty, we have confidence that your defense can establish reasonable doubt about you're being guilty."

Summers bowed his head, nodding it back and forth. Then he pushed his chair back and looked at the ceiling. Then he looked at Chris. "Suppose you do create reasonable doubt and the jury acquits. That doesn't establish I didn't murder these people. All it means is the state failed to prove I did."

"You could look at it that way. But however, your freedom, being acquitted of crimes you didn't commit is gained. Isn't that most important?"

"Take no offense Mr. Knight, but that sounds an awful lot like a defense attorney chalking up another success. Your victory is clear cut! You got your client off! I still must contend with people believing I got away with murder because I had a good attorney. I have to live with that cloud hanging over me, with the cloud that already hangs over me from the murders of my wife and daughter and the cloud that their murderer has been given leniency by the State Supreme Court. I'm not a violent man, Mr. Knight. But after the decision and what has happened to me since, I no longer remain neutral about the murder of Justice Baker. I've tried to ignore my feelings, but being cooped up here I keep going over and over what has happened since that decision came down and I can't escape feeling Justice Baker got what he deserved."

Chris remained silent and watched Summers body language. It was clear that Summers had changed under his ordeal. He couldn't be blamed for that.

But his new demeanor could complicate making his defense. Acknowledging Summers feelings, Chris changed the subject by starting his inquiry of the facts and circumstances that would form the basis of his client's defense, but not before making a mental note that he would really need Kelly's help on this case.

At 9 P.M. the group gathered in a dimly lit conference room on the thirty-third floor of a high rise office building in the middle of downtown.

"How about some more light?" one of the attendees asked.

"No!" came the immediate response. "There's a purpose in keeping the room dim. Just as there is in not using any of our names during our discussions."

"Really? And they would be?"

"Ensuring deniability. Making it more difficult and uncertain to recall who said what is a precaution. That's all. Any more questions?"

There was no response.

"Good! We have two items on the agenda. Knight's representation of Summers and the confirmation of Baker's replacement. Comments on Knight?"

"He's a good lawyer and dedicated. He'll do his best to get Summers acquitted."

"We all agree with that. What if he succeeds?"

"It means the police will have to keep looking."

"We have in place someone who will see that that effort is unproductive."

"How much assurance do you have of that?"

"He's been successful in providing the evidence the prosecution has against Summers. He should be able to steer a new investigation into enough dead ends to turn the murder of Baker into a cold case."

"And if he can't?"

"We cross that bridge when we come to it. If we come to it."

A different voice cut in, "What about taking this out of Knight's hands?"

"What do you mean?"

"What if before a verdict is rendered, Summers has an accident?"

"He's in custody," another voice interjected. "How can he have an accident?"

"Let me rephrase. What if Summers takes matters into his own hands?"

"Let's ask the professional?"

"If you mean me," a new voice responded, "it isn't out of the realm of possibilities. Despondent prisoners do take matters into their own hands."

"Yes. But can you pull that off?"

"It's not easy. But, yes."

"Wait a minute! If you are suggesting what I think you are, I'm out of here. I want no part in such doings."

"Okay! Okay! Calm down. We'll table that discussion. Let's move on to the new justice. What do we know about her position on our issue?"

"She refused or evaded providing her views on any cases pending before the Court, saying it would be inappropriate to comment since she would if confirmed have to study the cases and the precedents in order to make her decision."

"So we don't know how she will vote."

"That's right."

"After everything that's been gained so far, that's not good news."

"It is what it is."

Conversation ceased for several minutes. Then, "On that note, we're adjourned. Everything said here stays here. After I think over what has been said here, I'll be in touch with those of you as I think necessary. Goodnight!"

CHAPTER 38
TRIAL AND PUNISHMENT

Over nine months had passed since the murder of Justice Baker, less than five months since the death of Fleming Richards from anthrax poisoning, and twenty-one weeks since Ed Perry of CHASE had fallen in front of a Metro train. But it had been only six weeks since Jed Summers had been indicted for the murders of all three. The State deferred its prosecution of Summers for the murders of Richards and Perry, but intended to use the facts of those deaths in support of its case that Summers had shot Justice Baker.

The selection of the jury took a number of days of while District Attorney, Janet Newberry, for the prosecution, and Chris Knight for the defense made their respective peremptory challenges to exclude prospective jurors without stating a reason. In the peremptory-challenge phase of a trial, lawyers are permitted to remove prospects for any reason except their race or sex. There followed the tedious process of the lawyers and the judge in the case questioning prospects intensely in an effort to detect any biases they might have and so exclude them for cause. Of the 12 jurors selected, 5 were white, two Hispanic, 4 African American, and one Pacific Islander. Of the twelve, seven were women, and five men. They ranged in age from 32 to 59. Having reached this point, the jurors stood in the jury box, raised their right hands, and were sworn in.

That still left, however, the selection of eight alternate jurors, which began a week later.

The panel chosen came from a pool of 211 people initially summoned as prospective jurors for the case in which Summers was charged with the fatal shooting of Justice Baker in revenge for his having commuted the death penalty for the murderer of Summers' family.

The jurors chosen were not identified by name; nor would they be. Under rules and practices in criminal cases, it is customary and at times required that jurors be shielded from public pressure in cases that generate enormous publicity. Hence, all members of the jury pool were identified in court only by number.

When it was Chris's turn to exercise another of his peremptory challenges, he decided not to at that point thinking that the prosecution was being the more manipulative of the two sides. Chris offered to take all 12 prospective jurors then in the jury box.

"Your honor," he said, "the defense believes this is a fair and impartial jury and will accept the jury as presently constituted."

But prosecutor Newberry objected and a jury cannot be seated until both sides are in accord or until they reach the 20 challenges allotted to each. So, one by one, each side dismissed a jury candidate, and as that prospect stepped aside, another would take the vacant place in the jury box. As a defendant in a criminal case has the right to be present at all material stages of a trial, Summers sat through the process in varying states of disbelief, despair, and denial. Finally, however, a panel was selected.

District Attorney Newberry presented the prosecution's opening statement.

"Ladies and gentlemen of the jury, the defendant, Jed Summers, is charged with the murder of Chief Justice Bertram Baker. The prosecution will present evidence that will show that the defendant is guilty as charged. We will show that the defendant was motivated by revenge. Revenge for the Supreme Court's decision headed by Justice Baker commuting the death sentences of convicts on death row, one of which was the murderer of the defendant's family. Let me stop here to say that while Mr. Summers has suffered a terrible loss, that does not justify his taking the law into his own hands. It does not justify killing a member of this state's highest court. Any sympathy for Mr. Summers in this trial is grossly misplaced.

"The prosecution will show that Mr. Summers had opportunity. He is a resident of this city as was Justice Baker. He lived but five miles from Justice Baker's house where he was found shot to death in his bed. A coded note was found which when deciphered spelled out the motive for the murder. And Mr. Summers had the means. The gun that killed Justice Baker was found in his cabin hidden beneath a floor board under the bed in the master bedroom.

"The prosecution will also present evidence of defendant's background and familiarity with anthrax. We will show the connection between the death of the attorney who represented the murderer whose sentence was commuted."

"Objection, your honor," Chris protested.

"On what grounds, Mr. Knight?" asked Judge Bailey.

"May we approach, your honor?" Chris asked.

The judge waved his hand for Chris and Newberry to approach the bench. "Well, Mr. Knight?"

"Your honor, evidence of other acts is not admissible under section 404 of the Federal Rules of Evidence. The prosecution intends to use Mr. Summers' knowledge of anthrax to link him to the death caused by anthrax to persuade the jury that his character is such that he has a propensity for revenge. Rule 404 forbids this and I submit so does Rule 403. This is unduly prejudicial."

District Attorney Newberry responded, "Your honor, these facts can be introduced under Rule 404 to show motive, opportunity, intent, plan and knowledge."

"But, these are not facts that have been proven," Chris objected.

"Your honor, Mr. Richards died of anthrax poisoning. Another coded note was found in his office which when deciphered spelled out the defendant's motive of revenge. And bags containing anthrax residue was found buried behind a propane tank on Defendant's property. The attorney's killing is fully consistent with defendant's motivation of revenge," Newberry argued.

"I see,' said the judge. "I'll allow it. Objection overruled. I can handle your concerns Mr. Knight with appropriate instructions."

"Exception, your honor," Chris stated.

"Duly noted, Mr. Knight. You may proceed Ms. Newberry."

Chris returned to the defendant's counsel table and Newberry resumed.

"As I was stating, the prosecution will also present evidence of defendant's background and familiarity with anthrax. We will show the connection between the death of the attorney who represented the murderer whose sentence was commuted."

"We will also show that Mr. Summers was present at the same Metro platform when a member of CHASE, an organization opposed to the death penalty, fell in front of an oncoming train and was killed. His death occurred shortly after he appeared on a TV panel in which Mr. Summers participated debating the death penalty.

"Ask yourself ladies and gentlemen of the jury if it is at all possible that these three deaths are unrelated. Mere coincidences. You should conclude, after all the evidence is presented, that these deaths are related and resulted from the acts of one individual. An individual who wanted revenge. Revenge by the defendant who felt cheated of the satisfaction of seeing a murderer suffer the same fate he had meted out. Motive, opportunity and means. They all exist and all point to one person – the defendant. You must bring back a verdict of first degree murder. And note the irony. Once convicted, the defendant will not face the death penalty. He will be spared that fate because of the decision of the person he murdered. Thank you."

"Mr. Knight, will you be making an opening statement?" asked Judge Bailey.

"Yes, you honor."

"Proceed."

"Ladies and gentlemen of the jury, the most important principle you must rely on to assess the testimony and evidence the prosecution will introduce is that that testimony and evidence must prove beyond a reasonable doubt that Mr. Summers shot and killed Justice Baker.

The defense need not produce any testimony or evidence. The burden of proof is solely on the prosecution and that burden is heavy and justifiably so. Thank you." Chris concluded and sat down.

The prosecution presented its witnesses. The principle witness was Detective Dan Edwards and his discovery of the gun and bags with anthrax residue at Summers' cabin. When Newberry, said your witness, Chris rose to begin his cross examination.

"Just a few questions, Detective. What circumstances led you and officer Gaines to search Mr. Summers cabin a second time"

"We often revisit locations associated with an accused."

"Have you ever revisited a location that is or might be involved on a crime based solely on a tip?"

"A tip?"

"Yes, detective. Someone relays information that could be relevant to your investigation and you decide it supports revisiting a location where at first nothing relevant was found?"

"Yes. That occurs."

"Did it occur this time – that is for Mr. Summers' cabin?"

"Yes."

"Who gave you the tip?"

"It was a phone call. Anonymous."

"Did you make any effort to obtain the identity of the caller?"

"No."

"Why not?"

"The first concern is to obtain the information being offered. Trying to identify the source can scare the caller off."

"When you got the information, did you make any effort to identify the source of that information?"

"No."

"The caller hung up."

"Was the caller a man or a woman?"

"A man."

"What was the information the caller provided you?"

"I was told that it would be worthwhile to search Mr. Summers' cabin. When I said we had and found nothing, I was told, perhaps we didn't look in the right places or that things might have changed since our first search."

"Were you told where to look this time?"

"Not in so many words."

"What does that mean, detective?"

"Well, it was suggested we look inside the cabin."

"Were you told a specific room or area?"

"I recall a bedroom being mentioned."

"Any specific spot in the bedroom mentioned?"

"No."

"But you found the gun that you say was used to kill Justice Baker. How did you do that?"

"Markings."

"Markings?"

"On the floor. I could see the bed had been moved."

"What did you do after you saw the markings on the floor?"

"I moved the bed."

"Following the markings?"

"Yes."

"Then what did you do?"

"I tapped around and noticed a floor board that wasn't fully nailed down."

"Then what?"

"I lifted the board and found the gun."

"In your investigation of Justice Baker's murder, have you a theory or idea of whom among all the people you have interviewed would have had knowledge of Mr. Summers cabin?

"Well, we did talk to the lady that lived in the cabin next to the defendants."

"Did she suggest where to look in the cabin?"

"No."

"Anyone else come to mind that you recall might have the knowledge of where to look inside the cabin.?"

"No."

"What about the bags with the anthrax spores? Did your anonymous caller tell you where to look for those?"

"I don't recall."

"Did you tell Detective Gaines where to look for them?"

"I took the cabin. Gaines took outside."

"The bags were buried, were they not?"

"Yes."

"How did Gaines find them?"

"He told me he was looking around, came to the propane tank and noticed that the ground at one end seemed to have been recently disturbed. He dug around and called out that he had found the bags."

"Did he know they contained anthrax spores?"

"I don't know."

"What was done with the bags after they were discovered?"

"We brought them in as evidence."

"But you took precautions did you not?"

"What do you mean?"

"You went into the kitchen and got a container to put the bags in because you knew anthrax was dangerous if you came in contact with it."

"I suppose so."

"But if you weren't tipped off about the bags, how would you know they contained anthrax spores?"

"We were just being cautious."

"Has it crossed your mind that the gun and bags were placed there in order to incriminate Mr. Summers?"

"No."

"Has it crossed your mind that your anonymous caller may have been the real murderer of Justice Baker?"

"That's speculation. We act based on what our investigation produces. I can assure you we get a lot of anonymous tips that come from sources having nothing to do with the crime that they report on."

"But never from the perpetrator to throw suspicion on to someone else?"

"Not that I recall."

"Let me ask you this. Have your investigations led you to a suspect believed to be the perpetrator only to later be shown it was another that actually committed the crime?"

"Yes."

"How often?"

"I don't keep track of that?"

"But it happens?"

"Yes."

"You can't provide a number. But in your career, more than once?"

"Yes."

"Would it be fair to say several times?"

"Yes, I suppose so."

"So in your experience, evidence can point in the wrong direction?"

"Yes."

"And in your experience, people have been framed?"

"It happens."

"Would you say, finding the gun and the bags with anthrax spores is all too pat?"

"I don't follow?"

"Would you say that if Mr. Summers hid the gun in his cabin and buried the bags on his

property, he acted stupidly?"

"People who commit crimes often act stupidly. If they didn't, we wouldn't catch as many was we do."

"But in this case, the stupidity was blatant."

"If you say so. But, the defendant is not a practiced criminal. It's not unusual in that case, that they don't think about what they are doing or how it might make them look guilty or show that they are in fact guilty."

"That's all I have now, your honor," Chris said and returned to the counsel table.

"Redirect, your honor," District Attorney Newberry interjected.

"Proceed."

"Detective Edwards, is there any plausible evidence you have come across that suggests another motive for the murder of Justice Baker?"

"No."

"Have you come across any evidence that suggests the defendant is being framed?"

"No."

"Were any finger prints found on the gun you found in the cabin?"

"No."

"What does that mean?"

"It was wiped down."

"What about the bags with the spores?"

"The defendant is a pharmacist. He could take the precaution of wearing gloves."

"How long have you been on the homicide squad?"

"Twenty years."

"Thank you. That's all I have."

"Re-cross, Mr. Knight?" asked Judge Bailey.

"Yes your honor. Just a few questions.?"

"Proceed."

"Detective Edwards, your theory on the motive for Justice Baker's murder is based on revenge. Is that correct?"

"Yes."

"And if that is the case, it would be because of his decision on the death penalty?"

"Yes. Unfortunately, it's the only logical explanation."

"Would you say that a concern about the loss of hundreds of millions of dollars in investment, in losing a multi-million-dollar business, could be motives for taking the life of a judge?"

"I suppose so. I have no way of knowing. In any event, no such decision has been handed down by the Court or Justice Baker."

"How do you know that?"

"In the earliest stages of the investigation, we of course looked at the recent decisions of the Court and especially those where Justice Baker wrote the opinion. We found no cases of the type you mention in which Justice Baker was involved."

"Did you consider cases that were pending and undecided in which a multi-million-dollar business might be adversely affected?"

"No. We did not."

"What if there were such a pending case that depending on how it was decided, could have such consequences?"

"I'd be speculating. I know of no such case."

"But if there were one, would you agree, that preventing a decision being made that had such financial consequences would provide a motive to make sure the decision was rendered, even to the extent of using murder."

"I have never had a case in which a judge was attacked, much less murdered, because of a decision he or she might make."

"Fair enough. But in your experience has staving off financial ruin provided a motive for murder or other crime?"

"Put that way, I have to say yes."

"Would you consider this relevant to show motive for Justice Baker's murder? Pending for decision, a decision on which Justice Baker held the deciding vote was one on upholding the state's ban on fracking. If Justice Baker decided to uphold the ban, he would have been joined by four other Justices and the ban would be upheld. If the ban was upheld, oil companies, already in difficult financial straits, stood to lose hundreds of millions or billions of dollars and be forced out of business. Motive?"

"Objection your honor. The witness does not have to answer hypothetical questions," objected Newberry.

"Sustained," intoned Judge Bailey.

"Just a few more questions Detective Edwards. You responded earlier that you had been on the homicide squad for 20 years, correct?"

"Yes."

"Were those 20 years on this city's homicide squad?"

"No. I was on another for 5 years?"

"Different city or different state?"

"Both. A different city in a different state."

"What were the circumstances that led you to leave your former squad?"

"Looking for a new opportunity?"

"Detective, wasn't there an official reason for your leaving?"

"What do you mean?"

"Weren't you facing disciplinary actions for having failed to maintain a proper chain of custody in a murder case?"

"Objection! Irrelevant!"

"Overruled."

"In fact, the charge was lowered to failing to maintain the chain of evidence from the charge of having tampered with the evidence? Tampering in order to gain a conviction of a high-profile defendant?"

"Nothing was ever proved. I just decided to resign."

"Thank you. No further questions."

The gavel banged. "It's nearly 5 P. M. We're adjourned until 10 A.M. this coming Tuesday," Judge Bailey announced.

CHAPTER 39
DEADLY REACTIONS

Sitting in the rear of the court, a distinguished looking man in a dark business suit and wearing dark glasses rose at the conclusion of Detective Edwards testimony and quietly exited the court room. He walked with a determined step but without seemingly hurrying. He did not want to attract any attention. He left the court house, walked the two blocks to the garage where he had parked, presented his ticket. A few minutes later the four door Carbon Black Metallic BMW with its Black Napa Leather upholstery rolled up the garage ramp. The parky got out and held the door, "Can I ask what this baby cost?"

"Around one-hundred thousand," came the reply. With that, the man slid into the driver's seat and drove off. A block away, he pulled into the parking lot for a nearby motel, fixed the ear piece for his Blue Tooth and spoke the numbers for the phone he was calling. After three signals, a voice answered, "Yes?"

He backed the car up, turned back onto the avenue and drove on before he answered.

"I just left the court room. The trial is adjourned until next Tuesday. Edwards was on the stand and testified."

"How did he do?"

"On direct examination by the prosecutor he seemed convincing enough. The jury seemed attentive. But under cross examination there were difficulties."

"What happened?"

"This guy Knight, Summers' lawyer, is no slouch."

"What do you mean?"

"Long story short, he did a good job of laying the ground work for creating reasonable doubt."

"How so?"

"That's the dicey part. He got Edwards to admit he got a tip to go to Summers' cabin. He followed up by suggesting finding the gun and anthrax bags seemed a bit too pat, that it looked like a frame up."

"That was expected I guess. Is that all?"

"Not by a long shot. He focused on the prosecution's case that the motive was revenge for the decision on the death penalty. He then questioned Edwards on the possibility there were other motives than revenge."

"Like what?"

"This is the worse part. He questioned Edwards about a motive to keep Baker from delivering a decision upholding the ban on fracking. He cited the threat such a ban was to the oil companies and brought out that Baker's decision was expected to do just that, uphold the ban that he had established would cost the oil companies millions and billions of dollars. You could see the jury was paying attention. The result could be this guy Knight has made headway in creating reasonable doubt in the minds of the jury. But what is worse, that reasonable doubt is based on establishing another motive for Baker's murder, namely to keep the Court from upholding the ban on fracking."

"That it."

"Unfortunately, no. After the prosecution established that Edwards was in homicide for 20 years to support his testimony that he did not believe Summers had been set up, Knight went into Edwards past. He brought out that Edwards had to leave his position on his first homicide squad assignment under a cloud."

"What cloud?"

"Knight brought out that although the official record lists Edwards' failure to ensure the chain of evidence in a case, the real reason was he had tampered with evidence."

"How do you think Edwards will react to all this?"

"Can't say. If he keeps his mouth shut, the damage Knight did today may not get any worse."

"Why wouldn't he keep his mouth shut?"

"That's what I'll look into tonight. My concern, having dealt with Edwards before, is that he's fine when everything is working. But when things start to unravel and places him in a more tenuous position, he gets demanding."

"Demanding?"

"He'll want more money to continue to play along."

"How much?"

"I don't have a number, but it won't be small. But I don't see that as the biggest or the only problem."

"What?"

"Hold on, I'm pulling into my driveway. There. Okay, he could cave in and to clear his

name from being accused once again of tampering or planting evidence, he could threaten to turn us in."

"He'd be putting his own head into a noose."

"Not necessarily. He's smart enough to manufacture evidence that he had been duped and turn us all in and look like a hero instead of a goat."

"Perhaps, but I think he'd be taking a big risk."

"I don't disagree. The question is can we afford the risk?"

"What's your idea?"

"I'll arrange a meet with Edwards and see where he is. That is, how much it will take for him to continue to play ball. When we know that, we can consider satisfying him or whether we have to consider other options."

"Hold on. I just had an idea. Or another option anyway. Suppose we pin the Judge's murder on Edwards. His motive would be to extract revenge for his being cashiered by his first department and using planted evidence framed Summers, just to show he could do it and this time get away with it."

"I have to think about that. It seems awful risky and complicated."

"Okay, thinking out loud. First confirm that Edwards has no alibi for the night Baker was murdered. Then establish his access to Glocks. Then he is found shot to death with a suicide note based on his fear that his previous tampering would be a basis for pursuing him now and he confesses to framing Summers and takes his own life. Remember, it was Edwards who insisted on looking for survivors of the victims whose murderers escaped the death penalty and insisted the motive was revenge."

"It might work. But the good news is, we have some time and we may never need to go down that road. I'll know more once I talk with Edwards."

"When?"

"Tonight if I can catch him at his apartment."

"Let me know as soon as you know something."

"I will."

It was a little after 10 P.M. Raining, dark, perfect cover. But for the car's lights, the Carbon Black Metallic BMW was all but invisible. At that, one could not tell the make of the car with the lights on as all was invisible behind their glare. When the lights were off, the car disappeared into the gloom. The car was parked away from the light stands in the parking lot. The driver exited and walked to the lobby of the Crest Field Apartments where Detective Edwards lived. Inside he punched in the 10th floor on the elevator panel and exited going to Apartment 1010. Knocked. Edwards opened the door.

"Come in."

"Nasty night out there."

"Yes, suppose so. So why venture out?"

"This was not a good day."

"You're not talking about the weather."

"No. You know that. Your testimony."

"What about it?"

"You're the cop. You know what I mean."

"Suppose I do. So what?"

"We need to know how you feel. If you have any concerns. If you need anything."

"When I got into this, my past was not in play. Now it is thanks to Summers' attorney. I'm not happy about that."

"Understandable. What, if anything, do you want to do about it?"

"It's not what I want to do, it's what you and yours have to do."

"I see. And what would that be?"

"I could lose my job if we lose the case. If that happens I'll need enough for me to retire, retire in style."

"Obviously, that will be costly. How much?"

"I figure four million. Paid in full. Wire transfer to a foreign bank account, I'll set up. No installments. In addition, a fully paid first class airline ticket to the destination of my choice. I won't be returning."

"And if this demand is found to be too steep?"

"Then we have a problem. Or I should say you have a problem. I can flip and take you all down."

"You'll take yourself with us."

"Not necessarily. I've been accused of tampering with evidence. Well, just between us girls, I am an expert in that dubious discipline. And I have taken the precaution when I got involved with you all to create a paper and evidentiary trail that will show I was duped and misled. I'll look like a hero and you all will be going on a long and unpleasant 'vacation.' All at the government's expense of course."

"You have it all worked out. And you appear to have the upper hand. I will of course have to report this and get an answer whether we can meet your demands. They are steep, but not necessarily over the top."

"Good! Then we seem to understand each other."

"As I say, I understand your demands, even to the point that were I in your shoes, I would probably make similar ones. All that needs be done is convey these requirements and get you an answer as to how and when."

"I agree. Shall we call it a night?"

"Of course. I'll leave now and be in touch as soon as possible. Good night."

"Good night. Oh, one thing."

"Yes?"

"Time is of the essence."

In a chilling tone that Edwards noticed but ignored, the response was, "Oh, I couldn't agree more."

When the distinguished personage reentered his BMW, affixed the Blue Ray, he called. It was answered immediately.

"Well?"

Edwards' terms were relayed. A silence ensued. Then, "What's your recommendation?"

"First, are you prepared to meet his terms?"

"Not if there are reasonable alternatives."

"Okay. Let's start. I have confirmed Edwards was in his apartment alone on the night Baker was shot. A Glock is standard issue for police. Edwards had his pick of Glocks."

"Wait aren't they all registered to each officer?"

"Yes. But there are several in inventory. Edwards had easy access to these."

"Go on."

"Edwards is told his terms are acceptable on one condition. He has to see that Summers dies in jail – a suicide based on his depression. I have no doubt Edwards can pull this off. To ensure his acceptance, there's another million in his pocket."

"So, if I'm understanding, Summers suicide suggests he was guilty of murdering Baker. Case closed. Edwards suicide is his remorse for his past conduct. There is no one left to tie us to any of the crimes."

"There are of course the deaths of Richards the lawyer and Ed Perry of CHANCE. But by this time, everyone, including the authorities, have had their fill and will move on."

"Brilliant! But how do you handle Edwards suicide. There must be a note or something, mustn't there be?"

"Of course. But Edwards is a notorious pack rat. His apartment is full of his reports and writings from which a suicide note can be created that given the embarrassment of his confession will be gratefully accepted by the authorities as authentic."

"You're brilliant. Proceed."

"Not so fast. When this is done, I expect to be compensated fully."

"Name your price."

"The four million in a foreign bank account and first class airfare to a destination of my choosing."

"That's Edwards's demands!"

"Not relevant. Edwards's demands were based on his ability to upset the apple cart. Mine are based on eliminating the cart and the apples."

"I can't argue with that. Proceed."

"We will not be in contact, until the program has been completed. You will then be told the foreign account to which to wire the four million in funds and the, let's say $15,000 for the airfare. To ensure there is no thought of reneging, our conversations have been recorded. Should anything happen to me or should the aforesaid payments not be made, they will be furnished to the authorities after I am well gone without a trace."

"You do not trust me? I am abashed!"

"False indignation! In crimes of this nature, and with so much money at stake, only a fool depends on the trust of another."

"You seem the perfect Machiavelli."

"Perhaps. It is of no concern to me. I have my reasons."

"Then we are concluded. I will await your call that the deeds are done as planned. And you shall have your compensation."

"Yes. I shall or you shall face the unpleasant consequences that will occur."

CHAPTER 40
"ESCAPE"

He pulled the black BMW into the deserted parking lot of a rest stop on the Interstate. Turned off the lights and waited. Five minutes later another car turned and proceeded to park about 25 yards away. Another two minutes passed and the driver of the second car got out. Lit a cigarette and headed for the men's room. He exited the other side from where he entered and walked around the back of the building. There was only one street lamp and he quickly passed back into darkness. The door on the BMW opened and Detective Edwards slid into the front passenger seat.

"Right on schedule, detective."

"Force of habit, one might say."

"Let's get down to it." Edwards was then provided with the terms of the arrangement that he had demanded. Edwards nodding as each of the terms were set forth. At the conclusion, a moment of silence before the driver of the first car said, "Then it's settled."

"Not quite."

"What? These are your terms. There's nothing missing is there?"

"No! The terms are correct. It's making sure those terms will be complied with. I've been a cop too long to trust those I do business with on the side. No offense intended."

"None taken. What do you propose?"

"I want $100,000 in cash tomorrow delivered by courier to my apartment by 10 A.M. The remaining $3,900,000 must be wired to a foreign account I've set up. Here's the bank and account number."

"Very clever. But we can't be wiring funds before we have proof of the success of your venture, shall I say."

"I know. So with the wire, you have the bank hold the funds in escrow until it receives wired instructions to release them in accordance with instructions I will be giving. I will let you know what identity I'll be using to contact the bank so you know in what name to have it release the funds."

"You missed your calling detective. You should have gone into international finance."

"Yeah! If only! Do we still have a deal?"

"I'm sure things can be arranged as you require. The proof will be there tomorrow morning in the form of $100,000 cash and a record of the wire transfer will be couriered later in the day."

"That works."

"What are your plans?"

"Do you really want to know?"

"No, you're right. Of course not."

"Don't worry, you'll know I succeeded by watching the news or reading the papers."

"Makes sense. Anything else?"

"Just this. The next car I get will even more expensive than this one. Goodnight!" Edwards opened the car door and exited and walked back to his car staying away from the lighted spots in the lot. The first driver watched him pull away. Waited ten minutes and then left the lot headed in the opposite direction from Edwards. He clicked on his Blue Tooth and when he was answered explained what had transpired.

"Okay. I'll see the 100Gs are at his apartment in the morning. Give me the details on the foreign bank account." After he had the information, he said, "This better work!"

"There is risk in all important endeavors. But we have minimized them in this case."

"Yeah! I just wish it was your 4 million we were playing with."

"Well, you should recall, it will be when this is all over."

"Ha! Yeah! I forgot."

The next morning, Edwards woke early. Made coffee and started watching the clock waiting for the 10 o'clock delivery. He had arranged to take the late night shift so he could implement his plan that evening. By half past ten, Edwards was getting angry and scared. Then there was a knock at his apartment door. He tossed his cigarette into the sink and went to the door and opened it. The boy standing there was in a courier uniform Edwards didn't recognize.

"Mr. Daniel Edwards?"

"Yes."

"Sign here please."

"Thanks. This package is for you."

Edwards took the package, closed the door and bolted and chained it. "So this is what 100Gs weighs. Damn heavy."

He placed the package on the kitchen table, tore it open and gazed in amazement at the stacks of $20 and $50 dollar bills. After a few moments of awe, he carried the package into the bedroom and pulled out a suitcase. He transferred the money to the suitcase, closed and locked it, putting the key on a chain and the chain around his neck. Then he placed the suitcase in the back of his closet behind his suits and overcoats and closed the door. The money safely away, he walked into his den and sat down behind a small desk. He grabbed one of the pens from the coffee cup that held them and pulled a legal pad from the center drawer. He thought, "this is just like planning a bust." Details to consider and organize, no detail being too small and no limit on number of times he would review the organization of actions that were to be carried out.

Several hours later, he was satisfied he was ready. He replaced the pad containing his notes in the center drawer and locked it and put the key on the bookcase behind his desk, sticking it in the soil of the miniature Bonsai tree resting there. He turned and went to his bedroom and put on his workout jumper. When he had time before a big action, he found it relaxing to do a heavy workout. He'd be back in plenty of time to shower, shave and dress for his stint on the night squad at the precinct.

As Edwards prepared to carry out his plan, Chris Knight arrived at the precinct where Summers remained incarcerated. After going through security, the guard led him back to the holding cells. He advised Knight, "Good thing you came by today."

"How's that?"

"We got orders we have to move the inmates to our neighboring precinct."

"Why?"

"Don't really know. Only know we got the order. Must be for some upgrade or repairs.

The AC hasn't been keeping this place as cool as it should be. Anyway, we only have one inmate, your client Summers. So that may be part of the reason."

"When's the move?"

"Later tonight. Some think it's safer to move at night. Less traffic, no one around, you know. Here we are. Summers, your counsel is here." The cell door was opened and Chris entered. The door was closed with a clank and the key turned locking him in with his client.

"How are you, Jed?"

Jed looked up and Chris saw his eyes were swollen with black rings. He obviously hadn't been sleeping. He shrugged, but did not answer. Chris tried to encourage him by telling him that he thought the jury took notice of the testimony Chris had extracted from Detective Edwards. It seemed the jury understood that it may be cause for a reasonable doubt about his being responsible for Justice Baker's murder. Still Summers said nothing.

"Okay, look. I came to see how you were doing. Whether you needed anything I might be able to supply and to tell you about the case for your defense I will present."

Summers looked up. "There's a defense?"

"Yes. Let me outline for you. I will be calling Justice Baker's law clerk to testify about the cases pending before Justice Baker just before his death.

His testimony is important to establish another motive for the murder."

"And what would that be?" Summers asked, now paying attention.

"The case concerning the ban on fracking. I intend to show, that rather than revenge being the motive for Justice Baker's murder, it was to stop the ruling that would uphold the ban that would have serious financial repercussions on oil companies. Many, including those in this area, already under economic stress due to the plunge in oil prices. I have subpoenaed an expert on fracking and its impact on oil companies who will testify that if the ban on fracking was upheld, oil companies still around, but already in a financial tight spot, could go under. The purpose of this testimony is to undercut the prosecution's reliance on revenge as the motive for killing Justice Baker."

"I see, I think," Summers said and his dour expression changed for the better. "Is that it, then? My defense?"

"No there's more. I will also call the three people you identified that can testify to your character and Dr. Kelly Young to testify about your psychological profile. She'll testify that as a trained and accredited psychologist, it is her expert opinion that your profile does not indicate a tendency to any form of violent behavior and certainly not being able to commit cold blooded murder. I'm also going to call members of CHASE to testify that in all their experiences in dealing with the death penalty, they have never known any survivors of victims showing any tendency to seek revenge against any advocates of eliminating the death penalty. I will also call two witnesses that have experience in the violence perpetrated against abortion clinics and doctors and staff who work in them."

"Do...do you think it will do any good?" asked Summers with a hopeful tone.

"I honestly think so. But no one can tell what a jury is going to do. All I can do is present all I can that will raise a reasonable doubt in their minds that you are responsible for Justice Baker's death. Having said that, I think the defense that will be presented is solid. I want you to take courage by believing this."

"Why is my belief important?"

"It's obvious this ordeal you've going through has affected you. You exhibit aspects of deep depression, lack of sleep, black ringed, swollen eyes, bent posture. I can understand these. But what you have to understand is that jurors are affected by the demeanor presented in the court room by the accused. Your current demeanor can be taken as exhibiting your own sense of guilt."

Summers thought for a moment. "I see what you mean."

"Good. What are you going to do about it?"

"I don't..."

"Stop. You are not guilty! You know that, right?"

Summers said nothing for a moment. Then, "Quite frankly, I've been having doubts. The prosecution's evidence is damning. Perhaps I did do it and blocked it out of my mind. That would explain why I would have hid the gun and the anthrax at my cabin."

"But the fact is, is that you didn't do it. And Dr. Young and your character witnesses firmly believe, as I do, that you didn't do it and are incapable of such a violent act."

"Yes. I suppose so. But what do I do now?"

"Pull yourself together. Eat, sleep. Do some exercises. Straighten up your posture. Shave, shower, and keep as well-groomed as possible in this place. Ask for some books to read to keep your mind off of things until it's time to face them. When next we appear in court, dress as sharply as you can, suit, tie, etc. Think of it as attending a pharmaceutical trade show. Your demeanor should border on being defiant, squared shoulders, head held high, eyes looking forward."

"I... I think I can do that," Summers said with a faint smile.

"Good. I've got things to do, so I'll be leaving. But remember, you're an innocent man and your appearance and demeanor must convey that to the greatest extent possible."

"I understand. You've given me some of my dignity back. Thank you. I will do my best.

"Good. So long for now," Chris said and shook Summers hand whose grip was unexpectedly firm.

Edwards arrived at the precinct 15 minutes before the graveyard shift began at 11 pm.

He went to his desk and fiddled with some papers before heading to the cell block where Summers was being held. When he arrived, he showed his badge to the duty officer and said,

"I've come to transfer the prisoner, Sommers, 554637 and handed over the transfer forms.

The duty officer did a perfunctory check of the papers and said, "Right! Come on."

He led Edwards back to the cell block, pulled back the small window on the cell door and yelled, "Summers! Your transfer is here. Step back from the door."

"I'm on the cot," came the reply.

The duty officer entered first and put cuffs on Summers, hands in front. He grabbed Summers under his right arm and helped him up.

Edwards, standing just outside the cell, said with a satisfied smile, "Hello Summers. You remember me!"

Summers looked at Edwards and nodded. Edwards motioned for Summers to walk ahead of him. When they got to the entrance way, Edwards put his left hand on the back of Summers orange prison jacket and steered him to the right, through a hall way that led to the underground garage. As they entered the hallway, Edwards said, "I'll take it from here."

"Okay," said the duty officer and turned back to his station.

Edwards opened the door to the garage and said, "Look straight ahead, and don't try to turn around. Capisce?"

Summers nodded his head up and down.

Edwards released his grip on Summers' jacket collar and quickly drew his gun from his shoulder holster, and then put his left hand back on Summers" jacket and pushed him forward steering him to a police car at the far end of the garage. He opened the rear door of the car and bent Summers down as if to help him enter the back seat but shoved his head into the roof of the car stunning him. While he was dazed, Edwards turned him around so he was facing Edwards. Edwards put his gun into Summers' hands – safety on, then pulled Summers upright, turned the gun into Summers' chest, released the safety and pulled the trigger. The shot echoed around the nearly vacant garage. Summers slid to the floor. Edwards then dashed his forehead against the door frame enough to draw blood. Then he checked Summers. No pulse. He checked Summers' hands to ensure they had powder burns. Then he leaned over the trunk of the car and waited.

Edwards heard the garage door from the hall way open and the duty officer and another came out. Looked around. Saw Edwards at the far end of the garage and ran toward him. When they got there they saw Edwards was bleeding from his forehead and Summers' body lying in a pool of blood next to the rear door.

"What happened?"

"Damn fool grabbed my gun when I was assisting him getting into the car. We struggled. I was able to grab his hands that were around the gun and wrestling with him the gun got turned into his chest and went off. Damn fool! Damn fool!" Edwards repeated.

"Are you okay? Looks like you got a nasty crack on your forehead."

"Yeah. Almost blacked out. But hung on. Adrenalin I guess. Good thing, or I'd be a goner."

"Let's get back to the station. I'll call the ME. Leave him where he is, as is," the duty officer instructed.

Edwards put his right arm over the shoulder of the other cop and the three walked back to the station.

The ME arrived an hour later in a foul mood having to come out at the early morning hour. When he got to the scene, he wasted no time. The victim died of a gunshot wound at point blank range. Was dead when he hit the floor. Powder burns on his hands indicated he held the gun. A bruise on his forehead indicated a struggle like Officer Edwards reported. Later, it would be reported that both his and Officer Edwards' finger prints were on the gun. But for formalities, the case was open and shut. The accused was killed in a struggle trying to escape. Officer Edwards was injured in preventing that escape. All that was left to do was to notify the accused's legal counsel and the court which would dismiss the jury and close the case.

CHAPTER 41
DISBELIEF

It was 2 A.M. when District Attorney Newberry' i-Phone dinged. Sound asleep it wasn't until the third ding that she noticed. On the fourth ding, she picked it up and went into the bathroom so as not to disturb her husband. The message was "The Summers Case." She thought what prompted a call at this time about a pending murder trial was usually bad news for the prosecution. After swiping and entering her password, she accessed the message – "During the transfer of Summers to another facility, he tried to escape by grabbing the transporting officer's weapon. The officer resisted. In a struggle, the gun went off and shot Summers in the chest. He's dead. In subduing Sommers, the officer was slightly injured."

"Holy cow!" Newberry reacted. Then she sent this message: "Have all those involved in my office at 9:00 A.M."

"Roger that," was the reply.

Newberry went back to bed, shaking her head.

At 9 A.M. Edwards, the two officers on the scene and the ME assembled in Newberry's office. After being fully briefed, she said she would contact Summers' relatives. On learning he had none, she said, "Okay, I'll call his counsel. Apparently he is the only one to call."

Newberry dialed Chris Knight's office number. Chris's receptionist answered.

"Is Mr. Knight in?"

"Yes. Whom may I say is calling?"

"This is District Attorney Newberry."

"Please hold."

A short interval and Chris Knight picked up the call.

"Attorney Newberry! What can I do for you?"

"Mr. Knight, it's my duty to inform you that your client, Jed Summers, attempted to escape late last night when he was being transferred to another holding facility. Unfortunately, in his attempt, there was a struggle with the transporting officer during which Summers tried to take the officer's gun. In the struggle to take the gun away from Summers, he was shot in the chest and killed. According to the ME, death was instantaneous or nearly so. I waited to inform you until I had met with all those involved. That meeting ended only a few minutes ago."

Chris who was standing behind his desk flopped down into his chair. His disbelief kept him from responding.

"Mr. Knight, are you there?" Newberry asked.

"Yes! Excuse me. This is a shock. I don't understand."

"Well, Mr. Knight, as a prosecutor, I can tell you such an event is not that unusual."

"I know. This is different!"

"And how would that be?"

"In my last meeting with my client, I convinced him we could well win a not guilty verdict. His demeanor changed from one defeated to one who was confident in his innocence and that his defense had a chance of being successful. It makes no sense then that he would take such action. He was a mild mannered man. Resisting authority, no matter how unjust he may have thought it to be, would not have prompted him to challenge that authority. Certainly not in a violent manner."

"I see your point, Mr. Knight. But it's not relevant. The case against him will be terminated. There is nothing anyone can do beyond that. We will never know if he was guilty of Justice Baker's murder."

"I tell you now, Attorney Newberry, he was innocent. And my concern now is that proving his innocence was a threat to somebody."

"I have no understanding of your statement. We have investigated and have the ME's report. Summers' fingerprints were on the officer's gun and there were powder burns on Summers' hands. The officer was slightly injured in the struggle. We consider it an open and shut case."

"Yes! Yes! I understand you would. But it is not to me."

"I understand you are devoted to your clients. As should all attorneys be and not so often are. But it's your choice to do what you think you must if you decide to carry on in this case. Officially, this case will be closed." "I understand Attorney Newberry. Thank you for informing me."

Chris hung up and called Kelly and relayed the information about Summers' death.

"What? My God! How horrible? What can we do?"

"We can't do anything for Mr. Summers. We can try and do something to see justice is done."

"Chris. What do you mean?"

"I think Summers was murdered. He was murdered so the risk of his acquittal would not require the investigation of Baker's murder to continue. The fear being that if it were, those actually responsible would eventually be caught."

"But Chris, have you any idea who might actually be responsible?"

"Yes! Yes, surprisingly perhaps, but I do."

"Can I help?"

"Absolutely!"

"Then can you come home so we can discuss?"

"Yes! Let me put some things in order here and I'll be there in two hours."

"See you then," Kelly replied.

Edwards came in to Newberry's office a short time after her conversation with Knight to execute some forms. When he did, he stated, "Well, Summers saved the taxpayer's some money I guess. No long drawn out trial. No appeals."

"Normally, I would agree detective. But I'm not so sure."

"Really? Why not?'

"A short while ago, I called Summers' attorney to bring him up-to-date. His reaction was rejection of the idea that Summers would have tried to escape. I got the impression he was going to continue some efforts on Summers' behalf."

"Like what," Edwards asked.

"I have no idea. I only know that for Mr. Knight, Summers' death has not ended his efforts, whatever they may turn out to be."

'I see. Well he's welcome to his wild goose chases," Edwards responded. But it wasn't all that convincingly stated, Newberry noted.

Edwards left Newberry's office upset. Why the hell was this guy Knight refusing to close the book? One thing certain, he had done his job and entitled to collect his pay. A payment he could live on for the rest of his life. So what if Knight continued to snoop around. He'd be long gone. With that thought in mind, Edwards researched which countries had no extradition treaty with the U.S. He found several, but the one that best promised the life style he could now lead was Dubai. He made contact and delivered the message that in two months he would need a one-way first class ticket to Dubai. When asked why wait, he explained, "If I left now, it would raise suspicions and with Summers' lawyer still involved, it could cause problems. What I will do at the end of the two months is retire, I've got 20 years in anyway and I'll say that with Summers being shot while in my custody, I decided I have had enough."

"What about your retirement?"

"No problem. I'll arrange for direct deposit at a bank in some state that would be a logical choice for a cop to retire to, like Florida. Then I'll have the fund wire transferred to my bank in Dubai at various intervals during the year."

"Seems you thought this through."

"After 20 years on the force, you learn some things."

"I guess so. I'll take care of the plane ticket and since you completed the job, start arrangements to release the escrow on the account."

"Hold off on that too, until I am ready to leave. For the next two months, everything has to stay normal. I don't want to take any chances that somebody, like Knight, starts asking questions and gets a lead to follow."

"Makes sense. Two months and all will be done as we have discussed."

"Good! Goodbye!"

"Goodbye."

After the call with Edwards ended, the party with whom Edwards had made his arrangements, thought, "Perfect! The two-month time frame worked perfectly. But not the way Edwards planned."

Later the next day, Chris decided to call Newberry back. Chris could not get over his utter disbelief and shock.

"Janet, this can't be. It makes no sense."

"Chris, in my experience there's no way of predicting what a desperate person will do, one who's on trial for murder. Things like this happen. Fortunately, not very often."

"No! No! What I mean is that when I left Summers two days ago after our last conference there was a change. A major change. When the session started, Summers was dejected, despondent. He accepted he was feeling guilty for something he didn't do, but had given up hope and accepted he would be found guilty. When I left he was positive. Our discussion convinced him he had a chance. That the evidence I was going to present in his defense was sufficient to establish reasonable doubt. He regained some dignity. A few hours later he tries to escape and is shot. It makes no sense. No sense."

"Well we investigated the facts given us by the officer involved. The facts checked out."

"Who was the officer?"

"I won't reveal that right now. We are still confirming things."

"When will you?"

"We've scheduled a press conference later today.

"Will I be allowed to interview the officer?"

"Why?"

"Because I have to satisfy myself. Get rid of my disbelief. Perhaps, my guilt."

"Guilt?"

"Given what has happened, if it did happen as you say, I totally misjudged the state of mind of my client. I have to understand if that misjudgment was a cause of what happened."

"I know of no instance of allowing defense counsel to question an officer involved in the accidental death of his client. I'm thinking it shouldn't be permitted."

"Look! Can you ask the officer if he would agree to seeing me?"

"Hmm! I guess I could on one condition."

"What?"

"If the officer refuses, you drop it."

"Okay. I'd have little choice."

"I'll get back to you after the press conference."

"Okay. I'll be there at what time?

"Five o'clock."

"Thanks."

Chris hung up and called Kelly.

"Kelly, do you think it possible for Summers to have attempted escape after what I told you earlier about the results of our last session together?"

"No!"

"Do you think I misread his state of mind after that session?"

"No!"

"You know what you're saying and what I'm thinking then?"

"I suppose so. Like you said, Summers was killed and it was made to look like he was trying to escape to cover up his murder."

"Yes! And what's disturbing is that if he was murdered, it was at the hands of the officer who had him custody."

"Problem."

"Yes. Assuming our thinking is correct, what's the motivation?"

"I can think of only one. The one I was going to use in Summers' defense."

"You mean that Justice Baker's murder was not for revenge for his death penalty ruling, but for another motive."

"Yes. And the only one that makes sense is fear of his ruling upholding the ban on fracking."

"I agree. But how do you find the oil interests that would risk killing a state Supreme Court justice? And if you do, you have to prove the officer that killed Summers was acting on behalf of those interests."

"I know. But it ties together."

"Yes it does. But seeing the logic in this scenario is a long way from being able to prove it."

"I know."

"Chris, there's something else."

"What is that?"

"The person or persons responsible for Summers' killing are the ones responsible for Justice Baker's murder and logically for that lawyer Richards's death and Mr. Perry's. Whoever it is, has committed four murders. They won't hesitate to kill again. If you, we, go snooping around, you, we, become targets. One or two more deaths are hardly a concern."

"I agree and disagree. First, with the baby, you are not getting involved. Second, I'll only be interviewing those I believe have information that supports the motive of avoiding financial ruin. When I have enough information, I will go to the police and let them pick up the investigation."

"The problem is that you will be a target all the time you're gathering this information. If they find out what you're doing, you won't get to the police to turn over the investigation to them."

"I know. But I have to try. I'll be super careful."

"Your comment about the baby goes both ways. He or she needs a father."

"I know and I can hardly wait to be his or her dad. So here's my plan.

I will make discreet inquiries. If I become aware of any threat, I'll change what I'm doing or stop until things cool down or go to the police earlier."

"I in no way find that comforting. But I also know your mind's made up. So it's useless to argue with you. When you get home this evening, we will sit down and map out your investigation. I may not be able to be active, but I can go over everything with you and pick up on any oversights or judge whether the risk-reward factors are positive or negative on any action you contemplate taking."

"Perfect! I want that incredible mind of yours working on this and your analysis of facts and people my investigation turns up. I start with Justice Baker's law clerk and see if there are any more detailed facts in the Justice's files and court records on the ban on fracking. From there, I will research what oil companies will be affected by this state's ban. Then, I'll do what I can to establish relationships between the parties we know already and those we may discover."

"Sounds daunting."

"Yeah, I know. I'll be home after six or later. I have to go and pick up the police press release on Summers. Love you!"

"Love you too. See you in a bit."

When Chris hung up, he called Justice Baker's law clerk, explained what had happened and arranged to come by his office the next morning. Then he went to the police precinct for the press conference.

ith the Chief of Police, and some of her staff, District Attorney Newberry opened the conference saying, "We have called this conference to report that Jed Summers, on trial for the murder of Justice Baker, was killed last night trying to escape as he was being transferred to another facility. With his death, his prosecution ends. We have investigated the circumstances surrounding this incident. That investigation confirms what the officer transporting Mr. Summers told us had taken place is true. In essence, when Mr. Summers and the officer reached the police car that was to be used to take him to another facility, as Summers was climbing into the back seat, he wheeled around and grabbed the officer's gun. The officer was able to grip

Mr. Summers' hands holding the gun. During the struggle, in an attempt to wrest the gun from Mr. Summers, the barrel of the gun was turned toward Mr. Summers. While still trying to wrest the gun from Mr. Summers, it went off shooting Mr. Summers in the chest. He died almost instantly. Within a few minutes of the gun being fired, two officers arrived at the scene. The transporting officer was standing over Mr. Summers whose body had slumped to the ground. The officers noted that the transporting officer had sustained an injury to his forehead during the struggle. The transporting officer handed the gun over.

"The Medical Examiner confirmed that from the powder burns on Mr. Summers' orange prison jacket, he had been shot at close range. From the powder burns on Mr. Summers' hands and his fingerprints on the gun, the Medical Examiner confirmed that Mr. Summers' hands were on the weapon at the time it went off. The transporting officer has been placed on administrative leave with pay which is what the department regulations provide. I'll take a few questions."

"Who was the transporting officer?" came the first question.

"We're not releasing that information at this time."

"Why not?" was the follow-up question.

"We haven't completed our investigation. And who the officer was is not relevant. Next question!"

"Why was Summers being moved?"

"For his safety. Work had to be done on the facility where he was being held."

"Does Summers' attempt to escape prove he murdered Justice Baker?"

"It's a logical assumption. But we have not, need not and will not formulate a position on that."

"Excuse me Madam Attorney, but isn't that necessary?"

"I'm sorry, who asked that question?"

"Christopher Knight. Mr. Summers' defense counsel."

"This is a press conference Mr. Knight, you are welcome to attend, but I won't be answering your questions."

"Okay, I'm with the Daily Sun Newspaper," the reporter standing next to Chris spoke up. "I ask why it isn't necessary to formulate an opinion on Mr. Summers' guilt or innocence."

"The Department and our office have spent a lot of time and money in the investigation of Justice Baker's murder and also the deaths of Mr. Richards, the appellate lawyer and Mr. Perry of the CHASE organization. We have limited funds and man power. We have to use them wisely. Based on the case we built against Mr. Summers, based on his motive of revenge, the evidence found on his property, his knowledge as a pharmacist, we were confident of a conviction. Having no other evidence that pointed in other directions, we have no basis to continue investigating."

Chris scribbled a note and gave it to the Daily Sun reporter.

"District Attorney Newberry, your answer makes sense to a point, but what if Summers was acquitted? If so, it means someone else must have murdered Justice Baker, doesn't it?"

"It's possible I suppose," Newberry responded. "If there are no other questions…"

Chris hurriedly scribbled another note and passed it to the reporter.

"Just a minute please," the reporter said. "Suppose Summers was innocent and was being framed and knowing that, took a desperate chance and tried to escape. That would mean someone else murdered Justice Baker. If you close the case based on Summers' death, that means the person or persons responsible are still out there."

"We can't deal in possibilities or hypotheticals. As I said, we have limited resources. I know of no other motives for murdering Justice Baker than revenge for abolishing the death penalty."

With another note from Chris, the reporter asked, "What about the ban on fracking?"

"Fracking?"

"Yes. Court records show that a decision by the Baker Court to uphold or reject the ban on fracking was ready to be issued. It was widely expected that the Baker Court would uphold the ban and that would cost the companies relying on fracking millions, perhaps billions and would certainly have put some out of business. With Justice Baker's death that decision has not been handed down. No decision means fracking companies are still in business and avoided potential financial ruin. Wouldn't you say, that powerful companies facing ruin would have a motive to keep the court from upholding the ban?"

"Sir, that's a nice hypothetical and I know where you got it. It was one of the defenses Mr. Summers' counsel intended to present during trial. But again, we cannot act on hypotheticals. If someone comes up with some proof to support the existence of the hypothetical we will react. Until then, this case is closed. No more questions. Thank you all."

Newberry and her cadre then left the stage of the press room.

"Thanks," Chris said. What's your name again? Weren't you on the TV panel on the death penalty with me, Summers and Perry?"

"Yes. Good memory. William Nightingale. Bill."

"Of course!"

"Do you really think some oil company might be behind Baker's murder?

"I'm positive. But in truth I have no evidence so far. What I do know is that Baker's Court was expected to make a decision on the ban on fracking and release it as soon as things quieted down on the death penalty decision. And that decision was fully expected to uphold the ban."

"So where do you go from here, if anywhere?" Nightingale asked.

"I'm going to see Baker's law clerk tomorrow. He's consented to let me dig through some files to look for details that were not important to making the decision, but could be now because of his murder."

"Want some help?"

"You serious?"

"I'm a reporter. We're always looking for a good story. We also have resources you may not have. Your theory makes sense. I can certainly risk some effort to see if your theory can become proven fact. If so, it would rival Watergate."

"Great!" Chris said.

"Okay, while you meet with Baker's law clerk, I'll start digging in the newspaper's records. If we both find something, we can share and keep going."

"Bill. Appreciate this," Chris said, shook hands and they left the press room that was now empty but for them and one individual neither had noticed had remained after all others had left. This individual had listened intently to Nightingale's questioning of Newberry and just as intently to Chris' discussion with the reporter. He did not like what he heard nor would the person he would report to.

CHAPTER 42
A NEW INVESTIGATION

Chris showed up at the State Supreme Court Building at 9 A.M. Security was tight and it took twenty minutes for him to have his brief case and himself scanned. Once through, he had to lock his cell phone in a compartment. That done, the guard called Shelden Morris, Justice Baker's law clerk and announced Chris was through security and waiting for him to come down and take him back to his office. Morris exited the elevator, saw Chris waiting, walked over and shook his hand.

"Good morning Chris. Follow me."

They exited the elevator on the fourth floor and walked into the Chief Justice's office. Morris' office was to the right of Justice Baker's chambers. Morris maneuvered behind his desk motioning Chris to have a seat.

"I'm sorry to hear about what happened to your client. I wasn't anticipating that kind of end to his trial."

"Nor I. But thanks," said Chris. "You know why I'm here?"

"I think so, but tell me so we're certain to be on the same page."

"When I was last here, I was interested in other cases pending before the Court that were as controversial as its consideration of eliminating the death penalty. We agreed that the only one that could have serious consequences, serious financial consequences depending on how it was decided, was the case on whether to uphold the ban on fracking."

"Yes, I remember."

"With Summers' death, that decision and those it would adversely affect becomes far more important."

"Why is that?"

Chris explained his last conference with Summers and how his attitude toward his fate had changed and how that encouraged Chris himself that he was on the right track in believing revenge was not the motive for Baker's murder. Based on the results of the conference, Summers attempt to escape made no sense. Moreover, all Chris knew about Summers' character said he was not likely to try and overpower a police officer in an attempt to escape. Then continued.

"The officer involved was exonerated of any wrongdoing and the prosecution closed the case. When pressed at the news conference, the District Attorney made it clear she would not further investigate Justice Baker's murder despite the fact that with Summers' death before a jury verdict was rendered, it was possible the murderer was still at large."

"So, you're going to investigate and look for who you think actually murdered Justice Baker?"

"Yes."

"Why come here?"

"I want to look at the records on the fracking ban case. What companies had briefs filed supporting ending the ban. What companies filed Amicus briefs or sought permission to do so. What companies, organizations, individuals may have written the court?"

"Those records have been placed in storage. I'll have to write out a permission slip to allow your access. And you'll have to review them in our storage area."

"Understood!"

Morris pulled out a pad and completed it and signed his name. When completed he rose and Chris followed him out of the office. They took the elevator to the basement of the court house. Morris handed the permission slip to the man behind a wire cage, looked it over and said, "Just a minute." He turned and disappeared into another room. Several minutes later he returned pushing a dolly stacked with files. "Mr. Knight, you can review these at one of the tables behind you. If you want copies of anything, there's a per page charge. You can pay by credit card."

"Thanks," Chris said; then turning to Morris, said, "Sheldon depending on what I find, if I find something of interest, can I bring it to your atten-

ask you what you know about it and what you know about what
Baker may have known?"

"Sure. I don't promise I'll be of much help. But who knows?"

"Fine! I'll get started here."

"When you finished, tell the custodian and he'll call me and I'll come
and escort you back out."

"Will do. Thanks."

Chris sat down and pulled the first of the many bound documents to
examine. He thought he knew what he was looking for. The factual por-
tions of the appellate briefs that laid out the financial consequences if the
fracking ban were upheld and those if it was overturned. He also would
take note of the oil interests for which the briefs were filed. He would then
turn to any exhibits to the briefs that supported allegations of adverse financial impact if the ban was upheld. His goal was to create a dossier of
companies, their officers and shareholders, their finances, any public securi-
ties filings that would disclose a company's required disclosure to its shareholders of the financial impact on share values if the ban was upheld. He
would rank the companies by those threatened with the most serious financial impact, where their operations were located, with special emphasis on
companies whose fracking operations were concentrated in the state. When
his dossier was completed he would share his information with Nightingale whose newspaper background and access to public records might be
able to refine the search for the most likely company and its management
that would have few scruples about murder if it meant avoiding financial
disaster. He recalled that Honore de Balzac was credited with the observation that "Behind every great fortune there is a great crime." But others
found it also in Richard O'Conner's aptly titled book, *The Oil Barons: Men
of Greed and Grandeur.*

"Excuse me sir, but the court is closing. I have to ask you to finish up."

Chris turned around and nodded to the custodian his understanding.
"I'll just put these papers back in their file holders. Can I leave them here
so I can work some more on them tomorrow?"

"No sir. Sorry. But the files will have to be returned to the vault."

"I understand." Chris put the files back in order.

"I've called Mr. Morris. He's on the way down to escort you back to security where you can pick up your cell phone."

"Thank you."

These scenes played out again over the next two days until Chris had satisfied himself he had gotten all the information there was to get that related to his theory about the actual motive for Justice Baker's murder. Now he had to organize it and then meet with Nightingale to share his findings and hopefully have him find additional information that supported Chris's beliefs.

The man who hung back and listened in on Chris's discussion with Nightingale at the end of the prosecution's press conference on Summers' death, had arranged a meeting the next day to report what he had overheard. To ensure secrecy, the meeting was held at night at a private gated residence. A half block from the entrance the black car turned off its headlights. When it arrived at the gate, it turned into the driveway as the gates opened. Once through, the gates swung silently closed. The car pulled around to the back of the large mansion, parked and the driver got out and walked to the patio doors and entered a dark room and waited. He heard the whirr of the drapes closing and then the lights in the room came on.

"Well what's so important that requires this clandestine action? It's over. The plan worked as we planned. The only thing left is to take care of the one remaining detail and he's given us plenty of time to arrange for that."

"I want a drink. And you might also, once I tell you what I know."

"Help yourself. You know where the bar is."

The man with the message went to the bar, filled a glass with ice, poured himself a hefty scotch and a hefty swallow. Turned towards his host and said, "Your statement just now about only one remaining detail isn't accurate."

"Oh! And why not?"

Taking another hefty swallowing, the messenger related what he overheard after the press conference. His audience listened and when the report ended said, "You think this lawyer and reporter are serious trouble?"

"Yes!"

"Why?"

"This guy Knight is the lawyer who is challenging the interpretation of the Second Amendment."

"The Second Amend… What does that have to do with anything?"

"Nothing related to the current situation. What is relevant is that in his efforts on the Second Amendment, he and his wife were instrumental in the arrest, prosecution and murder conviction of a major figure of the gun lobby and the killing by police of the hit man, actually a woman, that was hired to lure Knight and his wife into an ambush and kill them. The police got to the scene just in time."

"So?"

"So. This Knight is tenacious and effective. He was defending Summers on a theory that the motivation for Baker's murder was not revenge, but to keep Baker from handing down a decision upholding the ban on fracking. When the prosecution said it would not be taking further action on Baker's murder, Knight had the reporter standing next to him ask a line of questions to establish that since Summers had not been convicted, Baker's murderer could still be at large. He's pursuing that now with the help of the reporter."

"So what? It's a wild goose chase."

"If it were anyone else but Knight and this reporter… what's his name… Nightingale, it well could be. But these guys are trouble. And consider this. That remaining detail you mentioned will not look so much as a tragic co-incidence as it would if Knight wasn't pursuing his theory about the case on fracking."

"You suggesting we let the four million go?"

"No. I've earned that."

"Then what?"

"Something has to be done about Knight."

"Suggestions?"

"None so far. Another accident like Ed Perry's comes to mind, but too coincidental. It's got to be random, totally random."

"You've just hit on it."

"I have? Enlighten me."

"What's more random than all the killings that have taken place in Orlando, San Bernardino, Dallas, Baton Rouge? Can we find someone with a death wish to take Knight out when he's in a public place?"

"Hmm! You may have something there. You have a candidate in mind?"

"No. But I know someone who could find one. Being in the oil business you have contacts with those from areas of the world where suicide attacks are part of the religion. Or maybe, we can get a gun nut juiced up to do the job. Now that I think of it, we may have a wealth of candidates."

"How soon can you put this together. We only have a month."

"You leave now. I'll start making contacts. I'll let you know when I have something put together."

A final swallow of scotch and the messenger put his glass on the bar and left the way he came in.

"His four million?" the host thought to himself. "Maybe these random shootings can solve a third problem – a real trifecta."

CHAPTER 43
TRIPLE DEADLY

The day after Chris completed his research of the court files on the fracking ban case, he called Nightingale. "Bill, Chris Knight. I wanted to let you know, I spent the last few days researching the records on the fracking case. I'd like to go over what I may have found with you and see if there's a path for further inquiries."

"You copy anything?"

"Yes. I have copies."

"I've got to finish a story. Let's say we meet at your office in two hours."

"That will work. See you then."

There wasn't a lot of time. A month to get rid of two people who were threats. The logical order was to first eliminate the threat to his wiring 4 million dollars to an offshore account. Staging this hit was the easier of the two with an explanation more easily based on common logic. The second elimination would be to prevent the discovery of a perfectly executed frame-up which in turn would jeopardize the 4 million dollar pay off. His serving on the board of CHASE had given him access to many who were accused or convicted of murder. From these contacts, he developed a dossier of hit men. One he had used to his advantage before and had now used to pull off framing Summers.

He arranged to meet the person he needed for the first hit in the swank lounge of the city's poshest hotel. A list of former and present guests read like a who's- who of corporate presidents, hedge fund managers, Wall Street major domos, top tier political figures, and the current crop of Hollywood and Broadway elite. Those considered masters in the deadly profession fit right in with such nabobs. Self-assured. Self-possessed with the muted excitement of playing God. He took a seat in a booth in the back of the lounge, ordered a dry Vodka martini and waited. Several minutes later, a tall, distinguished man in a perfectly tailored Italian made Brioni dark blue wool-silk suit appeared in the doorway to the lounge. Cast his eyes around and saw the man in the booth in the back of the lounge. As he casually approached, the man watching him thought business must be good knowing that the suit his visitor was wearing cost nearly $6500.

"Good afternoon. Have a seat."

The man slid into the booth.

"Want a drink?"

"No."

"I see. Down to business. I appreciate that." In low tones, the details and target were quickly outlined.

"That target will cost more."

"$50,000 is already a hefty sum. How much?"

"$25,000. All of it in cash."

A pause, then, "Alright! But there's another $5,000 on top for carrying out a step before hand."

"I'm listening."

After the additional service had been explained, the man said, "I can do that. I want the target's address, make and model of his car and license plate number. You have the information on the date and time of his flight?"

"Yes."

"The additional service will be done the night before he leaves."

"Your call, just be sure it's done."

"I do not like being warned. Don't do it again." He slid out of the booth and walked away.

"A master hit man. Absolutely," the host of this rendezvous thought to himself. He drained the last of his martini and left the lounge. "One down and two to go," he muttered to himself.

Nightingale arrived at Chris' office, was greeted by the receptionist, and shown into the conference where the table was piled with documents. Chris joined him a few minutes later.

"Hi, Bill. Glad you could come."

"Looks like you've been hard at it. You've reviewed all these?" pointing at the documents.

"Yes."

"What have you found?"

"A lot. The challenge is to sift it down so it points us in the best direction to focus our investigation."

"Nothing new there. That's been a constant problem for me. Give me the broad picture and then maybe we can narrow it down."

"Good idea," Chris said. He then told Nightingale he had found several oil companies that had their lawyers file briefs supporting the lifting of the ban on fracking. Checking on these, he had narrowed the best possible suspect companies by what they argued on the economic impact to their companies if the ban was upheld. There were three. But of those, the one that relied most heavily on allegations of financial doom was Universal Energy Company or UEC. The allegations were supported by affidavits of the company's Chief Executive Officer, Chester Gibbons, and its Chief Financial Officer, Russel Pederson. Moreover, UEC's main office is located in the city. The other two's headquarters' were located out of state.

Chris then continued, "These facts aren't sufficient to warrant the conclusion that UEC and its officers took the extreme risk of murdering a state Supreme Court justice. But they do warrant I believe that further investigation of the Company and its principle officers is where we start."

"I agree. The fact that UEC is here in town should mean the paper's archives will have stories on the company and its executives. I can get started researching right away. And the name 'Gibbons' runs a bell, but I can't recall why right now."

"Anything you can find; we can follow up on."

"Excuse me, Mr. Knight, your wife is on the phone."

"Something wrong?" Chris asked anxiously.

"No. The impression I got was, it was something good."

"Take the call Chris. I'm leaving to get back to the paper and start digging."

"Okay, talk to you soon," Chris said and picked up his desk phone. "Hello, Kelly, what's up?"

"Well I suppose I could have waited for you to come home, but I decided to call right away."

"Fine. What about?"

"You know that new restaurant that just opened. The one with a terrace for outside dining? The La Cote Basque Vigneron. There's a waiting list a mile long. But I just got a phone call and was told we have won reservations for two, two weeks from now. And our table is on the terrace so we can see the promenade and people watch."

"Sounds as if you won a jackpot, Kelly. Great news. We can discuss more when I get home."

"Oh Chris! I might be overblowing it a bit, but I thought with all that has recently happened, this was a happy surprise."

"I agree. I look forward to taking my beautiful wife and showing her off in the upscale and exclusive environment of La Cote Basque, whatever?"

"Your French is terrible. It's pronounced with a long 'e,' veny ron ron."

"I know. I leave the French speaking to you. You're the linguist in the family."

"Oh, I'm so glad you like the opportunity. Hurry home."

"I'll be there shortly. Love you."

A thousand dollars will pretty much get anyone a preferred table at the most upscale of restaurants. That was easy. So was announcing the prize to Mrs. Knight. Almost too easy. Regrettable at the same time. For such an auspicious occasion it would be a last supper.

"Never mind," he told himself. "It's time to finish the arrangements for eliminating the next threat." He sent a text message of the code numbers to punch in at the airport's baggage storage and this note – "Instructions for providing the special services agreed to. Please complete within no more than 48 hours."

"I have a problem and I think I have a solution. I want advice."

"What's the problem? Only then might I be able to provide the advice."

"I have agreed to pay $4,000,000 dollars for certain services. And I don't want to pay it. So what can I do?"

"Is there a contract?"

"No."

"Any other factor that establishes a legal obligation to make this payment?"

"No. This 'obligation' (making air quotation marks) is based on, how shall I put this… under the table agreements."

"You mean, illegal?"

"Such a harsh description. You have been part of this company's actions. You have always found, shall we say, 'loopholes' in the law to justify its actions. This is just a different variation on the same theme."

"What are you asking?"

"You were a former prosecutor. You dealt with the scum of society. You know murderers, killers. You know where to find them,"

"I… I don't like where this is going."

"You, sir, have no option. You have done things for me and this company that would get you disbarred, if not sent to jail. You did so to escape the paltry salaries that government prosecutors are forced to live with. Well, it's time you really earn the exorbitant salary I pay you.

You will find a hit man. You will negotiate the terms of his 'contract' and you will give me that information. You then will be released and have no further dealings. You see! I am being generous. You give me the information, and then you have no connection with what I do with it."

"I won't do it. I will put you in touch with someone and you make the arrangements. I will not be party to anything else."

"Very well. See you do it immediately."

Knight picked up the receiver on his office phone, "Hello."

"Chris, Bill Nightingale here."

"Hi Bill, what's up?"

"I've been going over the names of the oil company clients of the law firms that filed briefs on the anti-fracking case before the state Supreme Court. I then cross checked the officers of those companies. In addition, I looked into the clients of the law firms that filed briefs on the capital punishment case. From what we discussed about motives, I started wondering if there might be some kind of connection or cross-over among the anti-death penalty parties and the oil companies."

"Did you find anything?"

"I may have. The one interesting connection is between CHASE and Universal Energy Company. Do you know an Oscar Royce, ever hear of him?"

"Don't know a lot. I do know he's on the Board of CHASE. And he didn't take kindly to my request that members of the organization provide testimony that I believed would be helpful to the defense of Summers. Stormed out of the meeting when I had asked for their help."

"When the case was filed, Royce was Chairman of CHASE. While the appeal was pending, his term as Chairman expired. But when the amicus brief was filed for CHASE, he was the organization's representative that dealt with its law firm."

"I'm not sure how that's relevant," Chris questioned.

"Hold on and I'll try and explain the connection. Royce is a major shareholder kin Universal Energy and sat on its Board. Hence, he is well acquainted with its Chairman and CEO, Chester Gibbons. Following your theory, I checked and found that UEC has been affected by the drop in oil prices and stands to see its fortunes plunge further if the ban on fracking was upheld."

"Interesting. Is there more?"

"Consider this scenario, again based on your theory that the motive for Justice Baker's murder was to stave off financial ruin if the ban on fracking were upheld as was expected it would be. Then, there had to be a cover, a solid cover to keep suspicion away from oil companies. That's where Royce's connection with Gibbons comes in. Royce provides Gibbons with the theory that Baker was killed out of revenge for commuting the death penalty and helps frame Summers."

"That might explain why Royce stormed out of that meeting I had with the CHASE board."

"There's more. Years back, Royce was an officer in Special Forces. He's weapons savvy and did some code breaking. I found this in our archives on the early days of Afghanistan. Then I decided to cross check on the officer that killed Summers. I found out that he was forced to leave the police department he was at and come here."

"Let me think a minute, Bill," Chris said. "You have apparently established a connection between Royce and Gibbons which may have led to the frame-up of a survivor for Baker's murder. Then you have discovered that Edwards, the detective involved in Summers' death has a checkered career. If we could link Edwards to Royce or Gibbons, it would point to their involvement in Summers' ill-fated attempt to escape and blow Edwards story of self-defense out of the water."

"The pieces to the puzzle seem to fit. But it's a long way from being able to prove any of this," Nightingale observed.

"I know. But there's enough to justify continuing this line of inquiry. Do you agree?"

"Yes. But…"

"But, what?"

"If these guys are responsible, they're cold-blooded murderers. And they have a lot at stake. Enough to murder a state Supreme Court justice and most likely Richards and Perry. Meaning, they won't hesitate to take out anyone that gets in their way."

"I agree. We have to be careful. But I don't want to stop. You?"

"I'm in. This is one hell of a story and it will be written under my byline."

"Okay. What's the next step?"

"I'm going to snoop around this guy Edwards. See if I can find out any leads that might connect him to Royce or Gibbons or both."

"How can I help? Chris asked.

"If I come up with something, you can tell me if it's evidence that would be admissible in court."

"I'd like to do more."

"Well, why not contact the other members of CHASE. See what else you can find out on Royce."

"Good idea, I will. In the meantime, watch your back."

"I will. You take care yourself."

Chris put down the phone. What seemed like a workable theory to use as a defense now looked very much like reality.

CHAPTER 44
DOUBLE-DOUBLE CROSS

When the thrill of a kill was imminent, he indulged his narcissism. His microdot Armani shirt, cashmere blend jeans, velvet microdot jacket were accented by his Lanvin leather and Suede Skate shoes. Once last look in the full length mirror and he smiled, then left his hotel room to call on Detective Dan Edwards. Edwards' apartment was on the fifth floor of a high rise not far from the precinct where he worked. It was 10 P.M. Edwards heard a knock on his door, turned down the TV and wondered, "Who could that be? I never get visitors, especially at this hour!"

He went to the door and asked, "Who is it?"

"I have a message for you."

"From whom?"

"Oscar Royce."

"Who's that?"

"Do you really want this conversation to continue in the hallway?"

"Okay, okay, just a minute."

Edwards opened the door slightly. Saw a tall man that looked like he should be on the cover of GQ magazine. Stepped back and opened the door so the man could enter.

"What's this about? I don't know this Oscar Royce."

"You can drop the pretense Detective Edwards. I am fully aware of your dealings with Mr. Royce. It is he who sent me to see you."

"He did, did he? Tell me why."

"It concerns the arrangements that were made and the compensation for the completion of those arrangements."

Suddenly, Edwards got concerned. "He's not backing out," he blurted.

"No! Relax detective."

"Don't call me that. I'm resigning."

"We know. That was part of the plan as you know."

"Okay! What's this all about?"

"The payment you expect is scheduled to be wired once you leave the country. But, there's a condition."

"A condition? What the hell?"

"Keep calm, Detective. Mr. Royce is a careful man. He wants to ensure that your retiring so soon after having shot that poor Mr. Summers is properly explained, doesn't leave any of your superiors or others wondering about your reasons."

"Yeah. So how is that supposed to be fixed?

"You will write out, print and sign this statement addressed to District Attorney Newberry and mail it to her just before you board your plane."

Edwards read over the statement and looked at the man standing before him. "Are you nuts? This confesses to having killed Summers."

"Keep calm. Your confession will have no effect on your future. On the contrary, it will ensure your future."

"Oh yeah! How's that?"

"Mr. Royce has information that Summers' attorney and a newspaper reporter are piecing together facts that will point to the CEO of Universal Energy Company as being mixed up in the murder of that justice that Summers' was framed for. If that investigation continues, all those involved will become targets of the police. When that happens, everybody will be pointing fingers at everybody but themselves, cutting deals to save their own necks. That means you will be outed. This statement says you committed suicide because you couldn't face going to prison."

"You think I'm stupid. I sign this statement, and I sign my own death warrant."

"We knew you would think so, but you're wrong. Once the statement is signed, we will get you out of the country in a private plane that will take you to Dubai... I believe it is. You will also receive a new passport and identity papers that will be untraceable. In other words, you will be dead only insofar as the authorities are concerned and will be able to enjoy what you have earned without having to look over your shoulder."

"Suppose I buy this, when is all this scheduled to happen?"

"You will leave tomorrow night. The private jet will fly you to Nova Scotia. There you will receive your Canadian passport, driver's license and credit cards. Your new name will be Frank Reynolds. Retired. You have a small fortune you made through private investments. You will get your airline tickets for London and then on to Dubai. When you get there, arrangements have been made for you to stay at the Grosvenor House Dubai until you find your own accommodations on condition you do so within thirty days."

"Sounds good. But why should I trust you?

"Do you have a choice? But let me provide a better reason. Mr. Royce has had a disagreement with Mr. Gibbons, the CEO of Universal Energy Company. By your confession identifying Mr. Gibbons as behind the murder of Justice Baker, he evens that score and you get to spend your fortune in Dubai without fear of anyone's interference."

Edwards was wary, but as he thought it over, it was a solid plan and alleviated a concern he did have. As a cop for twenty years, he knew there were no perfect crimes and no statute of limitations on murder. If ever he decided he didn't want to stay in Dubai; with this plan, he wouldn't have to. He could go to the French Riviera, St. Moritz, Rome, anywhere.

"I'll do it. Give me the statement"

He was handed the statement and typed:

I, Detective Daniel Edwards, confess to having staged the attempted escape of Jed Summers. I shot and killed Summers making it look as if it happened in a struggle. I killed him because I was promised a lot of money. The money was hush money paid by Chester Gibbons, CEO of Universal Energy Company. Gibbons wanted Justice Baker killed to keep the Court from upholding the ban on fracking which Gibbons believed would ruin his company. Jed Summers was framed and the evidence found at his cabin was planted. The deaths of Fleming Richards and Ed Perry were also part of the plan to support the motive of revenge as the reason Justice Baker was murdered. I can no longer accept my failures as a police officer or tolerate any longer the crimes I have committed and the betrayal of the trust and honor of my fellow officers. If taking my own life provided any compensation for the wrongs I am guilty of, it will be a small comfort, but one I will not know of.

Daniel Edwards

Finished, he printed the statement and signed beneath his printed name.
"Should I date this?" Edwards asked his back still turned on Mr. GQ.
"No need." With that Edwards felt a small prick in his neck, felt suddenly dizzy and
slumped in his chair.
Mr. GQ started to search the apartment and quickly found Edwards service revolver. With gloved hands, the gun was put into Edwards hand. His slumped body was pulled erect, a pillow taken from the sofa to muffle the sound and the gun fired into Edwards right temple. Edwards slumped forward and fell to the floor. Mr. GQ placed the gun next to body the note resting conspicuously on the desk. Surveying his handiwork, Mr. GQ took the pillow, slowly open the door to ensure no one was in the hall and then took the fire escape stairs and was gone.

A few hours later, Mr. GQ reported in.
"It's been completed."
"Any problems?"
"None."
"You sure."
"Like clockwork."
"Good! Your money will be delivered and you will find it in the morning where we agreed."

Click

The next day, using a burner phone, a call was placed to Edwards' precinct. "Hello. I want to report there may have been a disturbance at the Arlington House Apartments. Something sounded like a gun shot."

"Who is this?" the duty officer asked.

Click

"Damn. Dispatch? Just had a call that there may have been a gun shot at the Arlington House Apartments. Send the nearest car around to check it out."

"Will do."

Thirty minutes later a squad car arrived at the apartments. Checking with the resident manager, they were told he knew nothing about any disturbance – no complaints and certainly no gun shots. The officers were about to leave when one stopped and said, "Wait a minute! Detective Edwards lives in this building. If anything went down, he would know. What's Dan Edwards apartment number? "Number 1010."

"Let's go. You come along too with your pass key."

"Okay."

When they got to the apartment, there was no response to its door buzzer nor to their knocking. "Open it up. You wait in the hall."

The officers entered. "Detective Edwards, it's patrolman Brady." No answer. They moved from the living room to the alcove on their right. Edwards body lay in a pool of dried blood, his right temple shattered. His service revolver lay next to the body along with a note. Brady picked it up and read it to himself. "Blessed Jesus!" and handed it to his partner. "Call this in and get a medical crew up here and give me the note back."

Having fingered Gibbons as the master mind behind the death penalty murders, Royce secured control of the account that held the $4,000,000 that was to be wired to the account that had been set up for Edwards. That accomplished, he revisited his plan to have Chris Knight killed. Knight was spot on in his suspicions that the motive for Baker's murder was not revenge. But with the suicide note of Edwards and his confession, was there still a reason to kill Knight? He no longer needed to make that case. Edwards "suicide" made that unnecessary. He smiled to himself and thought, "Well, Mr. and Mrs. Knight, you will be able to enjoy your outing at the chic restaurant on the terrace after all." But then he thought that when Gibbons is in custody, he could make a deal to rat me out. He would learn of Edwards death, seek to retrieve his wire of the $4,000,000 and find out it had been transferred. He would know by whom. He would certainly respond. If he made bail, which it was pretty certain he would, he'd be free awaiting trial to take his revenge against me and the cops and prosecution would be concentrating on me as the actual murderer of Baker, Richards and Perry. This would give Gibbons the opportunity to flee the country. Edwards' demands had educated him on countries with no extradition treaty with the U.S. Gibbons had nothing to lose. Oil prices were still well below $50 a barrel. The murder of Baker would certainly lead to a decision to uphold the ban on fracking. And efforts were now being made to ban fracking on public lands. Another killing was necessary.

Royce's years in the military had hardened his moral compass so that killings were just another means to achieve a goal. He was a hired killer for years and admired in his small circle for the efficiency of his hits and the high percentage of success he achieved. He preferred now to have others do the work, like Mr. GQ. But he knew it was risky going to the well once too often, and too soon. No he would have to handle Mr. Gibbons himself. As he reflected, he experienced the old exhilaration of risk-taking, of being in control. He could not deny that it was thrilling to kill. That in doing so he got to play God. And was Gibbons any less deserving of death than the enemies he killed in the service of his country? Having resolved his own debate, it was time to plan.

Royce was not the only one making deadly decisions. Gibbons had made his mind up to get rid of Royce when the deal was made to pay off Edwards for killing Summers. Royce had assured him Edwards would not get to enjoy his blood money, but made the mistake of letting Gibbons know that he, Royce, would "inherit" that money for arranging for the murder of Summers preventing anyone from finding out the truth about the death penalty murders. Now, Gibbons' corporate counsel did as he had been ordered and provided a hit man. Arrangements were quickly made to eliminate Royce.

Gibbons would arrange to meet with Royce to review their situations now that Summers had been taken care of. Gibbons' hit man would lie in waiting and take Royce out. Nothing fancy. Just a late night rendezvous in an isolated location from which only one would return.

CHAPTER 45
IT'S NOT OVER 'TIL IT'S OVER

District Attorney Newberry called Chris. Asked him to come to her office. "Mr. Knight, there have been developments in the Summers case I think you should know about. I would also like to get your opinion on what these developments might indicate."

"I can be there in two hours."

"Good. Security will escort you to my office."

Two hours later, Knight was escorted into Newberry's office.

"Thanks for coming Mr. Knight."

"Chris is fine."

"Okay. Chris. You know Detective Edwards is dead. Apparent suicide."

"Yes. I read it in the paper."

"You've dealt with Edwards. What do you think about his death?"

"Tragic?"

"No. I mean do you think Edwards would shoot himself?"

"I'm not sure I'm qualified to answer that."

"Here's the note the officers found next to his body. Take a minute and read it."

Chris did so. When he finished, Newberry asked, "What do you think?"

"Seems straight forward enough. Of course I didn't know his early background. You have a point in asking. What is it?"

"I worked with Detective Edwards for several years. He did everything he could to escape the bad reputation he acquired in his early days as a cop.

So Summers being shot in his custody and then his alleged suicide and confession don't jive. For example, I was aware he put in for retirement. You don't do that if you plan to kill yourself."

"I agree. But it's not impossible."

"Agree. But you were the one that believed revenge wasn't the motive for Justice Baker's murder. And according to Edwards' suicide note, you were right. And not only that, the note purports to identify the person responsible for having the Justice murdered. It seems all too neat."

"Have you brought Gibbons in for questioning?"

"No."

"Why not?"

"The contents of Edwards' note have not been made public and they won't be for a while. We have Gibbons under surveillance and that will continue. So far we've seen no suspicious activity. So, we want to investigate quietly a little longer. If Gibbons looks like he's going to travel, we'll step in then. But, we don't think Gibbons would get his own hands dirty."

"Hold on. You seem to be suggesting that Edwards was murdered and it was made to look like suicide. Am I right?"

"We think the kill was handled by a professional. And making a murder look like a suicide is as old as the hills. What is new here is that Edwards took the time to point a finger. Suicides seldom, if ever, are concerned with fixing blame on someone else. Their despondency is usually in total control of the thoughts and things that are driving them to kill themselves. The exception might be if the one named is responsible or believed responsible for say murdering a loved one of the suicide. There's no evidence that Gibbons even knew Edwards and vice versa."

"I follow. But where do I come in?"

"You got that reporter, Nightingale, to ask your questions at the news conference announcing Summers death. I should have thrown you both out, but let it pass. In any event, I suspect you and he started investigating to find facts to support your theory that since Summers hadn't been proven guilty of Justice Baker's murder, his actual murderer could be at large. Am I right?"

"Yes."

"Have you come up with anything?"

"We found reasons to believe that Gibbons' oil company would have had serious financial problems if the ban on fracking were upheld. We found out that Gibbons knew an Oscar Royce, former Chairman of CHASE and a former Special Forces Op who was weapon savvy, and familiar with coding. We're in the process of seeing if units like those Royce was in also had training in using biological weapons or defending against them. Also, when I asked the CHASE Board to assist in the defense of Summers, he got angry and left. None of this places Royce at the sites of any of the death penalty killings. But…"

"Have you found any evidence of Gibbons and Royce being in contact at any time that's relevant to Justice Baker's murder?"

"No, not yet."

"You were correct about the motive for murdering Justice Baker. You have verified ties between the firm and its CEO if Justice Baker's decision upheld the ban on fracking. You know Gibbons and Royce knew each other. My question is this. At this stage, if we go after Royce or Gibbons, they will dummy up, lawyer up, and call Edwards suicide note as a fabrication and part of a deliberate frame up."

"Sounds logical. And how are you thinking I could help avoid all that?"

"You have met and know Royce. You could approach him as Summers' counsel and let him know you also knew Edwards and that you have seen his suicide note naming Gibbons as behind the death penalty killings. That you know Royce also knows Gibbons and wanted to know if he had any ideas about whether Edwards was right in naming Gibbons. You're a defense attorney and your wife's a well-known psychologist. Royce's guard might not be up talking with you where it would be if we were asking the questions. You, and perhaps your wife, can read Royce's body language, his demeanor. Maybe he lets something slip. In any event this office thinks it's worth a try. We just need to know if you'll agree to give it a try."

Chris for a moment. "Let me get back to you tomorrow."

"Fair enough."

Chris left the District Attorney's office and drove home. He walked in the door and called to Kelly.

"I'm in the kitchen," she responded.

Chris went to the kitchen, gave Kelly a kiss on the cheek and a hug and said, "I have something to ask you." Chris explained his meeting with the DA.

"I see," Kelly said. "What's your thoughts."

"I'd like yours first."

"Well, do you think there's any danger?"

"Not really. The meeting can be in a public place. And the target is Gibbons, not Royce per se. If he wants to incriminate Gibbons he'll talk. If he doesn't, he'll clam up or deny everything. Either way, we're trying to get a reading on whether Edwards suicide was real or staged, whether Gibbons was involved."

"You said 'we,'" Kelly remarked.

"Yes. I was thinking two heads are better than one, especially such a pretty and smart one."

"Flatterer! Let's do it. It won't do poor Mr. Summers any good now, but if we could help find the real culprits, it would clear his good name."

"Never thought of that. But you are right. I guess that's why you're my better half."

"That's not flattery, my sweet. That's gospel."

They smiled at each other.

The next day, Chris called Newberry and told her they would contact Royce.

"When?"

"I was asked to attend the next meeting of CHASE and comment on Summers' death. Royce is expected to attend. I will bring Kelly along to offer her comments and observations. After the meeting, I'll ask if we could go to the coffee shop across from CHASE's offices and talk."

"When's the meeting?"

"Day after tomorrow."

"We'll be waiting for your report."

"Don't expect anything. That way if we get nothing, you won't be disappointed. If we do, it will be a good surprise."

"Got it. Good luck!"

Two days later at 5 P.M., Kelly and Chris arrived at CHASE's offices. They were welcomed and told to make themselves comfortable in the chairs behind the ones surrounding the conference table. Board members filtered in. Oscar Royce was one of the last to arrive. He looked startled to see Chris and Kelly, but averted his stare and took his seat.

The agenda was short and the meeting soon ended. Chris was introduced to give his comments on Summers. He emphasized that his death was all the more unfortunate because it prevented a determination of his innocence which Chris firmly believed would have prevailed. He didn't for a minute think revenge was the motive for the murder of Justice Baker or the other two deaths. And was hopeful that the police would drop their reluctance and reopen the case. He was certain the real culprit or culprits were at large.

The Chairman thanked Chris and announced they were adjourned.

Chris walked up to Royce with Kelly, introduced her and asked if he had time for a cup of coffee.

Royce looked at Chris for a moment and was about to decline, then thought better of it and said he could spare a short amount of time. They walked to the shop and took a booth toward the rear.

"Thanks again for taking some of your time. We will try not to keep you long."

"What do you want to discuss?"

"As you may know, my defense of Mr. Summers rested on an alternative theory for motive. Following up on that, we think we have identified a suspect with a motive that fits my alternative theory. His name is Chester Gibbons, the CEO of Universal Energy Company. Do you know him?"

"We've met."

"Can you share anything you know about him?"

"Like what?"

"Is his company doing well?"

"It's general knowledge that oil companies are hurting with the plunge on oil prices."

"If the State Supreme Court upheld the ban on fracking, would his company have been damaged?"

"Basic logic suggests yes. "I'm not invested in the company if that's what you want to know."

"Assuming the company was hurt, what do you think Gibbons would do?"

"Have no idea."

"Do you think Gibbons would have tried to stop the court from deciding the case on fracking?"

"If you're asking, would Gibbons have had anything to do with Justice Baker's death, I have no idea. But I will say, it's not unusual for these high powered executives to believe the laws don't apply to them as they do to the rest of us. I learned that in the military. And it was true enough of the time. The more stars on someone's shoulder, the more arbitrary they could be at times."

"Did you know a detective Dan Edwards?"

"Not personally. I read about his involvement in your client's failed attempt to escape."

"What if I told you that Edwards knew something about Gibbons that connected him to Summers and Edwards?"

"I would tell you, you have told me something I didn't know and still don't for that matter."

"In your military career, you were well trained on weapons?"

"Guilty as charged."

"Any other special disciplines?"

"Like what?"

"Codes, biological weapons or defenses?"

"Mr. Knight, I fail to see any relevance to your questioning. I have given you my time, but I have to go now. Good evening Mrs. Knight, it was nice to meet you." With that Royce rose and left.

"What do you think Kelly?"

"He's smart, shrewd and knows more than he's telling."

"I agree. Let's go."

CHAPTER 46
DEAD MEN TELL NO TALES

Royce left the meeting with the Knights, troubled. He was glad it had become unnecessary to make them victims of another random shooting. But he hadn't anticipated Knight's persistence in exposing the real motive for Justice Baker's murder and who was behind it all. If Gibbons was arrested, which seemed inevitable, he'd turn on Royce as the actual murderer. He wasn't keen on another killing. But he soon overcame his scruples. In the military he was paid to kill and kill he did, so much so he got used to it with no emotion or regrets.

"Time to plan," he thought. "What has to be done, t'were better it be done soon," quoting MacBeth.

"Hello! Is this Chester Gibbons?"

"Yes, who's this?"

"I was contacted by your attorney. He told me to contact you about some work you had in mind."

"You were told correctly."

"Then we had best meet to discuss the assignment."

"I don't think it wise that we meet anywhere that is connected to me," Gibbons said.

"I agree. There's a truck stop, about twenty-five miles down the Interstate, known as 'Martha's.' You know where that is?"

"No. But I can find it on GPS."

"Right! I assume you want this work done as soon as possible?"

"That's right."

"Meet me at the truck stop at 6 am tomorrow morning."

"Why then?"

"It's the busiest time. All the truckers are stopping for breakfast. It will be crowded and that makes is less likely anyone will remember two guys meeting for breakfast. You got some clothes that look like a truckers?"

"I started out as a trucker. Drove gasoline trucks. I'll fit in."

"Good!" I'll see you tomorrow."

"Wait. How will I recognize you?"

"I'll be wearing an army fatigue jacket and a cap that has "Go Army' on it. You?"

"I'll have a gray hoody on with a picture of the Grateful Dead. No hat. White hair."

"Got it. Until tomorrow."

"Just a minute. What do I call you?"

"Mr. Smith." Click.

Gibbons arrived just before 6 am. Parked away from the main building. Mr. Smith was right. The place was jammed with trucks and truckers. He pushed his way inside the restaurant and looked around. Didn't see anyone in a fatigue jacket or 'Go Army' hat at first. He maneuvered himself through the crowd to his left. Nothing. He turned and maneuvered himself the other way. Still didn't see what has was looking for. Then, "Wait," he said to himself, "there he is in the back near the kitchen."

Gibbons pushed through to the table and said, "Mr. Smith?"

"The same. Have a seat. Want some coffee?"

"Yes."

"Betty," he yelled. A matronly woman in her fifties, dirty blond hair tucked into a hairnet and topped with a tri-cornered cap, turned.

"Coffee!" Smith yelled.

"Keep your shirt on, I'm coming," she yelled back. She came to the table with the coffee pot and filled Gibbons' cup.

"Thanks."

"You're welcome," she said, turned and looked for others waiting for her to pour, and walked away."

"You know her?" asked Gibbons.

"Why?"

"Well, she came right away and there were plenty others trying to get her attention."

"Mom always did dote on me."

"That was your mother?"

"Yes. She's been working here ever since the old man passed on."

"And her name's "Betty?""

"No. It's not."

Gibbons was about to ask what her name was and let it pass. "Let's talk about what needs to be done."

"Your party."

Gibbons first explained who Smith would be up against. His military background, his knowledge of weapons and how to use them. He cautioned that the target was crafty, could not be easily fooled and was always on his guard.

"What do you know about his schedule?"

"Schedule? I don't follow."

"If I know his routine, it helps in the planning."

"Makes sense. But I don't know his schedule."

"Does he use a cell phone?"

"Yes."

"Do you know the number?"

"Yes. But why"

"It's easy to tap into his phone. Give me his number and I'll tap into his phone."

"You can do that?"

"Look it up online. Piece of cake."

"Won't he know he's being tapped?"

"Not a chance."

"I don't see how this will work. You're listening to his phone calls."

"The less you know about how and what I do, the better. Right?"

"Yes, but…"

"Okay. I'll tell you this. I listen in and sooner or later I'll learn about his schedule and his movements. I'll wait until one of his planned outings presents a best case opportunity. Then I make my move."

"That could take time."

"Not really. You in a hurry?"

"Yes! Yes, I am!"

"Well relax. It's never taken more than three days to get this kind of information. You wire the down payment that was agreed to with your counsel?"

"Yes."

"Well, count as an incentive that I want payment of the balance as soon as possible."

"I will."

Neither of the men knew just how quickly circumstances would hasten the events that had been planned.

The day following Gibbons and Smith's meeting, Royce called Knight using his cell phone.

"Mr. Knight. Oscar Royce here. I've been thinking about our recent conversation."

"Yes?"

"I won't mention anything specific on this call. Rather, I want to see if you would be interested in meeting with me again. It would have to be on my terms, and my scheduling at a site I designate."

"I'm listening," Chris said.

"You will come alone to meet me."

"Where?"

"Patience, Mr. Knight."

"Sorry."

"You will come alone to meet me at 11:30 P.M.sharp tonight. You know the Fountain of Pegasus in City Central Park?"

"Yes."

"Do you know the small memorial cemetery that is about one hundred yards from there that can be reached through the wooded path just behind the statue?"

"I can find it."

"I will meet you at the Bronze Vietnam War Solider sculpture in the center."

"Why all the cloak and dagger?"

"I prefer, 'precautions' Mr. Knight. But if you're not interested..."

"No. It's your party. I'll be there. Alone. Eleven-thirty tonight sharp."

"Good. I was confident I could count on you."

"Goodbye!" Chris said and hung up his home phone.

"Chris, what was that all about?" asked Kelly.

"That was Royce. He wants to meet. He wants to tell me more, but he wouldn't say what."

"When? Where?"

Chris told Kelly the time and place.

"Chris. Are you sure about this? It scares me."

"I'm not going into this without taking precautions. Our narrow escape at that country estate of that gun organization officer remains burned into my memory. I'll not walk into a potential ambush like that again."

"I'm going with you."

"You most certainly are not. Our first born takes over all considerations. But to help you rest easy, these are the precautions I'll be taking."

Chris explained his plan. Kelly was somewhat appeased but still fearful.

Having gotten Chris to agree to meet on his terms and place, Royce now had to pull together the second part of his plan. He called Gibbons. He told him about his meeting with Knight and that he was going to give Knight all the facts about the three murders and who was behind them.

"Are you crazy, Royce? Why are you doing this.?"

"I'm tired of the killings. I want out. You got me into this and now I'm going to make you take the wrap."

"Look! We can work something out."

"It's too late for that."

"No! No! Listen. Edwards is dead. That means I still have the $4,000,000 he was to get. And you and I can work the same deal."

"I..."

"Wait! I can have the money wired to a foreign bank account in your name or a name you choose. We can use the same escape plans Edwards was going to use."

Royce smiled to himself. The fool doesn't know I've already deposited the money offshore.

"I don't think I can trust you Chester."

"Yes, you can."

"Words!"

"Tell me how I can prove it to you."

Royce paused and there was silence on the line. Then – "You can prove it to me this way. I'll cancel the meeting with Knight. I'll just call and re-schedule for tomorrow night. Instead, I'll meet with you at the same spot, same time. You will have my airline tickets for the flight that leaves in the morning and proof that you transferred the funds. If you show up with these, I'll leave in the morning and won't return. Knight will have nothing to support his suspicions. And you have enough money to hire a stable of lawyers to get you off."

"Okay. I'll do it. We have a deal?"

"We have a deal. But one slipup and there will be no second chance."

"Yes. Yes. I agree. I understand."

"Tonight. Eleven-thirty sharp. Good bye." Royce hung up.

"Damn! Smith! Did he hear all that?" Gibbons thought to himself. He called Smith.

When Smith answered, he said, "You have some friends."

"Then you heard what Royce plans?"

"Yes."

"Well you can take care of him as we planned and right away. Tonight!"

"Not so fast. I appreciate that you have wired my down payment. But my price just went up."

"Up?"

"I'll be generous. I don't want the $4,000,000 you were paying to get rid of this Edwards."

"No?"

"I'll take half. Wired the next morning when the job is done."

"And if I refuse."

"It's your funeral."

"Alright. I agree."

"There's more."

"What?"

"You will have to show up tonight and keep that appointment."

"Why? That could wind up incriminating me."

"Precisely! With this kind of money at stake, I'm taking no chances. You can hire another hit man to take me out."

"I could do that anyway, but won't. What's my being there, tonight do?"

"Just this! You will be photographed at the scene along with the victim. Those photos will be placed in a safe deposit box with a full statement of what I know. If anything happens to me, the instructions are to give the statement and photos to the police."

"I wouldn't double cross you!"

"Yeah, right! Like you aren't double crossing Royce. You don't do what I said and show up, Royce stays alive and I make a deal with him about you."

"Okay! Okay! I get it. I have to get going to get all this arranged by tonight."

"Yeah! Get it all done. I will see you tonight, but you won't see me. So don't bother to try." Click

Chris had completed his precautions. Kelly felt somewhat relieved but was still anxious.

"Be careful Chris. I really wish you wouldn't do this."

"I know. And I'm sorry to worry you. But I'll be fine. It's quarter to eleven, I have to go. Love you!"

Royce got in his car as Chris was saying goodbye to Kelly. He had checked and rechecked his .38. He was ready for the last act in this drama. He reflected on the Latin phrase, *Omnia mors aequat.* death levels all things.

Gibbons had arranged for the bookings for Royce's flights out of the country and took the tickets with him. He also took the bank papers recording the transfer of the $4,000,000 to Edwards. Royce would take the papers. It would be dark. He couldn't risk any light to check them and even if he did, if Mr. Smith did his job, he'd be dead before he could react. He wouldn't have to transfer the $2,000,000 to Smith until the morning, not knowing that Royce had already transferred the funds to his own account.

Earlier in the day, Smith had paid a visit to City Central Park and checked out the wooded path and the area surrounding the Bronze Vietnam War Solider sculpture. He inspected three different locations that had line of sight to the memorial. All were secluded by the surrounding foliage. But he chose the location that was closest to a large gravestone with an angel sitting in front of a wall. If for any reason his position was compromised and faced return fire from Royce or he needed a better angle of fire, he could leap behind this edifice. He parked a mile away arriving at 10:30 giving himself time to get in position. Using infrared goggles he watched and waited for the parties to arrive.

First to arrive was Chris. This surprised Smith. Royce had told Gibbons he would call Knight and reschedule their meeting so he could meet with Gibbons. But then he remembered, the tap on Royce's cell phone never signaled a call to Knight. Obviously, Royce hadn't called Knight. But why? Smith mentally shrugged his shoulders and concentrated on the target area.

Next to arrive was Gibbons. He saw Knight first and shrunk back into the shadows before Chris could spot him. Royce didn't appear. Smith swept the area with his goggles. Then he saw. Royce had come in behind Gibbons. Gibbons was startled and let out a cry. Royce pushed him into the open area around the statue and Chris wheeled around and watched the two men approaching. Gibbons hands were in the air.

"Royce? That you?" Chris called out softly.

"It's me, Knight. And this here as you probably know is Mr. Chester Gibbons, CEO of Universal Energy Company and the man who ordered the hit on Justice Baker. For good measure, he had me take out Flemings and Perry. We corrupted Edwards. Had him kill your client, 'trying to escape,' as the papers so dutifully reported. Then I had Edwards killed. You and the misses were next in line, but with Edwards gone, it wasn't necessary. Not necessary until I overheard you after the press conference on Summers death planning to continue to look for the real killer of Justice Baker. You're a smart man Mr. Knight. Perhaps too smart."

"Damn it Royce! What are you doing? You're spilling everything. Why? Why tell him all this?"

"Not to worry Chester," Royce said with obvious menace. "Only one of us is leaving here alive."

"But, you can't. We have a deal. I've got your plane tickets and the bank papers of the transfer as we agreed."

"For such a big shot corporate guy, you're quite stupid. I transferred those funds myself after Edwards was killed. The papers you have are for an account with a zero balance. And those plane tickets, if that is what they are, are unnecessary for I have my own."

Gibbons face contorted in anger, disbelief and fear. Chris was frozen just listening as Royce unfolded the murderous story. Smith watched and listened. The revelations of Royce distracted his concentration.

"Now Chester, to use a Latin phrase that is most apropos for you, *Memento mori*. It means Chester, 'Remember, you must die.' After all, we all must. Just, in this case, some earlier than others."

At this Gibbons panicked, "Smith, god damn it, where are you," he yelled.

A shot rang out and grazed Royce's shoulder, who dove as soon as he heard the report of the gun. But for his training, experience and immediate response he would have been hit in the temple and killed instantly.

Gibbons froze. Then his senses returned briefly and he began to run. From his prone position, Royce fired once hitting Gibbons in the back between his shoulder blades. He crashed forward and lay still. Royce then rolled to his left just in time as another bullet ricocheted off the concrete path where a second earlier Royce had fallen. Righting himself, Royce fired at the spot where he had seen the flash of the rifle. He heard a scream of pain and knew he had hit the sniper. How bad; he had no idea and wasn't taking any chances rolling again to his left until he had the memorial between himself and the shooter.

While this unfolded in a flash, Chris dropped down and laid low. He inched backward trying to reach the wooded path leading to the memorial. Unable to get a clear shot with Royce behind the memorial, Smith leapt behind the graveyard angel icon and wall to get a better line of fire. Once there he couldn't distinguish who was who. He saw a body inching backward toward the path, then leap up and turned to run. To get a decent shot, Smith moved out from behind the gravestone wall and shot at the retreating figure. His shot hit its mark and the body pitched forward, fell and lay still.

When Smith showed himself, Royce leveled his gun and shot. He hit

Smith who fell back and as he did involuntarily squeeze the trigger sending a burst of shells skyward. Then silence.

Gibbons lay face down close to the memorial, moaning. Chris lay on the edge of the wooded path, not moving. Royce, rolled again to his left keeping the memorial between him and the shooter. Checking his shoulder, it bled, but was superficial. He rose to one knee. Then dashed to the memorial. A rustle of branches told him the shooter was on the move back into the surrounding wooded area. Question was: retreating or repositioning?

Smith had seen enough. What a fiasco? Still his form of "professionalism" required he finish the job. In his business, like others, reputation is key. Knowing he was up against a professional, extreme care was required. One last effort. Then "I'm gone!" he thought. He crouched behind the trunk of an oak tree and carefully looked back at the memorial hoping to spot his target. He reached to pull down his goggles, but they weren't there. "Damn!" Everything was quiet now. Then he heard a low moan. Who was it? His target? The guy called Knight? From what he could tell, his client was past moaning. He sat quietly. Breathing softly. Straining to hear a noise. A twig crack. A branch rustle. Anything to get a direction. Then he heard it. Someone crashing through the brush on his right. He fired off six rounds in the direction of the sound. Then stillness. He wondered, "Did I hit him? Should I move?" Wait!" he told himself. The next few minutes he crouched, sweat running down his forehead, into his eyes. He wiped them away, but they filled again. Then he heard another rustle, this time behind him. "Have I been outflanked?" he thought in panic. "Can't stay here. Have to move!" He rose on his haunches, tried to see into the darkness. Nothing. "Have to move," he said to himself. With that he burst from behind the tree in the opposite direction he fired at. He got one step, heard the crack of a gun, felt a sharp, burning in his left thigh, that twisted him around and then another gunshot this time hitting him between his shoulder blades. He pitched forward and fell losing his gun. He tried to rise, bringing his right knee under his chest and pushing with his arms to rise, when his hands were kicked out from beneath him and fell face down in the wet leaves and mud.

Someone rolled him over. He looked up. Is that an owl? An alien? His focus cleared and he saw it was a man with infrared goggles – his goggles. His head fell back. He heard, "Amateur!" A boom. Then all was quiet.

Having dispatched "Smith," Royce went back to the memorial. He first checked on Gibbons. Grabbed his right arm and turned him over. He was still breathing, barely. Royce removed the goggles, bent over and lowered his face towards Gibbons. "You shouldn't have tried to double cross me, CEO Chester," he said with derision. "You really don't know how to play for keeps." He pointed his gun at Gibbons head, then lowered and re-holstered it. He was already dead. Then he thought, "Knight. Forgot about him. He ran up the path. Gibbons shot him I think." He started up the path leading back to the Fountain of Pegasus. He found Chris lying on his back. "Still breathing. He pulled his revolver from its holster, then heard, "Stop right there! Make a move and you're a dead man!"

Royce could see no one, but re-holstered his gun. "Put your hands behind your head! Slowly! No false moves, then squat down!" Royce hesitated and heard "Now! Or else."

Royce slowly raised his hands and clasped them behind his head as ordered. Then slowly he sank down on his haunches. As he did, a figure emerged from the brush holding a gun pointed at him. Suddenly, Royce did a barrel roll and as he did drew his weapon from the holster. He was quick but the figure from the brush was a tad quicker and shot Royce in the chest before he could get off a round. Royce fell back with a thud, the force of the bullet shoving him a few feet along the path away from his shooter. He still held the gun and tried to raise and fire. Another shot rang out, hitting Royce in the forehead. It was over. Royce was dead.

After checking to be doubly sure Royce was no longer a threat, the figure turned toward Chris and leaned over. "You alright counselor?"

Chris raised himself on one elbow and made a small smile. "Sore. Sore."

"Sore?"

"Yes. This vest is a life saver, but the impact of the bullet still felt like I was wacked in the back with a baseball bat."

"Come on. Let me help you up," said Detective Whitmore.

"What took you so long?" asked Chris

"Sorry! We went down the path on the other side of the Fountain. When we hard all the fireworks, we came running back. By then we had to approach slowly so we wouldn't run into any stray bullets from the battle that was going on. We stopped. Advanced slowly trying not to give away our presence. Saw you on the path and that you were moaning. Knowing you were alive and the battle was still going on between Royce and whoever the other guy was, we waited. When Royce emerged and came toward you, we moved in."

"Glad you did. Have to thank you again for getting me this bullet proof vest. Wouldn't be here if you hadn't."

"You okay to travel? "I think there's a beautiful lady waiting to give you holy hell for being mixed up in this. Don't want to let her wrath get stoked by further delay in getting you back to her."

Chris smiled. "Thanks, Jim. I can travel. Let's go."

"Officer Cain will drive you home. We'll get your statement later."

"Okay."

EPILOGUE

Chris' back had a massive bruise in the middle of his back where he was hit. But it healed. He weathered Kelly's anger and scolding. She was entitled. Besides, after her fear and anger subsided, making up was always fantastic.

Jed Summers name was cleared. Detective Edwards suicide was recorded a premediated murder. Gibbons who was chiefly responsible for Edwards murder was dead and while the police kept a file open, they knew searching for an expert hit man had little chance of success.

"Mr. Smith," paid for his profession with his life. Small recompense for the lives he ended. But there was nothing more that could be done.

Oscar Royce was the wild card in all this. His indifference to murder obviously contradicted his membership in CHASE. Some surmised dealing with death so often as a military veteran made him want to do something to atone for all the deaths with which he was a part of. Some less kind, thought he joined to mock those opposed to the death penalty. These events would certainly not convince either side to change their positions. But there should be room for coming closer together.

The penalty must be reserved for crimes of depraved indifference to the pain, suffering and loss of both the victims and their loved ones who survive and are forced to live the rest of their lives unable to rid their minds and hearts of the tragedy and horror of such depravity.

Proof of guilt must be unassailable. The court has to ensure that the evidence is irrefutable, that defense counsel is competent, that prosecutors prosecute the crime and criminal and not for political ambitions or publicity. DNA evidence may have to be a requirement to show that the accused was at the scene of the crime. If other proofs establish guilt, but the accused's DNA is not present at the scene of the crime, that could weigh in imposing life without parole instead of the death penalty.

Appellate procedures must and can be corrected. There is no excuse for appeals lasting for decades. It's a situation that somehow has become ingrained in the system.

While no one wants to see someone who is innocent put to death, society has an equal interest in seeing that depraved individuals are not let loose to once again prey on innocent victims.

The constitutional provision against cruel and unusual punishment is intended, correctly, to protect those convicted of crimes. This book was written to give recognition that those who are brutally slain and those who survive them have, without cause, already suffered punishment that is extremely cruel and cruelly unusual.

THE END

ABOUT THE AUTHOR

H.H. Charles is a pseudo-name for Charles H. Helein, a practicing lawyer. His works are based on his experiences practicing law and living in the D.C. area. His first novel No Escape: A Maze of Greed and Murder covers the personal and political fallout of a proposal to legalize drugs. His econd novel, Dark Corridors: A Labyrinth of Loss, Lies, Lust, and Murder is based on true events on how big business gets its way in Washington through money, influence, cover ups, and murder. These novels were followed by; *Seeds of Anarchy* and *You, The Jury II.* He is currently working on his first non-fiction book, *The 44th Legacy*, a critique of the Obama presidency.